The Alternative Guide to the
London Boroughs

Edited by Owen Hatherley

Open House

Preface
Catherine Slessor

London has been done to death with guide books. You can find dissections of the capital to suit all tastes. Drinkers, thinkers, shoppers, clubbers, royalists, revolutionaries, ghost hunters, swimmers, occultists, epicureans, art lovers, bibliophiles, *roués*, *flâneurs*, puritans and pleasure seekers. Who needs another guide book?

But London can never be truly mapped, never totally pinned down. It's constantly shapeshifting, polymorphously reframed by politics, war, trade, industry, culture, money and above all, people. Immigrant or native, we all have our London stories. Mine began on a 1971 family holiday, as we trundled gawkily around the usual tourist sights. It was a world away from dreary Aberdeen where I grew up, the illicit thrill of technicolour Oz after monochrome Kansas.

Ten years later, as part of my architecture course, I worked in London for a year. I lived in Earl's Court, where the all houses looked like wedding cakes left out in the rain and you could zip around on the tube for just 10p, thanks to the Greater London Council's Fares Fair policy. In 1984 I permanently escaped from Scotland, blearily excreted at King's Cross from an overnight train, like thousands of others before me. I began my short-lived career in architectural practice by hand drawing the bricks in the walls for a swimming pool in Thamesmead. The bricks are still there.

Over time, I found I was better at writing about buildings than designing them. History records that I was interviewed for an architectural magazine job in a pub on Clerkenwell Green, in which Lenin shared drinks with Stalin. Twenty years later I held my leaving party from the same magazine in the same pub, but its hinterland was unrecognisable, bent into an utterly different shape by the questionable forces of gentrification, like so many London neighbourhoods.

Everyone who lives in London constructs a personal mental map of places, things, buildings, people and experiences. It's how we fathom the city's vast scale, enabling us to stay sane and navigate around a terrain oozing with possibilities and perils. Because for all her fragrant intrigue, London can be a harsh mistress. Of late, her world view has been coarsened by the impact of political austerity and now a global pandemic.

Proscription and hyper-vigilance are reordering communal interaction and transforming notions about what constitutes a convivial and inclusive public realm.

In normal times, much of London's architecture is routinely off limits, fuelling the popularity of the democratising Open House programme. Now, in abnormal times, it seem even more inaccessible. Hopefully, this will be a temporary condition. Being able to encounter buildings in the flesh helps you to apprehend not just their architectural style, but their social and civic substance with how they configure city life.

But buildings and locales can also be conjured by words, so this anthology, rather than guide book, is a richly textured magic show. A stellar posse of writers, many of whom I've had the pleasure of sharing drinks with, was commissioned to contribute vignettes illuminating the capital's 33 boroughs. From Havering to Hounslow, Haringey to Croydon, each is a diverting and unpredictable mind's eye walk. Together, this scintillating collection of mental maps, *billets doux* and tales of the unexpected will make you see London anew.

London has also been done to death with quotes, so I'll spare you the Samuel Johnson. But this from Bram Stoker's *Dracula*, though voiced by an undead fictional character, still resonates: 'I long to go through the crowded streets of your mighty London, to be in the midst of the whirl and rush of humanity, to share its life, its change, its death, and all that makes it what it is'.

Catherine Slessor is an architectural critic, editor and writer. Currently she is a contributing editor to the *Architectural Review* and was its editor between 2010 and 2015. She studied architecture in Edinburgh and worked for a short time as an architect before gratefully defecting into journalism. She has lived in London since 1984.

Each essay is followed by a selection of architectural highlights from the borough. These were written by [OH] Owen Hatherley, [MF] Merlin Fulcher, [EM] Ella McCarron, [RM] Rhea Martin, [NM] Nyima Murry and [PH] Phineas Harper and bear the author's initials unless otherwise credited.

Interspersed through the chapters you will find a selection of artefacts from the Museum of London's collection. The texts that accompany these images were written by George Kafka and Rosa Nussbaum.

London, Open City
Owen Hatherley

What does Open House mean when you can't leave your house? Since the first week of March 2020, I haven't left south-east London; while editing this guide, I have explored the capital vicariously. I am reliant on immuno-suppressants for a chronic medical condition, which meant I received the 'shielding letter' from the government, so between March and May, I was confined entirely to the flat I share with my partner in the London Borough of Southwark. Two surreal months of clear, silent skies, streets deserted but for walkers, mutual aid leaflets and weekly Thursday evening rounds of applause. In the process, my London was whittled down to a tiny grid of streets in SE5. As this guide goes to print, it's impossible to be sure to what degree Open House Festival will even properly go ahead, but what-ever happens, for many people it will mean exploring the area where they live. The bustling scenes I've seen over the years at Open House Festival – crowds of people in Lloyds of London or the Daily Express building on Fleet Street, spectacular reminders that yes, ordinary people are interested in architecture – and modern architecture at that! – may be replaced with distanced scatterings of people taking short strolls round their block to look at a local chapel, an old factory, a housing estate, a health centre. That assumption lies behind the places you'll find in these pages.

For all the disaster, the panic, and the imminent great depression, the lockdown has given us a sudden space to think, to concentrate on our immediate environment as time slowed to a crawl. This offers a new way of perceiving the city in which this festival takes place. Already, before this happened, London had started to feel unusual. A city that had become a giant property bubble felt on the verge of bursting altogether. A capital that last voted for the winner in a general election in 2005, that overwhelmingly voted to Remain in the 2016 referendum, and for Labour in both the 2017 and 2019 elections. London is increasingly a scapegoat, the home of a phantasmatic 'metropolitan elite' – a myth that sits oddly with the fact that more people rent, more people live in substandard housing, and more people work in casual, insecure jobs in the capital than anywhere else in the country. There are good reasons for hostility – London receives far greater funding for its infrastructure, culture and

Introduction

economy than anywhere else in Britain – but bashing London has become a weird national sport. Londoners outside of the capital often say they're from somewhere else when asked, just to avoid battling with nonsenses that we live in some sort of Sharia city state, that we live in a lawless crime-ridden dystopia, or that we all sit on millions in property wealth.

Many people live in London because here is where the jobs are. But most of us, I think, live here because we like it. It's freer, greener, denser, more complex, more interesting, than any other urban settlement on this island. And what makes London not just an interesting city but an almost miraculous one lies in how its 'convivial culture', as Paul Gilroy calls it – where you'll find the world in one street or housing estate, living together peacefully – can be found not just in the overvalued centre, but in its most apparently prosaic neighbourhoods, its most distant suburbs.

A lot of the appeal in Open House, in this enormously unequal but compressed city where the rich and the poor are cheek by jowl, comes in seeing how the other half lives. This can work both ways. My favourite memories of Open House come from juxtapositions in the same area – being able to walk from, say, Lord Leighton's outrageous Orientalist fantasy house with its opulent *Arabian Nights* interiors, up Portobello Road, to the housing estates of North Kensington, via the extraordinary Brutalist-baroque interiors of the former Czechoslovak Embassy and CZWG's fabulous green-tiled toilets in Westbourne Grove; or the next-door-neighbour Brutalist contrasts of Alison and Peter Smithson's now largely demolished Robin Hood Gardens and Ernő Goldfinger's now socially cleansed Balfron Tower, in Poplar. That trip was particularly uneasy, a class war *Through the Keyhole*. The flat in Robin Hood Gardens was a homely one, lived in by a council tenant from the north-east – customised and made her own, as the Smithsons would have wanted it. The flat in Balfron Tower had Mies chairs and bare walls, like a show home. A lot of people in Britain use the term 'a property' when they mean 'a home'. But, a lot of people who think like that are leaving London. At the start of lockdown, I watched out of the window as they were picked up by their parents. 'London is Open', ran the mayor's post-referendum slogan, but now it feels open in the wartime sense, too, as in Roberto Rossellini's *Rome, Open City* (1945) – a city in transition, on the cusp of something new.

So I find myself wondering, if I were to open my own house, or rather the 'ex-local authority' flat in a Southwark Council block that I rent, what would I be opening up? What would I want to show people? First of all, I'd want to praise the flat, without which my partner and I would have found lockdown incredibly bleak, as we work from home in the living room every day. Our block is one of two built soon after the end of the Second World War, mid-way up a late Georgian street, on the spot where

a VI rocket attack had instantly demolished several terraced houses.
It is three storeys high, pitch-roofed, faced in yellow London stocks,
and consists of eight flats with balconies, reached by short access decks
which are fluted in an art deco style that was then already out of fashion.
It is free-standing, surrounded on all sides by trees, some from the original
Georgian plan, with those closest to the windows dating from the post-
war rebuilding. It is architecturally mundane, but it quietly incarnates
the modernist trinity of *light, air and openness*. It has actively made my life
immeasurably better for the last five months. Not everyone has been so
lucky, but even so, London has a lot of places like this. Rather than being
celebrated, they have been pilloried. Yet there's nothing like a public
health disaster to reveal to people the importance of use values over
exchange values.

The communal garden between those two blocks built on that
VI bombsite tells another story. The open space was divided in two by
a metal fence, and then divided into eight small patches on either side
as allotments, presumably in the 1970s or 1980s when active tenants
associations started to come up with their own ideas for their own spaces.
But decades later, only one of the eight allotments is used, by one of the
three council tenants in these eight flats (or rather – his allotment isn't
used as such, but when the council's gardeners finally came to cut the
jungly undergrowth that had overtaken the communal garden, he stepped
in to protect *his* weeds from the chainsaws). The other five flats are
privately owned and extremely transient – at three years, we're already
among the longest established current tenants in the block – so getting
people together to convince the council to take the fences away so we can
have a single garden we can all actually use, rather than eight allotments
that nobody uses, is incredibly difficult. So often in London's housing and
planning, the problems of the 1970s have become such an obsessive focus
that the problems of the 21st century have been simply ignored.

But even then, the planning of this allegedly unplanned city has left
so many breathing spaces that can't be messed up. In walking distance
is Ruskin Park, Burgess Park, Camberwell Green, St Giles' Churchyard,
Peckham Rye, Brockwell Park; the places that tabloids have tried to
shame us out of (harmlessly) using as spaces of relief during the lockdown.
Alongside these is a density of three hundred years of architecture that,
even in the depths of quarantine, you can always explore – a permanently
open 'museum without walls', as Jonathan Meades called it. We've all
been trapped in that museum, and there's much worse places to be
stranded on this island.

For this guide I've asked thirty-three people – Londoners born
and bred and adoptive Londoners both – to write about their experiences

with their own suddenly open houses, in their own boroughs, in their own areas, locked down or not – the places they would take you and unlock their doors, if they could. They include writers, activists, historians, councillors, architects, journalists, and people who are none of these things. They take a variety of perspectives on the question of exploring London when the tourists have disappeared from the streets and the West End and the City from our mental maps, leaving us just with London as the place where we live. Along with that, you'll find all the things you'd find in the regular Open House festival guidebook in less challenging years – highlights from the thirty-three boroughs, little recommendations of places that might and might not be open during the Open House festival – I've written many of these myself.

I hope you enjoy this alternative guide. All of its entries are written in the hope that London can soon cease to be a bubble, a scam, a confidence trick – but instead, that it will, without losing its complexities, become a more simple thing: a place where people live.

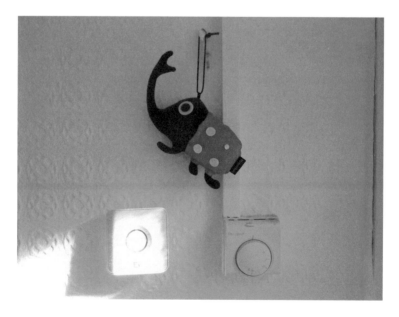

Owen Hatherley is the culture editor of *Tribune* and the author of several books, most recently *Red Metropolis – Socialism and the Government of London*, published by Repeater Books. Since 2015 he has been working on a gazetteer, *Modernist Buildings in Britain*, to be published by Penguin Books in 2021. Image: the doorway of the editor's flat, August 2020

She remained in Edgware, not knowing what next to do
Fatema Ahmed

When the kind of person who asks someone where they're from shortly after meeting them asks me that question, I always say 'London'. When they follow up, as they are likely to do, with, 'But where are you really from?' I say in my sprightliest manner, 'Edgware – you know, at the top of the Northern Line'. (Recently, but only if I think I can get away with it, my next move has been to ask in a concerned tone – 'And where are *you* from?'). As I write this in mid-July, it has been four months since I got the tube or any kind of public transport in London at all. This is the longest period of time I have spent in the suburb of my birth and the house where I grew up since before the Berlin Wall fell, and perhaps the very longest stretch since the late 1970s.

The reason I grew up here used to be visible from my front garden. In 1968, my father moved to Edgware to teach at a girl's grammar school. Orange Hill School was named after the road in Burnt Oak (one stop along the Northern Line or a short hop on the bus) where its counterpart for boys was located. In 1973, it turned comprehensive – a move welcomed by my father after his experience of moving between the extremes of secondary moderns and selective schools in Birmingham and Worcester. By the time my father died, in 2016, the school where he had taught was long gone. In the mid-1980s, Orange Hill merged with another comprehensive and all the constituent parts moved to a single site in Mill Hill. The school building – the last built by Middlesex County Council before its abolition – was demolished soon afterwards and its playing fields were sold for a cramped housing development by the end of the decade.

And at around the same time, I stopped being local in the same way. Starting secondary school meant taking the tube five stops every day and a zone 3–5 travelcard in term time. My two spells of living at home since university – in the early 2000s when I started working, and for a second time after my father's death – have both involved long tube journeys. I know every tree along the overground stretch of the Northern Line and sometimes still count the stops on the 13-minute journey between Edgware and Golders Green in seconds, but only when leaving here has been impossible have I realised that when I say where I'm from,

I mean this is where I am constantly getting away from. Over the last four months, trying to work out what Edgware actually is – and where it is – is the thing that has been getting away from me.

The extension of the Northern Line from Golders Green in 1924 and the completion of Edgware Way as part of the Watford bypass in 1927 are the reasons modern Edgware and its roads upon roads of 1930s houses exist. Before that, it's chief claim to fame had been as a resting place for pilgrims on their way to St Albans along Watling Street. In H.G. Wells' *The War of the Worlds* (1898), the narrator's brother is part of the exodus from London and Edgware is clearly still a village. One of my favourite paragraphs in any novel contains the lines: 'For a time he remained in Edgware not knowing what next to do [...] There was no fresh news of the invaders from Mars.'

Like the other Northern Line stations before Golders Green (and out of these Colindale was rebuilt in the 1960s and then again in 2010), Edgware tube station was designed by Stanley Heaps as an unshowy brick pavilion with a tiled roof and a colonnade. It's a modest structure but now that the art deco cinema has been demolished – along with all the other cinemas between Edgware and Golders Green – part of the public library has been turned over to (largely unused) office space by Barnet Council, and my post-war primary school fell victim to a particularly unfortunate PFI rebuild (and its grounds were of course sold off), it's the most constant local feature in my life.

Months of being confined to Edgware has made me feel that 40 years is too long to know anywhere in London and the place you're from most of all. I'm used to reaching corners all over the city to find that corner is under scaffolding with a new horror to come, but in the last few years I have seen so little of Edgware beyond my set routes that I've caught up on decades of change far too fast. The stretch of the A41 five minutes from my house is one of the few places that hasn't disappointed me (the manifestations of spring along the motorway verges were glorious); perhaps it can't disappoint because there was never anything there. The only other place that remains unchanged – and unrivalled – is also the only attraction I would recommend anyone go out of their way to visit: the B&K Salt Beef Bar on Whitchurch Lane, which is so confident in its excellence and so unfussed by the passing of time that it still has an 0181 telephone prefix on its minimalist shop sign. Strictly speaking, it is a few metres into Harrow – the borough of Barnet ends at the top of Edgware High Street – but since I have a London telephone number and a Harrow postcode, I feel more than entitled to claim it.

Even if you're not looking for a way out of Edgware, it always seems about to turn into somewhere else. I try to keep a tab on who the most

B&K Salt Beef Bar & Restaurant, Whitchurch Lane

famous person from here is at any one time, but there's so much disqualifying to be done. 'Oh, that's really Stanmore, or Burnt Oak, or Mill Hill' is usually the verdict. The 'London: North' instalment of Pevsner's *Buildings of England* cannibalises much of the earlier guide to *Middlesex* of 1951. The current volume edited by Bridget Cherry was published in 1988, and even 'with corrections' 11 years later was out of date in 1999. The section on my home borough begins condescendingly – 'Barnet has little immediate appeal for the architectural traveller' – and doesn't let up. My undeniable pleasure at finding mistakes regarding the places I know best is undercut by the fact that, on the two pages devoted to Edgware, which reads as if it was a struggle to get to two pages, two buildings (including the school where my father taught) have been demolished either totally or in part. A third – a Grade II listed pub called the Railway Tavern – is now derelict.

Apart from St Margaret's, a medieval church in the town centre, which was rebuilt in the 18th century, the only other notable pre-20th century building in the area used to be the Anglican Benedictine Abbey tucked between the A41 and Hale Lane, which is the road to Mill Hill. Much of its grounds were covered with large mock Tudor houses and private roads in the 1990s; only someone very lost could ever stumble across the site in passing. I haven't had any reason to go that way in a long time and, all too predictably, found on one of my first lockdown walks a large sign advertising the sale of houses and flats in 'Wildernesse House', formerly an abbey and cloisters designed by James Brooks. If anyone is willing to pay around £1.3m to live in part of a chopped-up Gothic Revival chapel in Edgware, which seems to be named on the same contrarian principle as Satis House (*chez* Miss Havisham) in *Great Expectations*, I would dearly like to know why.

If public – or semi-public – spaces in Edgware are fewer, there's more private space than there was. Most of the three-bedroom houses in my area are all frankensteined versions of their former selves – porches and loft conversions came in the late 80s, the garages were built over a decade later and now at least one house in every road seems to have had its roof removed entirely. Gardens are now driveways and lopsidedness prevails. I used to know the names of all our neighbours and we couldn't go anywhere without bumping into someone my father had taught, many of whom were the mothers of the children I went to primary school with. They often assumed that I was a grand-daughter and I refused to talk to any classmate who referred to my father as old (I wasn't a clubbable child). Our next-door neighbours were the last to move into this road before my father did. Their house was sold this year. My mother is now the street's longest-standing resident, but I don't think there's anyone who's keeping count except me.

But there is another story to tell about my part of Edgware. My contemporaries may have moved away long ago (not much sign of boomeranging here) and their parents are getting on – but families with young children are moving in everywhere. And lockdown led to an unexpected new development. I tend not to remember my dreams, but the ones I do hang on to are usually set in the Hampstead Garden Suburb, Kentish Town, or tube stations (my social-climbing subconscious aspiring to be in NW-something again – or just out of here). Not long ago, and for the first time, I dreamt about Edgware. The next time I speak in person to someone I haven't met before, and the question arises, I might take 'you know, at the top of the Northern Line' off my answer.

Fatema Ahmed is the deputy editor of *Apollo*.

East Finchley Station, Finchley, Charles Holden, 1939

A Charles Holden tube station outlier, not on the Piccadilly Line, and relatively messy in design, dictated by the need to integrate with what was then the North London Railway. Confused and blocky as a frontage, it is far superior on the platforms, with the stylish glass bubbles of its waiting rooms borrowed from Walter Gropius' 1914 model factory in Cologne. Eric Aumonier's splendid cuboid 'Archer' sculpture is perched on the edge of the viaduct; the sculptor would later design the angels in the stairway in Powell and Pressburger's ('the Archers') 1945 epic *A Matter of Life and Death*. Here, the archer points out from the heavenly air of the suburbs, towards subterranean inner London.[OH]

Grahame Park, Colindale, Greater London Council Architects Department, 1969–75

Grahame Park is a large 1970s housing estate in unpretty outer north London, with Brent Cross shopping centre and the M1 in one direction, and a massive redevelopment scheme on the site of a police training college in the other. Like so many estates of its era, the mistake is to walk, or worse still, drive its perimeter, where you'll find a dour collection of brick blocks with their services bunched up into hammer-shaped brick hammers on top. Walk into it, however, and you'll discover that it's one of the most humane, well-crafted and complex GLC estates, with terraces, mid-rise blocks and maisonettes linked together by tree-lined paths, plus Barbican-style

tile and brick paving underfoot. At the centre is a large 'town centre' of now mostly boarded up shops, several community centres and two churches – the design of both going in for conical, top-lit rotundas. The network of pathways – all at ground level – and the dark brick unite the various scales and shapes. The estate has been subject to regeneration for the last few years, with mixed results, though they include Peter Barber's very elegant Pegasus Court, with its 'Minoan' colonnade.[OH]

Mitre Inn, Chipping Barnet, 1633

By 1817, 150 coaches a day were passing through Chipping Barnet. The town became so famous for its coaching inns, of which The Mitre is probably the oldest remaining, that it acquired the nickname of the 'Town of Inns'. The Mitre retains its timber frame but has been refronted, with etched windows added in the 20th century.[Om]

Hampstead Garden Suburb Free Church and St Jude-on-the-Hill, Edwin Lutyens, 1911

Hampstead Garden Suburb was founded by social reformer Henrietta Barnett to be a model community where all classes of people would live together in attractive surroundings and social harmony. These twin eccentric Edwardian Churches, one domed, the other sporting a spire, are both by Lutyens and stand on either side of the central square. Both naves are barn-like with no clerestory but steep pitched roofs punctuated by vast dormer windows instead.[Om]

Phoenix Cinema, S Birdwood, 1910, refurbishment, Howes & Jackman, 1938

The Phoenix was opened in 1912 and is one of Britain's oldest cinemas. It has changed owners several times in its history, together with changes to its name and fabric. In 1938 it was remodelled into its current modernist facade and auditorium with art deco details. A community group took ownership to prevent it becoming an office block in 1985 and it has remained focused on serving locals with film screenings and events to this day.[Om]

Clitterhouse Farm, original architects unknown, 1890

With evidence of a moat and orchards around the original buildings, the area surrounding Clitterhouse Farm is recognised as being of special archaeological significance. The site has served as a dairy farm, sewage works, fever hospital, and housed suffragette Gladice Georgina Keevil. Community group, the Clitterhouse Farm Project, are now working to restore the site to a cultural resource conducting a feasibility study for the future of the farm with architects RCKa.[Om]

New Ground, High Barnet, Pollard Thomas Edwards, 2016

25 homes designed with the Older Women's Co-Housing, a group pioneering the idea of supportive community housing for women in later life. Architects Pollard Thomas Edwards worked with the group to develop a T-shaped layout focussed around shared facilities and communal gardens.[Om]

Pegasus Court (left, image by Pater Barber Architects), Hampstead Garden Suburb Free Church (centre), Clitterhouse Farm (right)

Clouds over Somers Town
Esther Leslie

Place yourself in the heart – or guts – of Somers Town, where Phoenix Road crosses Chalton Street, in a postcode more deprived than 84.6% of the others in England. Stand with your back to The Cock Tavern, the only *proper* pub remaining out of over thirty in this cat's cradle of streets. Scruffy, it deserves your backside, but have a heart too for this unfortunate spot, which offers uncommon consolation for the lonely wraiths who have cried rivers of beer on its carpets. It has long been the last halt for the Irish arrivals who turned left behind Euston station erewhile and did not stray much further than this expatriate patch of Sligo. The 1939 register of the civilian population in adjacent Levita House logs O'Brien, market van driver; Regan, gully man at St Pancras and lorry driver; Flynn, machinist for ladies' handbags; Fitzgerald, telephone and telegraph fitter, the wife a tailoress; McCarthy, railway porter; Burke, forewoman at H.M. Stationery Office and a boot repairer; Boyle, electrical wire man and motor body fitter. They followed riotous soldiers of the Light Dragoons, barracked here in the 18th century and, next, the potato blight escapees and navvies. They preceded the Irish who came to service the nearby hospitals and hotels after the Second World War.

Somers Town has been a trap, not a destination, not a stop on any bus or train, though it is an endpoint. Three railway termini, plus tube stations, off-load tens of millions of passengers to its edges yearly. Most move off unaware of the place that exists behind, above or beneath their feet. Transport skirts this enclave. When the frequent roadworks or burst water mains block and flood the roads or largescale redevelopment projects – such as HS2 or a future Crossrail station, to be called Euston-St Pancras – rip up the last old buildings, Somers Towners get stuck within the grid of streets, while thrown off-grid, forsaken in a densely historical place, abandoned by and abandoning history. This crossroads of Chalton Street and Phoenix Road is, like all crossroads, a charmed place between worlds, which is to say it may be a supernatural site that allows the past, its ghosts and hopes, to surface into the present. But this criss-crossing is also a vantage point to perceive a present in flux, the faintly glimmering traces of a once-was world overlaid by a shiny-new future undertaking.

Look left a little, across Phoenix Road: the greasy spoon, King's Café, used to be greasier, when it was called the Golden Tulip. In Shane Meadows' Eurostar-sponsored film, *Somers Town* (2008), its unlikely French waitress is a ticket out of the misery of a Somers Town cast only in shades of grey and racism. In its filmland, kaleidoscopic Paris fizzes as a freewheeling antidote to the dull cages of London lockups and poor quality housing, where work is a curse, but you are lucky if you can get it. Somers Town features as a place you are dumped in – only magic or luck lets you out. The film's sentiments were historically and politically asinine compared to those of *High Hopes* (1988), by once local director Mike Leigh: for all its caricatures, its ending poignantly elevates the viewer above the still Eurostar-less landscape of Somers Town, and muses on what Thatcherism did to the micro-logics of relationships, family, home and city and what hope might yet be discerned from a perspective nearer the clouds.

Next to the cafe, the fetish-wear purveyor, Breathless Latex Couture, has been there noiselessly signalling through glossy red and blue clingwear since 1998. It found an adequate home, at the arse-end of railway stations, an un-destination, anonymous enough. But what does it have to do with its building's distinguished past as a model housing estate, built by the council, with high design principles and a whiff of Red Vienna? Or those constructed by the church on the Sidney Estate, north along Chalton Street, with their predilection for priest-run gastro-pubs, nurseries, char-abanc beanos and art in everyday life, according to the motto: 'Housing is not enough'? Today the motto turns lamentful and it goes 'Not enough housing – for us, at least'. And there will be less and less, for Somers Town, as was, is being obliterated.

Look right along Phoenix Road. No. 42 on the corner – Pevsner men-tioned its canted oriels with swept roofs and arched windows. But between writing this and you reading it, it has been demolished. Now a memory, it housed, from 1931, a 'day nursery for fatherless children', countless kids' clubs and after-school tutoring sessions. On that footprint will rise another block for students, a population antithetical to historical ghosts, immune to being pulled into the quagmire of memory or long-term entrapment within the compact coop delimited by a square of fast car runs, Eversholt Street and Pancras/Midland, Crowndale and Euston Roads.

From the vantage of this crossroads, right, up Phoenix Road, there are barely traces of what was once the heart of Somers Town: Clarendon Square. This core of a speculative building project, begun in the 1780s, was designed as a higher-grade development for the professional and middle classes. The development, however, flung up in the shade of dusty brickworks, a smallpox hospital, slaughterhouse, soap boiling works and a House of Correction along a mucky river, attracted only those committed

Weir's Passage from Chalton Street, 1926, London Metropolitan Archives, City of London
(COLLAGE: the London Picture Archive ref 116311)

or condemned to the margins. In the new buildings, such as the 15-sided Polygon, were housed radicals William Godwin and Mary Wollstonecraft, as well as French Catholics fleeing the Terror, who ate their *boeuf à la mode* on Chalton Street. Later, in the 1820s, the Liberal Spanish and Spanish Americans came – their lurid tales of torture chambers and midnight trials, it is said, gave impetus to the literary revival of Gothic. Somers Town became a Spanish barrio, an abbreviated constitutional Spain, where publishers of political tracts mingled – sending out translations of Bentham and suchlike to influence the emergent Chilean republic, while Basque migrants gathered at the 'Tree of Guernica'. Nowadays, on the spot where the Polygon stood, there is Oakshott Court Estate, a 70s' council development, modelled on an Italian hill town, with each balcony possessing a piece of the sky – here still, at least, a dream of otherwise-otherwhere persists.

If it was obscured as an islet, offering cover to Romantics, anarchists and refugees in the 19th century and, in the 20th, squatters, Communist folk singers, pan-Africanists and filmmakers, it was not unseen. Somers Towners were dogged, time after time, by those who wanted to capture souls and improve bodies: social reformers and charitable types, priests of the churches, who built homes and missions, civic planners, lady rent collectors, Pearly aristocracy, medical professionals and nursery school pioneers. These sometimes made lives more liveable, and enabled tightknit communities to arise and to flourish. The newer ones to arrive, in the 1960s and 1970s, came from the Sylheti region of Bangladesh, to work in hotel kitchens and elsewhere. From the 1980s came Somalians, fleeing civil war. We tell fairy tales about community. Somers Town has had its share of horror stories too – and not just *Frankenstein*, whose author took her first steps here. However, Gilbert Bayes' undulled roundels for the spandrels of windows, featuring H.C. Andersen's *Wild Swans*, *The Princess and the Swineherd* and *The Tinderbox*, in Doulton's polychrome salt-glazed ceramics, could not be chipped off – unlike the washing-post finials of crows and dragons, trashed by irresponsible builders or stolen to be sold in auction houses. These items of communal luxury glow still as a gesture at that other, now almost impossible-to-imagine world of cradle-to-grave paternalism.

Look left, towards Brill Place, where a residential club once hosted railwaymen recovering from exhausting cross-country journeys. Now at the road's end, the Francis Crick Institute, a biomedical research centre, looms large. It slumped down on Somers Town – just as the British Library did on the former railway goods yard, when Bloomsbury wasn't having it. Somers Town crumbles from the edges. Facing the Crick are the self-proclaimed venture capitalists at Local Globe. From their cotton-cloud ceiling and rainbow chairs on yellow flooring they conceive, through mirrored windows, a future Palo Alto, if the all-too-analogue Somers Towners could be moved on and out.

Soon, on the park next door, formerly public land sold offshore by the council at a scandalously bargain price, a cloud-scraper 25-storey tower of 68 'luxury flats' will grab earth and sky and fling an obstruction into the free-roaming eye of any lingering Romantics. We ghosts of a defunded welfare state, social housing denizens, won't stop haunting in its broad shadow and reminding whoever will hear of those let-off words 'viability assessment' and so many dashed promises. But new lights will pale out our gloomy presence. The un-destination Somers Town becomes the other side of a bridge from the Eurostar, HS2, Crossrail 2, the new N1C, the UK HQs of platform capitalism, Cloud Computing and social media companies, whose reflected LEDs – up there on luxe-development round Granary Square – our elected leaders might hope to bask in.

Esther Leslie is Professor of Political Aesthetics at Birkbeck, University of London. Her books include *Hollywood Flatlands: Animation, Critical Theory and the Avant Garde* (2002); *Synthetic Worlds: Nature, Art and the Chemical Industry* (2005); *Derelicts: Thought Worms from the Wreckage* (2014), *Liquid Crystals: The Science and Art of a Fluid Form* (2016), and with Melanie Jackson, *Deeper in the Pyramid* (2018) and *The Inextinguishable* (2020). She is a long-standing member of the Somers Town history club, and is editor of *Spirit*, a journal about Somers Town.

The Regent's Canal

Visitors to Camden's markets can be forgiven for thinking that the Regent's Canal is a self-contained water feature, akin to a boating lake at a Disney theme park. But it is part of a 2000 mile transport network that has lasted over two centuries. Camden is one of five London boroughs that enclose this Canal. The Camden section descends via four locks from Cumberland Basin near Regent's Park to King's Cross, over a distance of under two miles. Today it serves both as a celebration of early 19th century architecture and as a transport system that supports construction and other needs. Canalside buildings have come and gone since 1820 but the canal walls, its twelve dual locks, tunnels, basins, lock cottages and many of its bridges have survived.

Two major landmarks still dominate the canal scene. The Interchange Building towers above Camden Lock Market, and at the lower end the Granary Building has become the centrepiece of King's Cross Central. These buildings are monuments to the interdependency between canals and railways.

The Canal is open to the public all year round, and still offers a welcome break from traffic and other urban stresses. Visitors are welcome to find their own way along the towpath, but they can book a guided walk – for further information, please visit the Regent's Canal Information Centre or the London Canal Museum.
Contributed by Ian Shadlock, Chair, Friends of Regents Canal

Sun House, Maxwell Fry, 1935; 66 Frognal, Connell Ward and Lucas, 1936; Frognal Close, Ernst Freud, 1937, all Hampstead

A collection of what would later be called 'case study houses' in close proximity in a very affluent corner of Hampstead, the first time that north London became the place for architects and intellectuals to try out their ideas on themselves before extending them on a wider, public scale. Of the three, the only one that would stand out as a design in any era is the house by Connell Ward and Lucas (here, largely Colin Lucas), a hard and complex design with hints of De Stijl – to the street, an elemental rationalist composition, to the back, a tight mesh of railings and cantilevered concrete. Sun House, up a private path nearby, is more of a standard 1930s International Style design, like one of the imaginary houses on a London Transport or Shell poster come to life, but still not entirely feeling real. In the other direction is Frognal Close, designed by one of Sigmund Freud's sons in a brown knobbly brick, already more insular and Anglicised. In Freud's houses you can see this radical import, this 'cultural Bolshevism' attacked by Nazis and English conservatives alike, gradually becoming just a regular English residential architecture of neat brick houses behind hedges in a cul-de-sac.[OH]

Cliff Road Studios, Camden, Georgie Wolton, 1968

Two elegant, precise blocks of artists' studios next to each other, by one of the major female architects in mid-century London. One block is a simple grid of rendered concrete and glass bricks, the other features thin, symmetrical ribbon windows with a projecting central volume, both on the same scale as the houses around. A decade or so later, Alan Colquhoun and John Miller would design similar schemes for Camden Council at Caversham Road and Gaisford Street. Cliff Road Studios were a restatement, unusual in that era, of modernism's first principles – clarity, rationality, and the air of the Parisian painter's studio – placed alongside a very new interest in London's mundane streetscape that comes from the bohemian culture of the later sixties.[OH]

Great Court at the British Museum, Foster + Partners, 2000

The courtyard at the centre of the British Museum was one of London's long-lost spaces. The departure of the British Library was the catalyst for recapturing the courtyard as a new public focus. At its heart is the magnificent Reading Room, which for the first time in its history is open to all. The glazed canopy consists of 6,000 individual steel members that are attached to each other by 1,800 connecting nodes. It has been built to an accuracy of plus or minus 3mm. The Court also forms a pedestrian link between the British Library to the river.
Contributed by Foster and Partners

Regent's Canal (left), Sun House (centre), Great Court (right)

We have been pondering our bookshelves more than usual this year, with two in five adults in the UK reporting the amount of time they usually devote to reading has doubled during the lockdown. Meanwhile, the shelves of many London booksellers have been gathering dust for months. Given Bloomsbury's long history of literary associations it comes as no surprise to discover that Camden plays host to more than its fair share, from the £1 bargain basement at long-standing radical and progressive Housman's (Caledonian Road, N1) to the antiquarian tomes that grace the windows of second-hand dealers on Charing Cross Road.

Running an independent bookshop is precarious at the best of times but when it comes to overcoming adversity Gay's the Word (Marchmont St, WC1N) has more experience than most. Founded in 1979, Gay's the Word was the first LGBT+ dedicated bookshop in the UK. Camden Council were initially reluctant to approve the lease but once the doors opened it rapidly became a vital hub for London's queer community, hosting meetings after hours for activist organisations including Lesbians and Gays Support the Miners. In 1984, amid a rising tide of homophobia in the early years of the AIDS epidemic, the premises were famously subjected to a raid by HM Customs and Excise leading to legal action against the shop's directors. This badge was worn by a supporter of the campaign to overturn the charges which garnered support from writers including Gore Vidal, whose works were among those seized. The case went to the European Court and charges were eventually dropped in 1986. Since then Gay's the Word has survived multiple acts of vandalism, burglaries and rent hikes.

The object you hold in your hands is a testament to the ways that books can transport us to inaccessible places. Open House encourages our readers to support their local independent book-shops and libraries to ensure they can continue to enrich our communities and provide space for new ideas to flourish. We recommend thelondonbookshopmap.org for an interactive guide to some of London's best independent and specialist bookshops.

Camden

Lapel badge, 1984–86, diameter 37mm, Museum of London (© Museum of London)

A Suburban Modernist Walking Tour
Joshua Abbott

The current borough of Enfield merged the Municipal Boroughs of Enfield, Southgate and Edmonton – and each of these brought their own characters to the new marriage. Edmonton was the industrial sector, home to factories and workshops. Southgate was the well to do, suburban area, made up of semi detached houses, and Enfield was the historic market town. Despite these different characters, all three areas had been altered by the encroachment of London in the first few decades of the 20th century.

The sprawling mass of Metroland, promoted by development companies with the promise of a slice of Eden for every Englishman, rapidly covered the fields of Middlesex in the 1920s and 30s. Development was haphazard, with estates being built next to small halt stations in the hope of luring clerks and shop workers out from the cramped city. The architectural default for these new suburbs was Tudorbethan, a mix of historical styles on the outside, with the mod cons of electricity and running water inside. However, this was also the age of art deco and modernism, continental flavours still finding favour with the British palate. By exploring the three different areas of Enfield, we can see how these new architectural ideas spread through the suburbs in the interwar years.

The Southgate area of the borough is home to two of the finest modernist buildings in the country. The Piccadilly Line stations of Arnos Grove (1932) and Southgate (1933) are probably Charles Holden's finest achievements, marrying form and function in an understated way. The stations were built as part of the extension to Cockfosters, hoping to capitalize on the spread of the suburbs towards Hertfordshire. As well as tube stations, Holden and Frank Pick, the CEO of London Transport, wanted the stations to be civic hubs, linking up transport networks and providing services. This can be seen particularly at Southgate, with its bus parade curving behind the circular station, and the masts designed to combine lighting, seating and timetables. Arnos Grove doesn't have the same level of connection as Southgate, but makes up for it with its exquisite design. Here, Holden combines brick, wood, steel and glass in a way that incorporates his Arts and Crafts training with stern northern European modernism.

Just a few minutes walk from Arnos Grove is another example of the influence of northern Europe on British modernism. The Bowes Road Clinic and Library (1935–40) is a combined swimming pool, library and medical centre, designed by the architects department of Middlesex County Councl (MCC), led by W.T. Curtis and H.W. Burchett. Their department was responsible for designing and building hundreds of schools, libraries, clinics and other public buildings in the interwar years, as the suburbs of London spread into Middlesex. They were not modernist ideologues, but were attracted by the ease of constructing steel-framed, flat-roofed buildings quickly and cheaply. The exteriors were influenced by the Dutch architect Willem Dudok and usually feature a central staircase tower and horizontal expanses of brick.

The more glamorous side of 1930s architecture can be seen nearby. The former ABC Southgate cinema (now a Jehovah's Witness Hall) opened in 1933, with its Moorish influenced art deco design by Major W.J. King, peering out onto the North Circular road. Back up the hill towards Southgate is speculative housing built throughout the 1920s and 30s. Brick and half-timbering dominates but in Abbotshall Avenue is a sliver of moderne; nine houses with curved sun trap windows and flat roofs built by brothers Frank and Charles Woodward from 1934–36. Underneath the white paint, these houses are actually brick, the Hollywood glamour only an inch thick.

Back towards Southgate station another 1930s staple can be found, luxury flats designed in the contemporary modernist style. Ellington Court (1936) is an early project by Frederick Gibberd, designer of Liverpool Metropolitan Cathedral and planner of Harlow New Town, amongst many others. The exterior utilizes the same rectangular brick design used by the MCC along with curving concrete door canopies. When completed, the apartments featured sophistications such as central heating, marble fireplaces and sliding doors. The apartment block has recently had an additional floor added to accommodate more 21st century luxuries.

To explore these buildings start at Southgate station, then head south on the High Street passing Ellington Court. Head west at the bottom of the hill, taking in Abbotshall Avenue, then south to Arnos Grove. After the station, walk east along Bowes Road for the Clinic, Pool & Library then a bit further along to the former cinema.

Further north, another walk can be made, exploring the same set of architects. Oakwood station (1933), although Holdenesque in appearance, was designed by C.H. James, who is usually remembered for his more traditional house designs in the garden cities of Letchworth and Welwyn.

Southgate station, bus sliproad and shopping arcade *c*.1960 (top, © Francis Frith Collection), Cockfosters station train shed (bottom, image by Daniel Wright)

The next and final stop on the Piccadilly line is Cockfosters (1933) by Charles Holden. Unassuming at surface level, this station's beauty lies underground, with a long train shed and platforms in exposed concrete, very much looking forward to post-war Brutalism.

In between these stations lie a couple of interesting interwar buildings. De Bohun School (1936) is again by the MCC, recognisable with its square staircase tower and continuous window bands. Next door to the main school building is the former library and health clinic, an example of the forward-looking vision of the county council. Around the corner is the Christ the King church and monastery, designed by Dom Constantine Bosschaerts, a Belgian monk, who had practiced as an architect before joining the Benedictine order. The building, only a small part of the original overall design, was completed in 1940 and consists of a reinforced concrete frame filled with white brick, and a tower with a recessed red cross.

To see these buildings start at Oakwood station, then head west turning onto Reservoir Road then Green Road, where you will find De Bohun School. Head through Bramley Sports Ground, passing the 1936 brick Clock Tower. Christ the King is a few minutes east. Then head through Cockfosters town centre to finish at the station.

Suburbia continues eastward, through Palmers Green and Grange Park, to the town centre of Enfield. Modernism is sparse here, but a couple of buildings stick out from the Neo-Tudor. In Grange Park we find another church, Grange Park Methodist (1938) by C.H. Brightliff. Not as starkly modernist as Christ the King, this church has a more Expressionist feel with its square brick tower, geometric patterned windows and Tree of Life murals over the doorways. Compare and contrast with the Nordic Classical St Peter's Church (1941) by Cyril Farey, just five minutes away. Just south of Enfield town centre is an interesting proto-modernist house, 8 Private Road (1883) by Arts and Crafts architect A.H. Mackmurdo. Built for his brother, Mackmurdo designed a stripped back house with roughcast walls and a flat roof, arguably as radical as anything his contemporaries C.F.A. Voysey or Charles Mackintosh produced.

These two buildings are about a 25 minute walk apart, in between are a variety of interwar detached houses; Neo-Tudor with half timber, Dutch Colonial with white walls and green pantiles and even some 1960s flat roofed houses in Walnut Grove.

We now come to the industrial part of the borough, containing Edmonton and Ponders End, which were built up with the railways expansion in the second half of the 19th century. Factories and workshops grew up around the River Lea and the Great Cambridge Road after its completion in 1924.

The vast majority of the factories built between then and 1939 have now been demolished. Nothing here matched the Golden Mile of Brentford's Great West Road, but the former Ripaults Factory (1936) is a nice example of the art deco era of industrial buildings. Designed by A.H. Dumford, the factory building is a long horizontal, balanced with a short rectangular tower, decorated with chrome strips and black trim.

Just south of the Riplault Factory is another MCC building, the former Enfield Technical College (1939), with its tall, rectangular tower, now part of Heron Hall Academy. Also in the area are two buildings by Edmonton Borough Architects Department, led by T.A. Wilkinson, one of the more proactive municipal architect departments. On Church Street is Edmonton Fire Station (1940), a fairly plain design with circular end towers and stone windows bands. Also by the architects department is the Queen Elizabeth Stadium on Donkey Lane, built between 1939–52. Despite its completion date, the building is thoroughly interwar, with a brick drum tower, overhanging concrete eaves and Crittall windows.

Once again these buildings are spread out. It may be better to visit them separately. The stadium, Ripaults factory and former Technical College can be visited in a 30 minute walk. The fire station is one stop south from Southbury station.

Joshua Abbott is a printer working in London and living in Welwyn Garden City. He has been running the Modernism in Metro-Land website since 2011, as well as conducting tours of the suburbs modernist and art deco buildings. His book *A Guide to Modernism in Metro-Land*, a guide to discovering the modernist treasures of London's suburbs, will be out on Unbound in October.

Industrial Past and Industrial Present

Enfield gave its name to both the Lee-Enfield rifle and the Enfield motorbike. Belling made the world's first radiant electric fire in a wooden shed that once stood behind the Hop Poles pub; the first commercial production of the incandescent lightbulb was here; and Ponders End became the centre of the UK electronics industry for much of the 20th century. The Ediswan Factory building is still here, unlisted, despite being the birthplace of the first radio valve and television cathode ray tube; for a beautiful Grade II listed factory site, however, the MAN factory round the corner in Southbury Road is an art deco stunner.

The maker spaces at Building Bloqs inherit this local tradition of industry and imagination: in one of the workshops they are building an Interstellar Portal, though it's decorational rather than functional. The largest film and TV studio in London, OMA, has just opened its doors this summer, and Metaswitch – makers of programmes for Microsoft Windows – are building an office in Enfield Town. The long history of market gardening around Crews Hill and the Lee Valley has morphed into craft beer and gin manufacture, award-winning Forty Hall English champagne, and the community cafe at the Dugdale centre championing locally sourced produce with its EnFood programme. 21st century 'factories' all.
Contributed by Enfield Council

Enfield Business Centre, RCKa, 2014

A modest refurbishment of a 1970s office building deploying a few strategic moves to great effect. The addition of a glazed entrance hall – its vaulted canopy now tipped with gold cladding – provides a multifunctional space on the ground floor opening onto a newly pedestrianised forecourt by architects We Made That. Doors and partitions were reused and repositioned to reduce building waste and cut costs.[Om]

Mevlana Rumi Mosque (formerly Passmore Edwards Public Library), Edmonton Green, Herbert Passmore and William Douglas Caroë, 1897

Originally built in the 19th century as one of the 24 libraries established by the journalist and politician John Passmore Edwards, this brick Victorian building has been adapted several times. It became a Sikh gurdwara for some years after the library functions were moved, then in 2008 was reopened as a mosque and community centre. The mosque takes its name from the 13th century Islamic theologian, Mevlana Jalaluddin Rumi while still bearing the Passmore Edwards signage above its door flanked by Ionic pilasters.[PH]

Friends Meeting House, Winchmore Hill, John Bevans, 1791

Many dissenting religious sects formed in the mid-17th century though these groups were severely suppressed. The Society of Friends, also known as the Quakers, was founded in 1647 by George Fox but anyone attending a Quaker meeting could be fined or imprisoned. Winchmore Hill, then an isolated village, was remote enough to not attract the attention of the authorities, proving ideal for an illegal Quaker group to put down roots. The first meeting house was completed in 1688, the year before a Toleration Act allowed Quakers to meet more freely. By 1790 the old Meeting Room was reaching the end of its useful life and a new one, the present building, was built in 1791 and is attributed to John Bevans, the earliest known architect who worked extensively for Quaker clients. It is a simple building of local yellow stock brick with a central double door under a bracketed cornice hood, flanked by large sash windows under gauged brick arches.[PH]

Padstow Road, Perry Mead and Hedge Hill, Peter Barber Architects, 2018

In the last four decades, British local authorities have largely refrained from building public housing in anywhere near the quantities they once did following the Second World War. Yet, while few boroughs have in-house architecture departments as they did in the post-war years, London's local authorities are once again tentatively building. Peter Barber, once an acolyte of Richard Rogers and now leading his own practice, is an architect whose council-commissioned work is especially compelling. In Enfield these three projects, Perry Mead, Padstow Road and Hedge Hill, reworked disused garage sites into characterful new housing. With an architectural language mixing southern European vernacular influences with Alvaro Siza-like compositions and arch-peppered brick facades, Barber seems to have hit on a rare recipe admired by contemporary critics and traditionalists alike.[PH]

MAN factory (left), Enfield Business Centre (centre) Friends Meeting House (right)

London's Next Big Opportunity
Aditya Chakrabortty

I was born right next door to Haringey, at North Middlesex Hospital, and I have been a neighbour to the borough ever since. When my mother took me from our home in Edmonton to her primary school in Hackney it was through Seven Sisters we drove. When she needed groceries on the way back, it was at Bruce Grove market we stopped. The streets taking us across to Tottenham then onto Stamford Hill were the first I ever saw, and when the time comes finally to shut my eyes they will probably be the last, too. It is not the grandest of inheritances – neither glistening emerald fields nor smart and shiny postcodes – but it is mine.

No boundary marks off Edmonton from Tottenham. You walk up Fore Street, past my old library (or one of them: as a child, I was a regular at three), over the North Circular and carry on past the tower blocks. Then Enfield peters out into Haringey, although the only clue to the changing of the municipal guard is a small sign half-hidden by bushes. Everything remains the same: the chicken shops, the retail parks, the traffic that speaks in inches. These two adjoining neighbourhoods are haunted by the same ghost – that of the light industry that decades ago thrived along this corridor and that buzzed away inside the surrounding giant sheds, before sending people off into the local houses, shops, pubs.

In place of the old furniture factories there is today an IKEA; the workshops have turned into warehouses and, as a council officer once said to me of Edmonton, working prosperity is now working poverty. It is a story the post-Brexit political classes will tell themselves about the North but that they don't dare admit of the UK's one supposedly-indisputable success story: London.

All this was unfolding during my 1980s childhood, yet growing up on the other side of the road, it seemed to me then that Tottenham had a quicker metabolism. It sent news – sometimes the bleakest kind, such as the deaths of Cynthia Jarrett and Keith Blakelock. It served up excitement, such as the jolt felt throughout my house in June 1987, as Bernie Grant became one of the first black Britons elected MP. It was the rougher, tougher, faster neighbour.

And the borough of Haringey offered other delights. When I had destroyed too many clothes, my parents would frogmarch me into Wood Green Shopping City, take me inside C&A and straight across to the discount rails, where my puppyish body would be cantilevered into and out of various bargain items of nylon. If you're thinking this is the stuff of pre-teen meltdowns then you are right. I had more scenes in the sale section of C&A then I did at the school Nativity.

Those days of ignominy came to an end after landing a Saturday job. Now I hunted for clothes and books in central London – heading into Seven Sisters station and running down the escalator onto the southbound Victoria Line. And if I was feeling especially flush I'd stop on the way back at Body Music, the then-sprawling reggae shop right next to the tube.

Think about these places: Broadwater Farm, Wood Green, and Tottenham High Road. What do they have in common? They don't feature in the architectural beauty catalogues. They boast neither art deco curves, nor eco-conscious fanciness. They are landmarks, not attractions; prosaic not spectacular; meant to be used, not gawked at. They don't feature in the news, unless it's for the wrong reasons. They are quotidian, vital, forgettable.

'The daily papers talk of everything except the daily,' remarked French writer Georges Perec. 'What's really going on, what we're experiencing, the rest, all the rest.' So it is with the buildings in which we live our lives: the drab, the banal, the essential – they all become background.

How we choose what we venerate and what we ignore is now the stuff of national news. This has been the summer of toppling statues, of chucking slave-trader Edward Colston in the Avon and (with any luck) sending down Cecil Rhodes from Oxford. Mere symbols, tut the critics; yet one of the things they symbolize is how the divide between importance and obscurity is decided by others, without consultation. And that line, in all its toxic arbitrariness, runs through lots of parts of our lives.

Politicians of every hue agree we need more public housing, yet don't actually build much. Government ministers cry out for 'shovel-ready' infrastructure projects to fund, yet starve of cash our social infrastructure – the youth centres, the libraries, the parks.

Everyone knows what happens when the hard infrastructure breaks – the lights go out, trains suddenly stop, bridges collapse. But the destruction of social infrastructure has a huge cost too. In his recent book *Palaces for the People*, American sociologist Eric Klinenberg lists some of the consequences: 'People reduce the time they spend in public settings and hunker down in their safe houses. Social networks weaken. Crime rises. Older and sick people grow isolated. Younger people get addicted to drugs…Distrust rises and civic participation wanes.' It's true of Donald Trump's America, of course, but it applies to Brexit Britain, too.

Friday night at Seven Sisters indoor market, November 2018 (image by Mario W.Ihieme)

What drives this process? A chronic lack of investment and a contempt for the things that really matter to people.

Which brings us back to Haringey. I have reported my *Guardian* column from here a number of times over the past few years and have noted how, in 2014, the council's then-director of regeneration described parts of Tottenham as a 'war zone', a remark she later described as 'taken out of context'. In 2017, she went with two senior council officers and two councillors on the cabinet to a four-day property fair among the yachts of Cannes, armed with a prospectus for potential investors in Tottenham and Wood Green. Titled 'London's Next Big Opportunity', it told would-be developers of the area's terrific transport links and 'bustling high streets'. But in this brochure flogging off an entire locality, something was missing.

Among the architects' drawings and artful photos of local residents and businesspeople, there featured not a solitary Black face. A page was devoted to a picture of a skinny white model – not, in my experience, a typical sight on Tottenham High Road – and another was given over to blokes clutching pint glasses and cabbages. But of Tottenham's single largest ethnic group, there was not a trace. Oversight or erasure? Those who suspect the worst point to the council's own 2015 assessment of its housing strategy, which concluded: 'There is a possibility that over time black residents may not benefit from the plans to build more homes in the borough... White households may benefit more easily.'

Another colour matters here: red. Almost since its creation, the borough of Haringey has been Labour-run. Just a short tube ride from parliament (that brochure got some things right), here is a one-party state – whose rulers are not always tempered by their voters. Local politicians have chased wild fantasies of privatising all council property, bulldozing them and building a shiny new town centre with lots of new homes – and no targets for social housing. Although that plan was derailed by massive protest, the attitude driving it was summed up for me by one local. The politicians in charge of her borough saw 'Tottenham as a giant brown-field site,' she said. 'But it's our lives.'

To see that point with painful clarity, go to Seven Sisters. Next door to where I used to buy records sit the ruins of a long-abandoned department store that is now a hub for Latin American migrants: an indoor market, a labour exchange, a community hall. Were the Latin Village in Brooklyn, it would be tourist gold. But in Haringey, traders have spent years facing displacement under a plan that originally envisaged a 'Pasta Express' and a 'Coste Coffee' and a market operator who called them 'bloody illegal immigrants' (he was only removed in late June, on separate grounds).

Nary a masochist would snub investment, but only a fool would not ask on whose terms it was being made. In any contest of the shiny against the dowdy, the novel versus the forgotten, the Opportunity Area and the warzone, it's easy to predict which will come out on top. Some of the same spirit has informed government policy on Covid-19 this year and been shown as badly wanting: think of all those ministerial boasts about 'game-changing' tests and 'world-beating' apps, which in the end were not a patch on the test-and-trace regimes of Kerala and Vietnam.

In 2012, the London School of Economics academic Suzanne Hall studied 199 retail units along Rye Lane in Peckham. This kilometre-long array of halal butchers and cheap clothes stalls was seen as 'a mess' by some of its middle class neighbours, who pined instead for bars and art galleries. Yet Hall found a thriving economy, where the 'slithers of space' taken up by tiny mobile-phone shops 'commandeered the equivalent rental per square footage to retail space in Knightsbridge'.

This was Harrods, on a high street in south London. It was also the entrepreneurial many-tongued multiculturalism boasted about by the capital's bankers and university admissions officers and marketeers – only one that couldn't readily be turned into 'London's Next Big Investment Opportunity'.

Much has been said this year about how the overlooked is now essential, and counting some of the lowest paid workers among the most valued. Something similar can be said for our cities. Let us judge them not on the income they generate but on the wages they pay, not for their gleaming towers but for the decent homes they provide. Let us judge them, in short, not for the world-beating activities in their centre but on how they treat the people who live on their edges.

Aditya Chakrabortty is senior economics commentator for the *Guardian*, where he writes a regular column. In December 2017, he won the British Journalism Award for Comment Journalist of the year. His work has also won a Social Policy Association award, a Harold Wincott prize for Business Journalism and he was also a finalist for an Orwell Prize for journalism in 2014, 2015, 2016 and 2017. He is a regular broadcaster on radio and television, appearing on Newsnight and Question Time, and tweets @chakrabortty. Aditya is now working on his first book, to be published in 2021 by Penguin / Allen Lane.

Hornsey Town Hall, Haringey, Reginald Uren, 1933–1935

A seminal building, insofar as it might be the first use of W.M Dudok's monumental version of Dutch avant-garde architecture as the appropriate style for British interwar bureaucracy. Dudok's style has been adapted to make his manner even more compromised – note the Georgian keystones on the windows to the main hall – but the quality of workmanship and the sense of generous but tasteful public splendour are all very admirable, as is the scale of the tall tower that marks it out from a distance. The detailing of the stairwells, with cast-iron screens and fluted marble columns, is gorgeous. Currently run as a community centre, but slated to become a luxury hotel. The Borough Architect's 1960s Library nearby is also worth a visit, with its sculptural pool, abstract mosaic and clear glass reading room.[OH]

Garton House, Hornsey, Alan Colqhoun and John Miller, 1980

Up on the hills of Hornsey, with views down to the Arsenal Stadium below and Canary Wharf beyond, this is in one of those areas you only really get in London – Victorian bourgeois villas, interwar tenements, Brutalist complexes, 70s vernacular low-rise flats and fussy 80s postmodernist council terraces, all threaded together with trees, pubs, grocers and streets – the sort of real but relaxed triumph that none of the narratives about urban planning have much room for. The buildings here are always decent, but only one of them is worth seeing as a major work of architecture. Colquhoun and Miller's high-rise council tower block on the top of the hill, built long after high-rise ceased to be fashionable and accordingly reserved only for single people, uses similar materials to everything around – yellow stock brick, glass, and brown wooden window frames (it originally had glass brick panels, which have sadly been removed in a recent renovation). That's what it is, baldly described, but the command of proportion is masterful. Colquhoun was a theorist and historian of some renown, and here all those Renaissance architectural textbooks have culminated in this effortlessly elegant grid, symmetrical, restful and pure. Look at the private high-rise next door to see the difference; Savile Row next to Primark, and it's the council tenants that got the finest.[OH]

Parkside, Finsbury Park, Sergison Bates, 2004–2008

When these three small blocks of Housing Association flats opposite Finsbury Park were finished, the *Architects Journal* put them on the cover as an explicit provocation – I don't think the headline was 'does it offend you yeah?', but that was the gist. It is now very hard to understand quite why they caused such animus, unless you recall what new London housing was generally like at that time – for a telling example, the explosive polychrome clad-flats designed by CZWG by Arsenal stadium are very nearby. This, though, is tough, dour housing recalling very ordinary post-war council housing; not the sculptural, Brutalist, coffee-table book stuff but concrete framed boxes with brick infill and modest walkways, only with more Georgian, vertical window proportions. More than ten years on, this has become the dominant aesthetic of London luxury living, the self-described New London Vernacular. Once again, nobody is quite so obsessed with fashion and quite so in denial of it as architects. But this scheme will stand even when it goes out of fashion again, as it will. From the park, it is scaled to look like a pair of Victorian villas, but up close you can see how geometrically strange it is, with what looks like a grid from a distance turning out to be a complicated system of turns and recessions to create balconies, extra sunlight, and secluded semi-public spaces for residents. The 'traditional' look is achieved not via appliqué brick cladding, but through vigorous and thorough construction, with a massive yet precisely detailed concrete frame, and satisfyingly chunky warm red bricks.[OH]

Hornsey Town Hall (left, image by Remi Wanless), Garton House (centre), Parkside (right, image by Stefan Müller)

Without Causing Offence to the Squares
Daisy Froud

When I was working at Harrow Civic Centre, for a few days in 2017 it became the headquarters of the Israeli cabinet. Visits turned dreamlike. One of those dreams where everything is ostensibly as it should be and yet, in small but confusing ways, is not.

In assuming a costume, the Centre's archetypal form became somehow hyper-visible. As it must have been to the location scouts of *7 Days In Entebbe*, scanning for somewhere institutional but groovy, severe but comfortable, to film their action thriller. On the one hand, the mid-20th century civic order beamed loudly with pride and polish: the varnished panelling, the open-tread stairs, the public art, the leather trimmings, the troughs of glossy pot plants. Less flatteringly, the stereotyped bureaucratic maze of this architecture was simultaneously under a spotlight (in this case literally: ranged along the facade, peering in windows like Triffids). When all signs are in Hebrew, if you can't read Hebrew, then every room off every corridor is potentially committee room 5A.

Opened in 1973, Harrow Civic Centre is today frequently a film set – a useful, if lightly disruptive, revenue source for economically constrained times. ('During the filming, some inconvenience to the civic centre users is inevitable, mostly due to the parking suspension last week, but the civic centre has been working smoothly', observed local blogger Harrow Monitoring Group.) But it debuted on celluloid even before it was operational, as the star of a 22 minute Super 8 silent feature: *The Building of the Harrow Civic Centre, 1970–1972*, a work of dynamism, new beginnings and optimistic civic dreams.

The film opens with a panning shot of an architectural model: a series of rectilinear white pavilions with grey roofs, trimmed by landscape, connected via walkways, and encircled in a lover's knot of tarmac. Everything is a neat 'block', apart from the Chamber: 'staff block', 'office block', 'theatre and halls block'. In the scenes that follow, there are lots of men, looking at, and busy doing, things. Older ones, low on hair but big on overcoats, nod beneath signs that read 'Erection of Civic Centre'. Bare-chested younger ones, with hair but without site helmets, carve a huge underpass through soil, and wedge vast rebar frames into place for foundations, which they fill with soupy streams of concrete. Others, in shirtsleeves and ties, jump onto machinery and gesticulate in approval. They all smoke. At ceremonial moments, there are women too, in hats like sugar-spun cakes, sitting on orange plastic chairs, and holding programmes in white-gloved hands.

In this film, demolition balls swing joyfully through Victorian gables. An intertitle explains: 'The 11 acre site of the complex was previously occupied by residential units, most of which had deteriorated to a very low state, and the construction of the Civic Centre at one stroke cleared a dilapidated area and injected new, vigorous life into the environment'. In this it is again typical of post-war development of its type, as 'town halls' were replaced by civic complexes across the UK from the early 20th century onwards. Historian Peter Larkham describes how expansion in scale, complexity and service provision of local government led to compulsory purchase and comprehensive clearance, sometimes of entire quarters of towns, in order to accommodate, with appropriate municipal grandeur, all necessary functions in 'single-use precincts'.

Although the burghers of Harrow had dreamed of this since the 1930s, the catalyst came with Harrow's departure from Middlesex to become one of the 32 new Greater London boroughs under the 1963 Local Government Act. An architectural competition was launched. Basil Spence led the jury. Of 68 entries, that of Eric G. Broughton – designer of Enfield Civic Centre – was judged to best meet the brief: 'a scheme which would satisfy the avant-garde without causing offence to the squares'.

And so the camera starts to roll. The Mayor waves, and plants a shovel. The old is razed, and the new is dug. And then, at 13:12, we glimpse the new Centre – it's suddenly UP! And after all that mud and tar and aggregate and cement, it's so gleaming and so white! The image still impresses: elegantly organised storey-upon-storey of bright reinforced concrete panels. Above a cloud of rubble, a modern civic castle floats against the sky, with a hint of castellation, and a cloister-ish row of ground floor arches, and even a tiny water feature moat. The real moat is yet to come: a sea of cars that will flood around once it is open for business. And that remains dominant in today's first impressions of the Centre, as you pick your way through to the entrance.

All the people in the film seem to be white too, save for one construction worker. Which is striking; Harrow today is one of the UK's most ethnically diverse local authority areas – with the highest population of Indian descent nationally, and the highest density of Gujurati Hindus – as well as number one for religious diversity. (It's said if any two people meet, there's a 62% chance they'll be of different religions.) This monoculture locates the film firmly in the past. Most of Harrow's first generation of South Asian heritage residents settled in the borough in the years after 1972 – the same year the Centre was completed – following their expulsion from Uganda.

While accounts make clear that migrants were not immediately made welcome at either personal or institutional levels, today the borough's diversity is a source of pride. I remember the figures above less from reports, more from people sharing them when I ran the recent 'community engagement' process for Harrow's planned *new* Civic Centre. Diversity was seen as integral to Harrow's identity, to be celebrated by both programme and architecture. The design team, rightly, was queried about their Eurocentric precedent images. Lovely as these Scandinavian town halls are, people said, there are also great civic buildings in Asia and Africa – can we take inspiration from some of those too?

The new building, by Gort Scott Architects, is destined for a more accessible – and compact – site on the High Street of nearby Wealdstone, contributing to wider regeneration of this 'deprived' town centre while allowing the Council to make necessary 'efficiencies'. In a reversal of the 20th century narrative, the scale, and spatial demands, of local government are contracting. If this project goes ahead, the current Centre site will revert to housing, named 'Poets Corner' after the estate demolished there in the 70s.

Imagining a new Civic Centre meant a proper conversation about what 'we', in 2020, mean by, and require from, one. This was something both the Council and – importantly – the citizens of Harrow were very much up for; Harrow is one of the most proactively civically-minded places I've ever worked, if that can be measured by numbers of voluntary groups, civic and resident societies.

The dream of a Civic Centre endures, but different from before: more communal, less bureaucratic. Opinions inevitably differ about what happens there, and how it looks, but some things were clear. (1) Fewer people will go there for services. Though it's vital that when they do, particularly when vulnerable, that they feel welcome, and can easily locate the help they need. (2) While the pomp of Chambers and Halls is no longer a priority – civic activity (and civil society) needs space – and inclusive, *affordable* space – to thrive, space for people to meet, plan, and celebrate, and to make what they do *public*. And (3) above all, a Civic Centre in 2020 needs to be in the ownership – and for the free use – of the people, not just 'the Council'. Interestingly, formal or constitutional politics was rarely brought up. But in a discussion about the building's appearance, and the need for it to have a 'front' – or not – an intriguing point was made: 'If the Mayor wants to launch a campaign, or someone wants to protest, where do they go to stand? In front of the Civic Centre! One, you need space for that and, two, the building needs to be recognisable in the photographs.'

LONDON BOROUGH OF HARROW

The New CIVIC CENTRE

Construction work on Phase 1 commenced on 2nd February, 1970, and Departments took up occupation on 27th November, 1972. The building contract, worth nearly £1·8m, was awarded to Messrs. F.G. Minter Ltd......

......this is the story of the work between 1970 and May 1973.

Stills from *The Building of the Harrow Civic Centre, 1970–1972* (London Screen Archives and Headstone Manor Museum)

Council Departments

the end.....
of the beginning

Of course, Harrow's people have, have a long connection to the culture and industry of photography. Kodak Eastman was one of the borough's biggest employers. Their first non-US factory opened there in 1891: the largest outside the States – employing 6,000 people by the 1950s – and the last in the world to close, in 2017. When speaking to me of the desire to protect Harrow's skyline from development, for many Harrovians this related not necessarily to preservation of generic space, but to a wish not to crowd views of the Kodak Chimney – a much-loved, centenarian, 213ft industrial steel 'spire'. (The factory itself is now demolished, replaced with housing by Barratt: 'Eastman Village'. But they've kept the chimney, as part of the village energy centre.) This being the case, it's perhaps no surprise that the first breaths of the Civic Centre were captured on Kodak Super 8 film, and that Mr. R.W. Raby (public relations) instinctively reached for his cine-camera as the workmen reached for their tools.

When I was working at Harrow Civic Centre, my favourite spot was in the formal first floor entrance lobby, by the open-tread stair, where nearly 1,000 glazed tiles are arranged in a gloriously, gaudy grid over the landing wall. This is the Kodak Mural, a 1974 gift to the people of Harrow, designed by Pentagram and made by ceramicist Kenneth Clark. Each colourful tile captures a graphic fragment of Harrow past – faces, buildings, signage, words, numbers – applied via a special photographic screen-printing technique. 1,000 memories brightly frozen by technology, heralding the promise of a new civic future. Roger Bannister, Byron, Winston Churchill, Dave, 13th Harrow, Bingo 1st Floor, fish and chips, Gay, Danger, 25p. You should go and see this ceramic mural sometime. When the Centre is demolished, I'm sure they will save it.

Daisy Froud designs tools and processes to support collective decision-making about future buildings and the future of existing places. She has an MA in Cultural Memory, and is a Teaching Fellow at The Bartlett School of Architecture, where she specialises in spatial politics and the role of non-professionals in architecture and planning.

2, 4, 6, 8 and 10 Valencia Road, Stanmore, Douglas Wood, 1934; 1–6 Kerry Avenue, Stanmore, Gerard Lacoste, 1937

Emerge at the northernmost end of the Jubilee Line, cross the road and you'll find a reverse L-shape street of big suburban villas, whose builders decided to let themselves go a little and experiment with the new forms that had just been introduced to Britain by Central European exiles. They didn't do so in a particularly rigorous way – no free plans, no pilotis or Corbusian roof terraces here, just a shift in the design of semis towards smooth white surfaces, cylindrical glazed stairwells, an air of modernity rather than nostalgia, and in some of the Kerry Avenue houses, asymmetrical, sprawling layouts. They exude the suburban values of exclusivity and luxury to a much greater degree

than your average mock Tudor house, because these houses are *special* – around them, the half-timbering goes on until it subsides into the green belt.[OH]

Kenmore Park School, Curtis and Burchett, 1938

Middlesex County Council had a 'progressive' architects department in the thirties, and built many schools, libraries and suchlike in the north-western suburbs, such as the great little Arnos Pool, but it's their schools that have survived best. Built just before the war, they're straightforward Dutch brick modernism, of the sort that you'll find in abundance in the suburbs of Amsterdam, Rotterdam and Utrecht. Bulky, often curved forms, beautifully detailed, pulled into asymmetric yet monumental profiles with simple playgrounds, all in very ordinary residential areas. Unusually for interwar suburbia, there's no garden city dreams of a lost Eden, which makes schools like this into a glimpse of what most British architecture in the interwar years might have looked like were it not for a collective paroxysm of nostalgia and fear. All of the Middlesex schools are worth a glance, but this is the most convincing – a brick prow at the centre of a rather wan housing estate, with cubist stairwells and long flanking wings, transplanting the shabbier end of Harrow to Hilversum.[OH]

St Paul's Parish Church, Nugent Cachemaille-Day, 1937

A suburban instance of proto-Brutalism. Grey rendered walls give Cachemaille-Day's brick structure the muscular air of later post-war municipal architecture. Behind its skinny lancet windows the nave is restrained and barn-like – a more frugal gesture in the direction of Grundtvig's Church in Copenhagen, a masterpiece of brick ecclesiastical architecture completed only a decade earlier.[PH]

Northwick Park Hospital, John Weeks, 1970

Not long ago, the capital's last surviving paternoster elevator, connecting ten storeys of Northwick Park Hospital,

was standing idle, long since decommissioned by hospital administrators. However, amid the Covid-19 pandemic, conventional elevators are nearly impossible to virus-proof so, thrillingly for architecture nerds, London's only paternoster is now back in action ferrying doctors and nurses around Weeks' pioneering seventies wards. Pioneering, because Weeks was exploring a new approach to healthcare design in which each department was organised independently, with its own appropriate built form, and then connected to a central 'hospital street' with corresponding channels for pipes, cables and other services. Each of these departments was left with a 'free end' for future enlargement – able to grow and change over time giving the hospital a sense of permanent incompleteness but great flexibility.[PH]

Kenton Library, Curtis and Burchett, 1939

Built in the Middlesex County Architects Department's style, which gave distinctive architectural form to the London suburbs. One of the best examples of interwar library design in London. An unusual feature is the large garden which is accessible to visitors.[Om]

Heath Robinson Museum, ZMMA, 2006

Beloved by many architects, cartoonist Heath Robinson once lived near to the site of this purpose-built museum in Pinner Memorial Park which displays a collection of his work. The air conditioning ducts and lighting runs are suitably eccentric, recalling the many whimsical contraptions Robinson depicted.[PH]

Valencia Road (left, images by Julian Osley) and Heath Robinson Museum (right, image by ZMMA)

"Bloom's"
TM
WORLD-FAMOUS
KOSHER FOOD PRODUCTS
STREET LONDON, E1 7RA 130, GOLDERS

The way that London eats has changed dramatically during the Covid-19 pandemic. Empty supermarket shelves and queues outside foodbanks became regular occurrences, while footballer Marcus Rashford successfully pressured the government to continue providing school meal vouchers for qualifying children outside of term time; a scheme that was otherwise due to be cancelled.

Perhaps in future, post-pandemic cities will rely on more locally sourced supply chains for their food. In the first few months of the pandemic, small independent stores saw a 69% increase in sales as supermarkets were felt to be unsafe. There are already a surprising number of food production facilities operating on different scales within London. These include Dagenham (Central Park Nursery, RM10) and Hackney City (Goldsmiths Row, E2) farms and the businesses at the Cedar Way Industrial estate (N1C) in Kings Cross which supplies fish, meat, muesli and much more to schools, offices and the like across the city.

Elsewhere independent restaurants have begun offering takeaway or collection services so their regulars can enjoy socially distanced fine dining. For example, classic East End cafe E. Pellicci (Bethnal Green Road, E2) begun offering their famous lasagne to be picked-up and heated from home and new Kurdish Camberwell favourite Nandine (Vestry Road, SE5) have been sending out their mezze boxes by bike. We love this takeaway soup tub from Bloom's Whitechapel, a Jewish eatery first founded by Lithuanian immigrant Morris Bloom in Brick Lane in 1920, which also had a branch in Golder's Green. Bloom's closed down in 2010, but there are still plenty of Jewish spots offering takeaways, including Beigel Bake (Brick Lane, E1), Reubens (Baker Street, W1U) and Monty's Deli which delivers a full reuben sandwich pack – sauerkraut and all.

Barnet

Bloom's food packaging, c.1994, 70 × 110mm, Museum of London (© Museum of London)

The View from Archway
Jude Wanga

It starts at the Archway Bridge. Facing south, on a clear day, or a clearer night, you can see the whole of London laid out before you. How will the future look? Will you work in Canary Wharf, glittering to the left? Or is it the BT Tower for you, shining bright on the right? Then you turn around, facing northbound, looking out to Highgate and the A1. Will you go north, leaving London behind for pastures new?

These are the thoughts that crossed my mind aged 9. Islington has been my home and sanctuary for thirty years. Arriving as a three-year-old asylum seeker from Congo, I had no idea how important a borough of many faiths, races and faces would be in shaping the person I would eventually become. Where you spend your formative years can play a big part in the values you assume, and there was no better setting for a curious child than the pavements of the London Borough of Islington.

Walking across the bridge towards St. Joseph's Church, where my siblings were confirmed, where my neighbours got married, down towards Whittington Hospital, where my uncle was hospitalised and my godchildren born. I pass the Whittington Cat – a memorial to the friend that came with Dick Whittington on his journey to London to find riches. Archway marks the spot where Dick heard the bells of Bow calling him back to London, having already given up. In 2020, you can't hear the Bow bells, but you can see the whole of London – only the Tory north is beyond in the other direction. Memories flood back of hours spent exploring the myriad ways to see London, when all you have is a child bus pass and a lot of time.

Growing up in the unfashionable parts of Islington, where beautiful Victorian houses like those of Canonbury Square make way for the sensible social housing of the Elthorne Estate, we couldn't afford day trips to anywhere that wasn't free. But the bus. The bus could take us all over the borough. Hop on the 4 and follow its byzantine route through Tufnell Park, back to Holloway, down to Finsbury Park, up through to Highbury and down to Angel. Islington Poor to Islington Rich. Islington Hidden to Islington Celebrated. Nag's Head Market to Chapel Market. Whittington Park to Barnsbury Park.

I think about the person I would be today had I grown up anywhere else. What is it about Islington? The birthplace of gentrification carries two different identities – to the media and outsiders, it's latte sipping guardianistas and 'metropolitan liberal elites'. It's Highbury Park and Upper Street. To me, Islington was playing cricket in Wray Crescent. It was summers spent in Elthorne Park – in the sand pit, at the swings and the slide, in the football pitch – playing football, watching boys play football, flirting with boys who were playing football. It was finding all the shortcut entrances into the park (there were six), and the best way to go through the park at night as a kid whilst avoiding the loitering, drinking adults.

It was walking to the church, St Gabriel's, for mass. And then for eucharist class. And then for confirmation. And then for choir practice. Islington was Goldie House, where I grew up in the forgotten end of Archway. Hornsey Rise they called it. A massive sprawling estate. Goldie House was a home, a sanctuary. Growing up working class in north London meant you didn't have a garden. Goldie House had a communal green area. 'NO BALL GAMES ALLOWED' read the sign, but ball games were played anyway. Champ. Football. Rounders. Cricket. Everybody knew everyone. Auntie Diane and Jason at number 18. My best friend Sacha, her mum Tina and brother Leigh at number 20. Gaby at Number 28. Rana at number 48. On the drains we played marbles and on the concrete we played Pogs. On the trees, we built a communal treehouse that Sacha, Jason and I painstakingly cultivated into a place of real pride. We even tried to convince our parents to let us sleep in it, their refusal a sharp reminder that ours was not the idyllic middle class countryside childhood. Real monsters lay outside the protective bubble of our council estate. But within that bubble, oh what lives we lived! What joys we had! What memories we made!

It seems bizarre to have such an affinity to bricks and mortar, but to live in Goldie House in the early 1990s was to find a community of people that society would never allow to be cultivated again. We came from all walks of life – cockney Londoners, Irish immigrants, Bengali asylum seekers, Congolese refugees, Greek migrants. We were all there. We laughed together. We cried together. One summer, Little Stuart and his friend managed to get the tap in the block open and we had the mother of all water fights. Everyone's doors open. Buckets, cups, water balloons, super soakers. Mums, children, big sisters, older brothers. Everyone was a wet mess by the end. Towels were handed out as children were dried off by one and all. It was pure, unadulterated joy.

There were hard times, of course. It was the 90s after all. Water fights and summer barbecues masked unemployment and poverty. It would take years to realise the reason one neighbour's child always wore the same

Elthorne playground and the view from Goldie House (images by Jude Wanga)

clothes everyday was because they literally only had two dresses. Or why the Bengali family that lived on the side of the estate just up and vanished one night. Deportation wasn't part of my vocabulary back then, yet the threat of it loomed over so many of my friends. And when times got hard I had my sanctuaries outside the glorious estate. I had church – St Gabriels with its vibrant mixed congregation and vivacious Irish priests and nuns. Spending my weekend with Father Kevin watching football in the afternoon before performing at 6pm Mass.

Occasionally, in those moments when my faith was wavering, I would walk a little further down the road to a small park opposite the famed Whittington Park. I would sit there on the swings and listen to my walkman and read books, or cry, or feel sad, or miss my parents. This was my space to feel and navigate daunting emotions I had no idea what to do with or how to approach. Emotions that felt like they could swallow me whole and leave me irreparably damaged.

Were there times I wished I lived as the other Islington half did? It would be a lie to pretend we didn't play at having more. Occasionally, in dreams where all things are possible, I would dream that it was not a first floor flat on an estate that I lived in, but in one of the big expensive houses in Thornhill Road. I would occasionally fantasise about the bicycle I would ride to school, with the brand new school bag. And as I grew older, so did the fantasies. Because, as much as I loved Islington, my Islington was forever tinged with an outline of hardship only visible to the working class eye.

And when the time came, I moved out. All of five minutes down the road. It turns out, like the prodigal son, Islington has to set its children free only to watch them all return one by one. For thirty years I have lived in this beautiful, polarised, occasionally pretentious and always brilliant borough. One of the saddest thoughts I have these days is not of my friend next door who only has two dresses, but of how the hardship remains, with families forced to downsize due to the bedroom tax, first time parents moved far from their families as social housing makes way for affordable housing, which is affordable for only the richer half of the borough, not for those raising kids on the estates of Islington; your Mayvilles, your Marquises, your Manchester Mansions and your Goldie Houses.

The social housing estates that gave us Akala and Lady Dynamite will soon give way to market price rents, middle class renters and their upper class rentiers. The working class families will slowly make way for the professional couples and families with the money to pay the rising rents, descending to capitalise on the schools that these communities worked hard to make so stellar. One day it will simply be too expensive for me to live in the borough that housed me, raised me, guided me and educated me. But until that day arrives, I will continue enjoying hour long bus rides on the 4 to Waterloo, and summertime picnics with my childhood schoolfriends and godchildren at Waterlow Park. I'll make the most of Whittington Park as I attempt to start running again, and you'll no doubt find me playing the organ in a reopened St Gabriel's Church at a future advent Mass. Islington is now in my blood, my childhood, the foundation of my adulthood and the root of my faith. I'll not go lightly.

When Sammy Cahn wrote the lyrics to *My Kind of Town*, I doubt he knew it would become my anthem for Islington, but mainly for Hornsey. Because Islington really *is* my kind of town. The Chapel Market, Islington is. The Union Chapel, Islington is. The tennis courts of Highbury Fields, Islington is. Seven Sisters Road, Islington is. Fonthill Road, Islington is. The Archway library, Islington is. A borough that won't let you down, it's my kind of town.

Jude Wanga is a human rights activist, campaigner and writer who lives in Islington. In 2010 she was the focus of the BBC documentary *The World's Most Dangerous Place for Women*, focusing on the use of rape as a weapon of war in the Democratic Republic of Congo. She has written for various national outlets and is a UK ambassador for Women for Women International. She is currently an editor at *The New Socialist* and an interpreter working in asylum and immigration law.

Gordon House, Highbury, MJ Long, 1987

A purpose-built artist's studio designed by MJ Long, renowned as the principal architect partner on the British Library with Sandy Wilson. The studio is a detached structure with an independent entrance in what was the garden of a terrace house with a double-height painting studio overlooked by an upper balcony originally dedicated to graphic work. Now a work-live space owned and used by artist Andrew James. To our knowledge, the Gordon House has never been open to the public but we hope it may be for a future Open House festival.[Om]

Finsbury Health Centre, Lubetkin and Tecton, 1938

This is a building of enormous significance, being both one of the great propaganda coups of modern architecture – a well-publicised, attractive showcase of both modernist and socialist social planning, that would even feature on a Second World War poster – and one of the founding buildings of the NHS, free at the point of use a decade before Aneurin Bevan introduced a similar system across the country. But visiting Finsbury Health Centre is an uncomfortable experience. It is tiny, far more monumental in photographs; its facade is almost hidden by the trees that were planted to import some healthy air into noxious Finsbury; it is dilapidated, having nearly been sold off a few years ago

and with the local NHS trust not having the funds to restore it properly. To add insult to injury, it faces a hideous street of postmodernist suburban houses covered in 'Beware of the Dog' signs. So it's a hard building to enjoy, but it does still manage to communicate, particularly through its casual levity: the little roof terrace, the neo-Victorian typography and the light, elegant tiling, all of which avoid the heaviness and pomposity of 30s bureaucracy. It promises that health and equality are about being carefree.[OH]

Tremlett Grove Estate, Upper Holloway, LCC Architects Department, 1964–68

An unusual little London County Council estate in a close in a dense Victorian area. Clipped glass cubes, displaying the Americanophilia that went alongside the Dutch and Swiss obsessions in neighbouring Camden – Chicago or Montreal as a model for modern living just as much as Europe. Its lightweight, brightly coloured classical grid frames a neat green square, all with a precision that suggests Skidmore Owings and Merrill or Mies van der Rohe gone municipal.[OH]

Falcon Court, Philip Boyle, 1970

A three-storey residential concrete and brick terrace, back turned to the street and overlooking the rear gardens of a parallel row of older townhouses. To the north, the terrace terminates in a four-storey block completing the enclosure of a semi-private court which the terrace's name reflects. Its architect is now the UK co-ordinator of the modernist conservation group Docomomo.[Om]

15 Clerkenwell Close, Groupwork + Amin Taha, 2017

Clerkenwell Close is a quintessential London conservation area, in that nothing truly awful has been allowed to happen, but aside from the baroque church at the centre of it, nothing particularly interesting either. It has been maintained, nothing more. It's not so surprising that Amin Taha's building has been so controversial – threatened, for a time with demolition for allegedly breaking planning rules – as it really is a challenge to how conservation areas are meant to work. With fake load-bearing brick on either side, it's held up with a giant grid of limestone, some of which is chiselled to a clean finish, and much of it left as rough as possible. Taha was asked at one point in the planning process whether he couldn't have treated the limestone just as a facade, a smooth skin wrapped around a steel frame, so that it wouldn't have this effect of giant mass. Well he didn't, and we should be grateful. But a lot of the things that make 15 Clerkenwell Close so much fun are actually made possible by conservation's constraints, from the Mediterranean, Greek-ruin roof garden to the grid that follows the line of the neighbouring buildings. Rather than seeing the past as a static picture, it incorporates it as archaeology, with its basement office full of traces of the buildings that were there before. There is an aspect of wind-up about it all, nerous and rich – new ideas about how to build in historic areas of London could start from here.[OH]

Gordon House (left, image by Billy Bolton), Falcon Court (centre), 15 Clerkenwell Close (right, image by Tim Soar)

Barking and Dagenham, City of London, Hackney, Havering, Newham, Redbridge, Tower Hamlets, Waltham Forest

Where is Becontree?
Verity-Jane Keefe

'Becontree? I live in Becontree? I've lived in my house for coming on 60 years and I never knew that – I thought I was proper, PROPER Dagenham Verity' She tells me she loves Dagenham, and now she loves Becontree and we go our separate ways.

This is not the Conclusive, Exclusive Complete Story of the Becontree Estate, nor a history lesson in social housing. These exist. This is a slice of a place at a certain time. The estate is 99 years old in part and up to 113 in others, with various teenage and younger buildings infilled throughout. The Becontree Estate is huge. Not just big by housing estate standards, it's big by small town standards. It covers a third of its host London borough's footprint and has at points been part-Ilford, part-Barking, part-Dagenham, part-Barking and Dagenham, part-London, part-Essex. Divided across historical boroughs, an outer London experiment in large scale planning and mass post-war house building made up of ten or twelve wards depending on which map you look at and splitting across two historically solid, Labour constituencies.

But what *is* Becontree? Where is it? And *why* is it there? The London County Council (LCC) were under huge pressure after the First World War to deliver mass good quality housing and had identified a large swathe of land, some 3,000-ish acres to the east of the city, out of their normal county council boundary next to Dagenham. Farmland, market gardens, close to the river – the site was perfect, if there's such a thing as a perfect site for 29,000 new homes.

Tap out, leave the station, look left and right along a tired looking but very busy shopping parade. A sign for an allotment down an alleyway. Groups of young people in bright green uniform and different coloured t-shirts joke and laugh outside the sweet shop. Keep walking. The remains of 'Dave's Reptiles' on the corner, St George's flag flapping from a first-floor window. Cars, cars, cars, more cars. A former library, closed but in use for something, past a former Councillor's house who I was once told 'Was so far left he's fallen off the fucking edge' Labour Party to Socialist Labour Party to no Party. I meet said ex-councillor on the same street a few years later – 'The BNP, UKIP, NF – we've got to do something or these bastards will

take it all!' These words have stuck with me. Trust in Ford visible in the distance
on a showroom forecourt. The southern border, fuzzy and green with the sound
of the A13 racing by.

Becontree: a tube station, a housing estate, a place, an ancient site of
gathering. There is so much more to the area than meets the eye, beyond
the suburban sprawl and sheer scale of ambition. The Fiddlers, Chequers,
Parsloes, Dagenham, Heathway, Martins Corner, Clifford Corner,
Andrew's Corner, Valence and Green Lane – places named after much
loved local landmarks that have since been demolished, after pubs, old
shops, parks or shopping areas, place names that all blend in to one another and over each other. So far, so complex. It's no wonder that people who
live within the invisible boundary of this place within a place that contains
loads of other places, don't really have a joined up sense of place.

Becontree can be viewed through a lens to tell the story of Barking
and Dagenham, but also a wider, national story. It has no clear cut beginning, middle or end, no estate maps announcing your arrival, location
or departure, just streets upon streets of houses that might all look
similar. But stop and look closely and you can begin to unpick not only
the last hundred years of social housing, but some of the huge social and
political forces that have changed the urban, suburban and rural landscape. Industrialisation, de-industrialisation, immigration, East End drift,
trade unionism, work, workers' rights, the left, the right, the far left, the
far right, regeneration, neoliberalism and some hefty changes to housing
policy and notably and visibly, The Right to Buy.

I'm on one of the main long roads, an Avenue with fast moving traffic heading
north. Essex Plumbers, Country Driveways, Mark's Landscapes, City Bouncy
Castles. Vans lining the pavements with multiple geographic identities. Shared
porches and entrance ways cut in half and boxed out or boxed in. The Becontree Arch
becoming a Becontree Half Arch shared with a double-glazed box. Driveways instead
of plaques for prize-winning gardens. Nostalgia balancing with practicality and mixed
tenancies and home ownership. NO BALL GAMES signs on every amenity green
and patch of grass around. A scheduled civic centre at the centre of the estate and
borough is now houses, with the built Civic Centre housing Coventry University.
Coventry in Dagenham near Becontree in Essex in London. Walking past cat slide
roofs and dormer windows, giant palms, small palms, gnomes, dreamcatchers.

Celebrated at a distance by many an architect, planner, historian or social-
housing hobbyist, they have it on a pedestal. 'Ah Becontree, now there's
a place I'm interested in' I was told when I was out campaigning for the
last election in Dagenham – 'Where is it, am I close?' 'You're in it pal...'.

Becontree Estate (images by Verity-Jane Keefe)

Barking and Dagenham   E

Maps, plans, black and white photographs are pored over, accompanied by the big-hitters of facts: '27,000 houses built! 100,000 residents! The largest housing estate in Europe at one time – no, THE WORLD! 91 different type of houses!' How many of these enthusiasts have spent time in Becontree is another thing entirely. These facts and statistics are all impressive, and the houses are still standing strong and looking less uniform and more eccentric and individualised than ever – HELLO PEBBLEDASH! AFTERNOON GRECIAN COLUMNS! Oh hi, owl-statue-as-post-mounted-CCTV camera!

'A tour of Becontree is demanding even for the enthusiast.' Wise words Pevsner, wise words. A walk from north to south, east to west or around the perimeter can be exhausting and at times disorientating. The first terrace was completed in 1921 – Chittys Lane in the north of the estate – and the ribbon was cut 14 years later to mark the completion in Parsloes Park. You can walk through the last 100 years and think ahead to the next on one of these walks. But why would you care about this archi-planning-celeb-status if you're just trying to live and exist? Becontree is everything and nothing at the same time.

I'm in an industrial estate walking the course of a former river on tarmac, right on the eastern perimeter. On match day you can hear football chanting coming from Dagenham and Redbridge. A council vehicle depot, a dance school, YESSSS Electrical Dagenham, singing from Grace to Grace church, a Tesco in a former pub. Further in, there's mock Tudor cladding on one side, pargetting of a swan on the other, red hot pokers and for sale signs. A former Housing Divisional Director once told me the key to identifying council properties was to look for a certain style of brown door, replaced via a Shape-Up programme of improvements. These brown doors are private, council and rented now. Back to another main avenue, with promises of Crossrail at the very top, just beyond the northern border.

A mass monoculture of majority white working class East Enders moved to Becontree and were all issued with the exact same London County Council Tenancy Agreement, complete with tenants handbook outlining handy hints for the housewife, pruning guides, suggestions of how to keep a garden looking tip-top – with visuals showing what not to do if you were in any doubt – and contact details for housing officers, painting teams, groundworks departments and the rest. Those early settlers were fairly unsettled as schools weren't completed right at the beginning, and there were very few pubs and community spaces. Faith spaces, a small amount of pubs, community centres and schools started to open and then in more recent times, adapted to change or closed.

The LCC became the GLC and soon tenancies were all transferred to Dagenham, and the East End drifters blended and morphed into a local population. London expanded, outer London formed and Becontree's geography has slowly shifted to become more urban and it's demographic more mixed. Where it was once surrounded by fields, the borough and the city have absorbed it within its own perimeters. Becontree came first, Ford soon followed, with more and more industry providing work for the community and beyond for a long time. People purchased their homes, some via the GLC's own model of Right to Buy and then Thatcher's version came alongside the mass unemployment of the 1980s. A perfect storm which feels like it's still brewing, both nationally and locally.

As we prepare our vocal chords, gear up to sing Happy Birthday to Becontree in 2021 and congratulate it on making it to a hundred, we might look to the next hundred years before blowing out the candles. Not just what Becontree might look like, but the future of (council) housing, and the urgent need to build good quality houses for everyone. How can we take this radical blueprint, learn from its successes and failures and apply it to the future of living in London and beyond? Becontree is more than its houses, it is home for approximately 100,000 people. The borough has already weathered one change in working culture via deindustrialisation, but how will it fare post Covid-19? A normal, ordinary place with all the challenges that a decade of austerity has thrown at it, plus everything that has come before and is happening right now, it is not perfect and is made up of many contradictions, but there is visible evidence, and plenty of bus stop conversational anecdotes, to prove that there is more than enough to see here and talk about beyond the statistics – including the ever-evolving and active community of individuals that live in these houses so often admired from afar.

PS The history of Becontree is well documented at the brilliant Valence House Local Studies Centre and Archives bang splat in the middle of the estate – go there, virtually or physically.

Verity-Jane Keefe is a visual artist working predominantly in the public realm to explore the complex relationship between people and place. She works with moving image, text and installation, has an ongoing, accidental love affair with outer London, and is currently lead artist for Living Together, a project celebrating the upcoming Becontree Centenary.

Barking Station, British Railways Eastern Division, 1959–1961
An aggressive but straightforward Brutalist terminus, designed by John Ward for the British Railways Eastern Region, whose post-war rebuilding programme was one of British Rail architecture's few successes. It's placed in a high street and displays the important 'here is the station' signifiers – you have no doubt what the big building is. Like a miniature version of Rome's Termini station, it's basically a big, wide, cranked concrete roof, with a glass hall beneath. All extremely simple – a glassy open hall under a heavy roof, with such strength and integrity that it can survive however many branches of Upper Crust are chucked into it.[OH]

The Folly, Barking, Muf Architecture/ Art, 2010
Barking Central, designed by AHMM architects, so exemplified New Labour architecture that it became the basis

for parodies by artists like Matthew Derbyshire and Scott King – meanly proportioned single-aspect flats smothered in lime green barcode facade razzledazzle. Muf, hired as artists and designers of what planners insist on calling 'public realm' (a pompous term which always ought to be prefaced with 'BEHOLD, THE,') made this place a lot more interesting than it would otherwise be through insisting the square being kept open and unencumbered. They then created, out of various pieces of waste attached to a bare gable wall, 'The Folly', a ludic and lurid piece of instant history which by now, many people in Barking will probably think has been there forever. It features steps to nowhere, pieces of Victorian salvage, a stone sheep at the top, and grass growing out of it. Behind, vans load and unload the goods for a supermarket.[OH]

St Patrick's Church, A E Wiseman, 1940
Better known for designing cinemas than churches, Wiseman took on the design of this striking interwar church marking the creation of the new parish of St Patrick's in 1938. Building work had started before the Second World War began and, unlike many buildings of the time, was allowed to continue during the war. St Patrick's is constructed on piers with a reinforced concrete frame and faced in buff Dutch bricks. Approaching the building from Denham Way the view is dominated by the impressive, symmetrical east facade with its imposing drum tower flanked by low curving transseptal vestries and a Lady Chapel in a bold composition. The exterior, though embellished with subtle details retains an ultimately utilitarian dignity, comparable to a metroland tube station, or grand electrical infrastructure. The church has undergone a few changes, perhaps the most regrettable is the blocking of the clerestory windows to combat heat loss, restricting the light flooding into the building which is what the architect had originally intended. The interior exploits the contrasts between concrete, wood and brick. It is the chancel though that is most striking. There is a fan shaped

reredos above a stepped wooden backdrop to the altar with curved brick side panels. The reredos has a painted sky either side of gilded ribs giving colour and drama to the building. The charismatic decoration perhaps shows Wiseman deploying the architectural tactics of his usual stomping ground in cinema design.[PH]

The Eastbrook, Dagenham, architect unknown, 1937
This Grade II listed neo-Georgian building has been barely altered or tampered with over the years. Outside the tall chimneys, red brick and sprocketed eaves, hint at the nostalgic interwar design features of oak and walnut bars and panelling, fireplace and glazed windows. The combination of it all conjures a wistfulness of Merrie England, while the number of different function rooms nod at how the pubs of this era were positioned as hubs for a neighbourhood; the neo-Georgian architecture, rejecting the opulence of Victorian architecture, aimed to create modest places of recreation, hosting different activities alongside boozing.[Om]

Barking Station (top left), The Folly (bottom left), St Patrick's (top right, image by Marion Hull), The Eastbrook (bottom right)

Living in the Barbican During Lockdown
Helen Thomas

I am a child of the Black Country, of the suburbs of Dudley and Wolver-hampton. Images of the denuded Long Mynd and the hills flowing into mid-Wales overlap in my mind with the slag heaps of the freshly-closed local colliery. In the same analogous relationship, the layered open landscapes of the Barbican and Golden Lane estates in the City of London remind me of the fields around my grandmother's house in rural Gloucestershire. Moving from Islington with a small child just after the trauma of 9/11 in 2001, this tranquillity at the heart of the capital was appealing.

Both estates were constructed on an empty site that had been created in a single night in 1940, when incendiary bombing destroyed the ware-houses, factories and dwellings described in the novels of George Gissing. In 1952, an architectural competition was held to find the architect for the Golden Lane estate. This was won by Geoffrey Powell, who teamed up with Peter Chamberlin and Christoph Bon to become Chamberlin, Powell and Bon, architects of both the Golden Lane estate, which was built first, and the Barbican estate, begun in 1965.

These two estates are like two villages, situated side-by-side but quite different in character. The dwellings of Golden Lane – especially those that meet the ground – unfold into the gardens, pathways and courts contained within its permeable boundary. Neighbours can see and meet each other easily – there are three different community spaces on the estate, and the swimming pool enclosure is a transparent lantern at its heart. The Barbican, on the other hand, is more formal; the gardens, terraces, high walks and podium are monumental, many are public, and life is more anonymous. When it is full, around 6,000 people live in the more than 2,000 flats and houses. Like many other villages in Britain, the Barbican has its own grocery shop, hairdressers, police station, Indian restaurant, playgroup, and church. It also contains a national arts venue that attracts many visitors from outside the estate, some of whom are also interested in the Brutalist concrete architecture. The Barbican Centre, with its three cinemas, concert hall, theatres, library and art galleries has a huge multi-level foyer which, when open, is usually full of people sitting at large tables, tapping on their laptops, using the free wifi.

During the almost twenty years that I have lived in one of the three Barbican towers, the city around – the soundscape and the views from our windows – has changed a lot, but this has been a slow and incremental process compared to the transformations to life caused by the spring lockdown of 2020. During that time it was very quiet; above the hum of fans moving huge volumes of air in and out of buildings, birdsong could be heard. The gates to the Barbican Centre were locked shut for months, barring many of the routes through the estate and disrupting the flow of the podium as it weaves among the various housing blocks and institutions such as the City of London School for Girls, the Museum of London, and the Guildhall School of Music. This separate realm floats over the streets below, which are usually very busy with cars and buses driving by, pavements full of people. The podium makes the Barbican different to other housing estates in London, and I think the whole world. It is a safe and quiet place, a perfect territory for small children to own, with fields of flowers and lots of secret, beautiful places. Some of these are open to everyone, some of them are for the people who live here.

There are many layers between the podium and the street level, which continue underground. These can make visiting the Barbican very confusing for visitors, and in the past, a yellow line on the ground helped them to navigate their way from the Barbican tube station to the arts centre. The drawing of the Barbican Centre on the next spread is a section cut through the middle as if it were a big cake. It gives a good sense of the many levels that the estate has, and how any sense of a natural ground made of earth doesn't exist here. On the far right of the drawing is a little car coming down a ramp towards an underground car park. Above this internal space is a palm tree in the conservatory, constructed to hide the vast fly tower of the Barbican Theatre. On the other side of the fly tower the conservatory continues, and below it the balconies of the auditorium extend into the underground cave of the theatre. The layered foyer steps down on the left-hand side of the drawing and curving above it is Frobisher Crescent.

I live in Cromwell Tower, situated at the end of the Beech Street road tunnel. The view from the front door looks up Whitecross Street, which on a normal weekday is filled, from early morning until midday, with the aroma of fresh vegetables and food cooking for the lunchtime market. The public entrance to the tower is from a forecourt at street level. In the foyer, a striped yellow line on the floor marked the zone protecting the Cromwell Tower porters at their reception desk during the two metre distancing phase of lockdown. When we moved in, one of the porters at the time told us stories of playing on the bombsite on which the tower was built as a child; he and his colleagues have long been replaced by a new cohort. Originally, the tower was supposed to be accessed from the podium, so we have two levels of entrance foyer, but the upper one can only be used by the residents. The foyers were restored by architects Witherford Watson Mann around ten years ago, and I like the exposed brickwork contrasted with the filmy curtains.

In our flat, the kitchen is like a long galley and the architects worked with a shipbuilder called Brooke Marine to design the kitchens, which have their ship-like idiosyncrasies. There is a little pull-out table which is very useful, and the unusual row of four electric burners creates a useful space for moving things around. Some flats still have the original garchey waste disposal system, which is why there are two sinks. The bathrooms, too, are special, lined with white tiles that are brick-shaped on the floor, and the bath is huge so that it is possible to float full-length in it. Some flats have the specially designed Barbican basin that is built into the wall and designed for tiny spaces, which is also used in the Barbican Centre lavatories.

There are three flats on every floor of the towers. Each flat extends the full length of one side of the tower's triangular volume. This is a clever shape that sometimes appears to be solid and heavy and at others paper thin, depending on the angle you view it from. Our front door leads into a triangular lobby that mimics the shape of the tower. This dark and mysterious place has an atmosphere that visitors often find interesting. The flats are acoustically separated from each other by a fire escape stair. The strange object in the centre of the lobby often causes confusion, but it is simply where the lift button is. In the morning, when the postman is delivering mail and the cleaner is collecting the rubbish the lift can take a long time to arrive. One of the lobby doors leads to the incredibly tall and scary main fire escape stair. Long balconies stretching the full length of the flats lead either to the fire escape stairs or to the smaller flights going down to lift lobbies one or two stories beneath.

Across the street from the forecourt at street level is a restaurant, boarded up for lockdown, and two cinemas, also closed. My route to Golden Lane takes me halfway down the tunnel to where the street begins. Walking around the corner one Sunday morning, on the way to the swimming pool, I had a new encounter with an elaborate work by Banksy, made to celebrate Jean-Michel Basquiat. So, although the art gallery was closed during lockdown, there was still some art to see at the Barbican. Another of my favourite works is the 'Minatour' by Michael Ayrton, which has travelled around the estate's labyrinthine world during my time here, displaced by construction work, finally resting in a garden on London Wall.

Many people who live in the Barbican like the various rules that control life here. In addition to the laws of the land, there are numerous bylaws that define how to behave on the podium and in the gardens.

Barbican Centre: perspective section (© John Maltby / RIBA Collections)

Lockdown brought additional, unwritten rules into play, open to interpretation and changing how the landscapes of the Barbican were used. Chatting, socialising and general loitering were discouraged, and so cyclists on urban safaris zoomed along the high walks and across the podium, ignoring the 'No cycling' rule, while at the same time benches were removed from the communal gardens to prevent sunbathing, and all of the playgrounds were taped up. Nevertheless, the massive, corporeal character of the Barbican estate always remains the same, and open to as many interpretations as it has residents and visitors, each of whom brings their own associations, memories and preconceptions to bear upon their experience of this unusual place.

Helen Thomas is an architect and writer with a PhD from the University of Essex in art history and theory. Recent books include *Hopkins in the City*, 2019; *Architecture through Drawing*, 2019; *Drawing Architecture*, 2018.

Ibex House, Fuller Hall and Foulsham, 1933–1937

A great cruiser of streamlined, strip-windowed, glazed-stairwelled offices at the south-eastern edge of the City, before it starts to crumble into the East End. Its curves of yellow and black faïence and Crittall windows are all retrofuturist period charm, but the industrial scale of the building takes it somewhere other than seaside pavilions and Odeon cinemas, into an H.G. Wells world of perfectly functioning machinery and lacquered hairstyles. There are some obvious cribs from the tile-clad ripples of Berlin's pre-Hitler Shell-Haus, but what it really resembles is a miniaturised version of the proto-megastructural Starrett-Lehigh warehouse in Manhattan. As early as this, modernism in London's financial centre was about American dreams, not European realities.[OH]

St Mary Aldermanbury Garden, Christopher Wren

The City of London is home to around 150 small parks and gardens with several incorporating the ruins of former churches. One of the most enigmatic of these green spaces is St Mary Aldermanbury's Garden, built on the site of a church which Christopher Wren rebuilt after the Great Fire of London but was later gutted during the Blitz. The surviving stones were transported to Fulton, Missouri in 1966 where they were rebuilt in the grounds of Westminster College leaving only the church's footprint in London. Today the ruin is enlivened with charming shrubs and trees forming a garden. It is a perfect spot from which to enjoy the Grade II* listed McMorran and Whitby-designed Wood Street headquarters of the City of London Police, and the nearby surviving tower of St Alban, Wood Street which is now a private house.[MF]

60 Queen Victoria Street, Foggo Associates, 1999

A speculative office block next to James Stirling's notorious Number 1 Poultry, showing a darker shade of postmodernism. Like a lot of City office blocks of the 80s and 90s, Peter Foggo's work here continues the proportions and scale of the Victorian and Edwardian buildings that survive in the City in fragments, after the ministrations of the Luftwaffe and 'planning'. While most buildings of this sort try to recapture Victorian architecture with a kitschy melange of grilles, pediments, reconstituted stone cladding and gee-gaws, 60 Queen Victoria Street opts for a more original fusion of retro and high-tech. The facade treatment is defined by the washed-out, blue-grey bronze cladding, metal screens like prison windows, and an exposed structural steel frame. There is nothing else from this era in London that approaches its sinister elegance, or risks its practically fetishistic, S&M approach to materials, more H.R. Giger than Edwin Lutyens.[OH]

Holland House, Hendrik Petrus Berlage, 1916

This small building for a Dutch shipping line, now round the back of Norman Foster's 'Gherkin', is the only evidence in Britain – after the decline of Charles Rennie Mackintosh at any rate – of the early development of the modern movement, which otherwise arrived here almost fully formed fifteen years later. Berlage, from his Amsterdam Stock Exchange onwards, favoured a pared-down Gothic whose minimalism increasingly emphasised structure and repetition rather than craft and irregularity. Holland House shows his work at a dreamlike stage close to the Expressionists of the Amsterdam School. A steel frame mirrored by a grey-green tile grid, and a geometric wipeclean interior like Frank Lloyd Wright designing a Victorian public toilet. Industrial and intense, and with a stylised relief of a ship at the corner, it seems to have been almost completely ignored at the time, and is easily missed today.[OH]

The Museum of London, Powell and Moya, 1976

Soon to move to a new site at Smithfield Market, the Museum of London was designed as part of the redevelopment of London Wall by Phillip Powell and Hidalgo Moya. With its chunky concrete pillars and exterior of glossy white tiles, the museum speaks to the architecture of the adjacent Barbican while also setting itself apart. Located above a roundabout, the metaphor of motion is apt for the museum, whose layout creates a single route through the museum as a 'walk through time'. Perched above the road and the historic Ironmongers Hall, the museum's entrance level connects directly to the Barbican's highwalk network, allowing the whole site to be traversed away from traffic. A major redevelopment by the architects Wilkinson Eyre took place in 2010.[JA]

Ibex House (left), 60 Queen Victoria Street (centre), The Museum of London (right)

A Walk with my Baba through Stoke Newington

Aydin Dikerdem

Earlier this year, a journalist tweeted about how much they hated Stoke Newington. This launched a debate about which parts of London middle class professionals no longer wanted to hang out in. Unsurprisingly, absent from the narrative were the migrant communities that had made these areas home before hyper-inflated property prices and rent became the backbone of national economic policy.

Since some of my earliest memories are walking the streets of Stoke Newington with my Baba (father) as he pointed out which political faction ran what – and to my frustration, continually stopped to greet various people – we decided to put down an oral history of the neighbourhood and the hidden history of the Turkish speaking communities – whether Cypriot, mainland Turkish, Kurdish or Alevi – that call it home.

We start sitting on the grass slope outside the Clissold Park cafe. Long before the 2012 class war couscous fight, Turks used to meet in the semi-derelict Clissold House, a late 18th century neoclassical villa built for the anti-slavery campaigner Jonathan Hoare. In the 1980s this was 'a hang out spot, but it was rough, and the business was constantly swapping hands between different families'. I tell him this journey cannot just be him pointing at things and sighing that Turks used to run it.

We are meeting an old friend of my Baba's, Cavli, who was the head of the Turkish Students Federation in the late 1960s and early 70s. 'When I arrived, you knew how many Turks there were in this country by looking at the Embassy visitors book. And if you were a student, they warned you to keep away from a trouble-maker called Cavli'. In 1972, Cavli helped establish the Union of Progressive Turks, which operated out of 10 Jenner Road off Stoke Newington Common. It was a magnet for recent arrivals and served as a community centre where people came for advice and socialised. 'It was basically a front for the then growing left wing movement in Turkey', my Baba says, 'but still we were very few in number compared to now' he explains. We head through the park towards Newington Green down the most southern part of Green Lanes.

The first generation migrants were mostly Turkish Cypriots, who had access to London through the colonial link with the British Empire. This was a predominantly nationalist community and the strip we are walking through is associated with right wing nationalist and Islamic groups. It was here that in the early 1970s the famous Sufi 'guru', Sheikh Nazim Adil Haqqani, established himself. An important figure in the history of British Islamic life, Sheikh Nazim built a following that ranged from British hippies exploring mysticism to the ethno-nationalist groupings of the Cypriots (and most famously, the Greek Cypriot Yusuf Islam, formerly known as Cat Stevens). In 1976 the Sheikh partnered with Ramadan Güney, a leading Turkish Cypriot community figure and founder in the 1950s of the nationalist paramilitary group Volkan, purchasing 16 Green Lanes, Newington Green, which later became the London Islamic Turkish Association. 'Looking back on it, some of the things happening then would come back to bite us' Baba exclaims, referring to the synthesis of far right nationalist politics and Islamist politics that now makes up the powerbase of the reigning Turkish President Erdoğan.

Of course different factions lived next door to each other and this stretch would also become the centre for the distribution of Turkish newspapers led by Faruk Zapcı, which later evolved into a publishing and community bookshop under Celal Sönmez. Olay Gazette's offices, Britains biggest Turkish newspaper, still remains on this strip, which has continued to maintain its Turkish character, alongside the best Lahmacun in London at Ustun.

We curve around onto the corner of Newington Green. 'From this corner, the Varan and other Turkish buses used to leave. If you wanted to go to Turkey, you would come here on a Sunday, buy your tickets and off you went. The first proper Turkish restaurant Hodja Nasruddin was around here too,' nods Cavli. Baba explains that when he first arrived in London they had to go to an Armenian restaurant in Camden (where they couldn't speak Turkish) in order to get food that reminded them of home. 'The park is also where we used to celebrate May Day and things like that' smiles Baba, 'we were provoking the right by doing it next to their area'.

We cross over into the park to find a small memorial to Kağan Güner. He was a socialist artist involved in Attaturkçu Düsünçe Dernegi (a secularist organisation that supported the ideas of Turkey's founder Kemal Atatürk) who died in 2011. He started some of the first Turkish artist organisations and put on local exhibitions. We come back out facing the Newington Green Meeting House – 'the birthplace of modern feminism', exclaims Baba to Cavli, referring to Mary Wollstonecraft, who was a member of the Unitarian church there. The three of us head off onto Mathias Road, down Boleyn Road and then up Crossway towards where Kingsland High Street meets Stoke Newington Road.

A boarded up Turkish social club on the corner of Ormsby Place – *tavla* being the Turkish word for backgammon (all images by Aydin Dikerdem)

We arrive facing the dome of the second Nazim-Güney Mosque. Established on the old site of the Dalston Synagogue in 1977, the red brick building is home to the UK Turkish Islamic Trust. We take a left turn and start walking up the strip. 'After On iki Eylül (September 12th) things change' Baba says. He is referencing the 1980 coup d'état that saw the civilian government toppled and replaced with a military junta. Around half a million people were imprisoned by military courts (my grandfather among them), with torture and executions widespread. 'You see the first major migration of mainland Turks into the capital, most of whom are political refugees. And where do they come? Here.' Baba explains. 'Everywhere you went you could see left wing revolutionary political slogans in Turkish, from Dalston to Stoke Newington.'

There are, of course, still plenty of Turkish businesses among the High Street's now famous bars and clubs. We walk past the art deco façade of the former Konak Cinema, now Hackney Arts Centre, which used to show Turkish films after midnight. When I was growing up it was a classic Turkish pool hall and 'football club'. Each coffee house represented a different area in Turkey, Baba explains, and during the 90s they became football clubs because of the introduction of satellite dishes, which meant you could get Turkish football, and could claim a different business rate for being a 'social club'. Some were also gambling dens, hiring Eastern European women clad in miniskirts to serve endless cups of tea. A number of of them still remain hidden down the backstreets.

We head on up to another art deco façade, now a Beyond Retro, this large purpose-built textile factory was established in 1929 by the bespoke interwar tailor Simeon Simpson. On May Day 1983 it opened its doors as Halkevi Turkish Community Centre and would become the beating heart of community life for the 1980s generation. My Baba was amongst one of the dozen or so founders, the most famous being Nafiz Bostanci, who led the work of supporting recent migrants and asylum seekers. Things were complicated though. 'You have to understand that by the 1980s it was the political left that organised the community'. Halkevi was run by the Orthodox Turkish Communist Party (TKP) but there was a rival faction that had developed – İşçinin Sesi (Workers Voice). The splits mirrored political battles back in Turkey and pitted former comrades at the Union of Turkish Progressive against one another. 'There were frequent beatings, stabbing, violence basically between the two factions here in Stoke Newington,' Baba explains. 'One night I couldn't come home because I'd been tipped off that they were watching our flat.'

We keep walking, Baba points out the offices where the Claudia Jones Organisation operates, Claudia Jones being the Trinidadian communist and founder of Notting Hill Carnival. I ask about the relationship between the area's Black Caribbean community and the Turkish speaking community. My Baba sighs, 'One of the main problems we faced at the time was even conscious workers maintained petty racism. But there were places where communities came together.' He points down back towards Dalston, 'Centreprise was a brilliant example of that'. The iconic radical bookshop run as a collective, Centerprise became a cafe, meeting place and community hub where organisers brought together Black and Turkish youth and ran cultural activities. Surely there was a shared struggle, I ask? 'The Union of Turkish Progressives and the TKP were formally and ideologically of course on the side of liberation organisation here, but our own experience of working was completely insular and Turkish, typical exile politics. And we spent more time combatting other factions than building alliances with other migrant communities.' It sounds disappointingly familiar to politics of anti-racist organising today.

We continue walking up Stoke Newington Road, past the bright blue Aziziye Mosque, which opened in 1984 and was the first Mosque established by mainland Turks. It inhabits the building of the former Apollo Picture House, and when the cinema opened in 1913, the Baptist Church directly next to it launched protests against films being shown so close to a house of worship. By the 70s it was a seedy cinema called the Astra that showed uncensored B-movies and 'skin flicks'. It's a nice twist that it's now literally become a place of faith. As we walk past the Stoke Newington Police Station, Baba exclaims, 'If you want to know what this lot were up to back then, look up Duncan Campbell'. Back when Dalston's Sandringham Road was known as the 'Front Line' the *Guardian* crime correspondent uncovered a corruption scandal at the Stoke Newington police department ranging from drugs being planted to officers selling confiscated drugs. It rocked the area and led to a huge libel case that the Metropolitan Police lost. The reputation of the force was so bad they demolished the station, and the new building was designed to seem more welcoming and transparent. It is also worth mentioning that it was not just political factions that were at war with each other. The Turkish heroin trade also entered London in the 1980s and remains to this day. Turkish gangland killings peppered the local press and were part of the neighbourhood's bad image. Middle class British people did not want to live here.

We take a left onto Church Street. Cavli, who by the 1980s was living in East Germany, stoically remarks, 'Well this has changed a lot'. I can't tell if he is being funny. We walk down dodging the baby strollers and al fresco brunchers. 'When the wall comes down, the political left begins to lose it's grip on the Turkish community and is slowly replaced by more Islamic organisations. And of course you then have the huge wave of Kurdish migration in the late 80s to mid-90s. It's really important. That's where people like Nafiz head off into the Kurdish struggle'.

Aziziye Mosque and Stoke Newington Baptist Church

One of the most important remaining community centres in the area, Daymer, reflects this change, and took the place of institutions like Halkevi. 'How long is this piece?' Cavli asks. Around fifteen hundred words, I reply. 'Well you'll need more if we are to talk about the Kurdish struggle'. He is referencing the long-standing oppression of Kurdish people in Turkey, and the continuing struggle for equality, human rights, and more recently, the protection of the autonomous Kurdish territory in Rojava.

We drop in on a friend of my Baba who runs one of the French delicatessens facing the old Stoke Newington Town Hall. Huseyin Kaplan represents that later generation, a leader in the British Alevi Federation up in Enfield. When the area began to change many re-located to Enfield but maintain a foothold in Stoke Newington still. He shows us images of a huge open-air cinema they have been running for the community at their centre. We walk past the Rose and Crown, 'the SWP pub' chuckles Baba and we're back at Clissold Park. 'We're still here, and some people have done very well. But the politics has changed so much. Like back in Turkey, the Left are now working on Kurdish struggles, voting HDP. A story for another day perhaps?' We can head up to Haringey for that one, where the revolution still lives.

Aydin Dikerdem works as a Community Organiser in London and is a Labour Party Councillor in Wandsworth. Growing up he moved between his Mum in Battersea and his Father in Hackney, two areas that have changed drastically in his lifetime.

Haggerston School, Haggerston, Ernő Goldfinger, 1964–1967

A tough and generously scaled inner city comprehensive school, and while it's another example of the category error of painting the concrete work of the architect responsible for the best concrete work in 20th century Britain, everything else about the building's upkeep is heartening, right down to the gardens and play areas. The vast assembly hall and the pathway leading between the two buildings of the school are especially strong – unsentimental, spacious, full with civic pride.[OH]

OtoProjects, Dalston, Assemble, 2015

The sort of thing they call in the more intellectual parts of the trade 'expanding the field'. Built by volunteers out of packed earth, waste, and wood, this is anarcho-hipster rusticism for the 'project space' of the Dalston free jazz and experimental music venue Cafe Oto, placed into a wasteland behind a fence, surrounded with rubbish. There is nothing else quite like it – a post-apocalyptic garden shed, built with such mob-handed clumsiness that you can imagine it housing the characters in Russell Hoban's *Riddley Walker*.[OH]

Gillett Square, Hawkins\Brown, 1993

First master-planned by the Hackney Co-operative Development in 1995 and imagined as a new town centre for Dalston, Gillett Square has been an incremental development over some 25 years. This process has allowed its design to respond and adapt to the changing ambitions of its community, as though improvisation was baked into the architecture. Gillett Square is one of few contemporary British public spaces where visitors don't feel they have to be actively consuming to be present. Yet commerce isn't totally eradicated from the square, which is lined with trees on one side and bounded by ten kiosks for local businesses on another. Most afternoons, a pop-up playground is constructed by volunteers – the high octane play of children offset by an older crowd lingering, loitering and watching the world go by.[ZC]

Gibson Garden, Stoke Newington, Henry D. Davis and Barrow Emanuel, 1880

Turning off the busy A10, as you enter the claggy one-way system around Stoke Newington, there behind the wrought iron gates is Gibson Garden. It's a strange little pocket of preserved Victorian London with cobbled streets still intact. Gibson Gardens is configured in an L shape and lined with four-storey, robust brick Victorian houses. Built in 1880 by the Metropolitan Association of Dwellings of the Industrious Classes, this was one of London's first social housing experiments. It housed the workforce of the Industrial Revolution, raising living standards, health standards, even productivity standards. Yet you didn't have to be active in the industrial workforce to be considered in the masterplan, as the strip of cottages in the middle was for the elderly relatives of the tenants – the original granny-annex. Gibson Garden is now the sort of place councils are hankering to recreate in their placemaking strategy sessions. Children-chalked hopscotch, four storeys of window ledges be-decked with terracotta plant pots brimming with geraniums and a patchwork of community-built flower beds. My bedlinen and your knickers, drying side by side.[ZC]

Dalston Eastern Curve Garden, J&LGibbons, EXYZT, Muf Architecture/Art, 2010

This garden was created on the derelict Eastern Curve Railway Line, to offer green public space in a built-up area, where few people have their own gardens. A spacious timer pavilion which now houses a cafe, pizza oven and seating areas opens onto a naturalistic garden sloping north-east down the curve of the site.[Om]

The Bath House Children's Community Centre (formerly Dalston Children's Centre), Hackney Downs, Matrix Feminist Design Co-operative, 1985

The state-funded Dalston Children's Centre was established by an all-women group of parents and childcare workers in the 1980s. Having already worked to develop their temporary premises, the Matrix Feminist Design Co-operative became the architects for the conversion of a former baths building in Dalston. With early drawings being criticised for an 'aura of completeness', Matrix developed the method of using large-scale, movable models to involve the clients in the design process. Now called the Bath House Children's Community Centre, the conversion continues to operate as a volunteer-led charity.[IA]

OtoProjects (left, image by Assemble), Gibson Garden (centre), Bath House Children's Community Centre (right)

Romford, the Suburban Vanguard
Tom Wilkinson

Coney Island was an embryonic Manhattan, according to the architect Rem Koolhaas, a place where developments that would later characterise the metropolis were first essayed on a smaller scale. In a similar vein, we can see Romford as the petri dish of British urbanism. But whereas Koolhaas found Coney's pasteboard dream-worlds reflected in Gotham's spires, the parallelism we are concerned with here is altogether less surreal: the Romford model is rather one of hard-nosed commercial interests in unison with hard-bitten local government. And the ersatzery produced by this duumvirate does not aspire to fantasia but to a version of the quotidian urban setting optimised for sales and rent-gathering. The result is an answer to the unasked question, 'what if out-of-town shopping ate the high street?', which has since been enthusiastically reaffirmed in 'malls without walls' such as Liverpool One.

Romford attained its avant-garde position via a rear-guard action. In the 19th century the historic Essex market town was absorbed into the city by the suburban railways, like so many of London's satellites. Nevertheless, it continued to thrive as an independent industrial and commercial entity, the former thanks to the huge and ancient brewery that once occupied much of the town, the latter to the even older market that continues to this day, and which so appealed to the architecture critic Ian Nairn. Writing in the mid-1960s, Nairn regretted the traffic that choked its bustle and asked: what if arcades were driven back into the town off its main streets, providing havens for its shoppers? 'Then Romford could become an exciting place on every day of the week.'

Nairn's dream came true, but not perhaps in the way he had envisaged. The borough solved its traffic problems by girdling the town with a ring road, which certainly has its merits – an old information film shows the centre jammed with buses, whereas much of it is now car-free. However, this also turned Romford into an island accessible from its hinterland only via dismal underpasses. Meanwhile, the centre was devoured by malls. Today there are five of these, and much of the remainder of the town is a carpark, offering no fewer than 6,000 spaces.

Romford's seemingly unstoppable mallification began in the 1960s and intensified in the wake of Thatcher's deregulation of out-of-town shopping, when Havering attempted to compete with the lure of Lakeside in the neighbouring borough of Thurrock. This strategy was a partial success, if we measure these things in terms of footfall, jobs and rents. Nevertheless, while it may seem churlish to criticise a place that has, after all, managed to resist the hollowing-out of other suburban centres, thereby retaining an unusual identity and vitality for a London satellite, one might well ask – at what cost?

On first acquaintance, the cost seems high indeed: Romford's charms are obscure to the point of invisibility. The market place has two notable older buildings, an uninteresting Victorian church and a much better pub, but the remainder is blighted by decades of bad commercial architecture. Across the square, which is (of course) a carpark when the market isn't on, a glowering 1960s Debenhams faces a cheap-looking 1990s neo-vernacular mixed-use megastructure. This idiom is also applied to the market's point de vue, a paper-thin pseudo-market hall with a ground floor colonnade, the fanged maw of the intestinal subway.

The pedestrianised South Street is, if anything, worse. Although the buildings here are less overbearing, they are still of poor quality and, furthermore, many house the chain bars that comprise Romford's 'night-time economy'. Though lately rivalled by the flashier nightlife of Brentwood, Romford still draws an enthusiastic weekend crowd that reminded me starkly of my own teenage years in a market town. This is fun for a lot of people, but not for a lot of others – let's just say I wouldn't walk down South Street holding my boyfriend's hand. It should also be noted that Havering is the whitest borough in London, thanks to the *Drang nach Osten* following the Blitz and later waves of white flight.

This demographic composition gives the place an unmistakeable cockney twang, which it is easy to romanticise. Indeed, this tendency has a venerable history, from Ian Dury's song *Razzle in my Pocket*, about shoplifting pornographic magazines from South Street shopping arcade, to Underworld's more recent love-affair with the town – the singer has referred to Romford as 'my Manhattan'. The Welsh duo have lived here since their 1990s heyday, and their most famous song, *Born Slippy* is named after a greyhound that ran on the local track, the survival of which amenity itself speaks volumes. The song's lyrics sound like an ambiguous celebration of the town's more obvious characteristics: 'lager lager lager... mega mega white thing'.

Both of these representations are the work of what could uncharitably be called class tourists (as could Nairn), but despite their grimy romanticism the trajectory Romford travels between these songs – from working-class 60s shopping centre to raucous watering hole – is not inaccurate. Ironically, it was the closure of the brewery that marked this transition. When Ind Coope shut up shop in 1993 after 300 years of operation in the town, much of the population's erstwhile place of work was demolished and transformed into a mixed-use mall called The Brewery – in and around which they are more than capable of organising the proverbial piss-up.

Romford's most interesting architectural features are traces of this transformation, which is emblematic of the UK's metamorphosis as a whole over the last half century. A lost fragment of the brewery façade lingers on the High Street, in which the local museum is embedded, and an enormous concrete chimney remains marooned in the carpark of the shopping centre that replaced the factory. The architects of the centre have wound the ramp leading up to the rooftop parking level around this feature, giving it the look of a waterpark flume, elegantly summing up the relationship between the town (and the wider country's) past and present economies: parasitic growth and moribund host. Sprinkled else-where around the carpark are large, brightly coloured metal sculptures, insect-like forms evidently intended to alleviate the barren landscape. In this they succeed, albeit to menacing effect.

Thankfully, Romford has more to offer beyond the ring-road, in the form of its famous garden suburb at Gidea Park. Many of the houses here resulted from a 1910 competition that attracted some of the best architects working in Britain at that time. The two contributions by Parker and Unwin are particularly good, their Arts and Crafts exuberance constrained by a harder-edged rationality. However, whatever the merits of its individual components, Gidea Park does not cohere: its proposed centre is missing, and, as the project of a local Liberal politician, it delib-erately rejects the radically reformed landownership of Ebenezer Howard's Garden City ideal. Instead it is just more suburban sprawl, albeit prettier than average.

On the western fringe of the town can be found, to my mind, an even more striking domestic experiment, a solitary early attempt to densify the suburbs. Despite its drastic 60s reshaping, Romford was never a high-rise town. The centre contains a couple of office towers, but these are the tallest points in a vast steppe of semis and commercial ribbon development. On the border with Barking and Dagenham, however, stands Bedwell Court: an austere four-storey sentinel marking the cross-ing point into Havering. This miniature Brutalist castle, all grey brick in concrete frames and jutting concrete balconies, is strikingly dissimilar to the houses that surround it, and the wastes of Becontree to the south. What happens inside is even stranger: a glass-topped atrium with walkways flying across to the flats' doorways. In its hard-wearing spatial exuberance it is not dissimilar to Hermann Hertzberger's extraordinary Centraal Beheer building in the Netherlands.

Bedwell Court (all images by Tom Wilkinson)

Gidea Park

River Rom

Havering

E

After this fanfare, what comes next can only be a disappointment, but Romford needn't remain that way. As a recent report by the borough identifies, there is plenty of room for improvement – however, the changes it suggests are extremely timid. What could Romford (and by extension the British town) be like, if it weren't so dependent on the rates from vast shopping centres? Well, some of these could be cracked open, or built upon, starting with their carparks. There is no green space to speak of in Romford, and the River Rom runs culverted beneath the tarmac, emerging only briefly and almost unobserved beside a run-down industrial estate. Imagine what an architecture practice like Muf could do if set loose on this post-industrial landscape, perhaps excavating the carpark around the looming chimney to reveal a cratered waterway, and greening the ruins. Following the precedent of Bedwell Court, more and denser (and better designed) housing would also improve the centre, giving it a life apart from out-of-town shoppers and drinkers. In view of the virus-exacerbated retail crisis, it is well worth thinking about the coming changes creatively rather than them being thrust upon us willy-nilly. With a bit of imagination, Romford could become a model for an altogether happier urban future.

Tom Wilkinson is a Leverhulme Early Career Fellow at the Warburg Institute and History Editor of the *Architectural Review*. His book *Bricks and Mortals: Ten Great Buildings and the People They Made* was published by Bloomsbury in 2014.

The Trackway and Rainham Marshes, Rainham, Peter Beard Landroom, 2009

This gently sloping bridge provides significant improvements to an important rambling and cycling route, linking Rainham village to the River Thames. Its ramp, perched on many jaunty legs, forms an elegant new threshold landmark appropriate to the scale of Rainham marshes and a much-rationalised walk down to marsh level from the astonishingly ugly and over-engineered pedestrian bridge spanning the Eurostar line. The timber columns support a composite deck with structural engineering by Jane Wernick Associates. The trackway is the most prominent of numerous adjustments Landroom made to paths and tracks that tread carefully across the marshes including wayfinding signage, seating, interpretive elements and informal play areas. Beard's designs sit somewhere between landscape, infrastructure and architecture, feeling both tough enough to seem at home in a semi-industrial setting, and sensitive enough to allow rambling families and bird watchers to appreciate them.[PH]

Railing Hall, Rainham, East Architecture with Mark Pimlott, 2014

East Architecture have been working on projects within the village of Rainham for many years supported by the GLA. One of their more curious additions is this steel structure, designed with artist Mark Pimlott. A wall, constructed from off-the-shelf railings, defines a public garden intended to eventually become overgrown with plants. The form lightly references the grandness of the nearby historic Rainham Hall, a National Trust property.[PH]

Upminster Tithe Barn

A 15th century box-framed barn with a reed-thatched roof run as an eccentric museum of memorabilia. The Barn is a scheduled ancient monument commonly known as 'The Tithe Barn' although there is no evidence to suggest it was ever used for the collection of tithes.[PH]

The Queen's Theatre, Hornchurch, borough architect R.W. Hallam and project architect Norman Brooks, 1975

Opened by Sir Peter Hall, a robust example of 1970s civic architecture. The auditorium seats 506 people in a raked, continental-style layout with an orchestra pit accommodating up to 24 musicians. The musicals Tommy and Blood Brothers both started at The Queen's Theatre before transferring to the West End.[Om]

The Round House, Havering-Atte-Bower, original design attributed to John Plaw, 1792

When it was built The Round House, an oval stuccoed country villa of three storeys, was described as providing 'all conveniences of a country seat in miniature'. In the early 20th century the Round House was occupied by the Revd. Joseph Hardwick Pemberton, a famous rose-grower and President of the National Rose Society who grew and hybridised roses there, including the Alexandra Rose as well as various Musk and Shrub roses.[Om]

Cold Blooded Reptile Centre, Rainham, original architect unknown, refurbished by Designed by Good People, 2015

Actively eschewing an online presence and forbidding photography or filming inside, the Cold Blooded Reptile Centre is an enigmatic presence in the village of Rainham. Behind its painted *trompe l'oeil* windows, hundreds of snakes and lizards writhe under ultraviolet light in a cave of reptilian wonders. Watch out of the Komodo Dragon. The reptile centre moved premises to its current home after it was burned to the ground in 2012. It was then treated to a facelift by Designed by Good People who were also commissioned to upgrade the frontage of Rainham's Phoenix pub and Kings Kebabs.[PH]

Rainham Hall, 1729, refurbished Julian Harrap Architects, 2015

Rainham Hall is a remarkably intact Queen Anne style merchant's house built in 1729. The Hall and its cluster of associated buildings are situated in the centre of Rainham Village next to the Norman church of St Helen and St Giles. The Hall has been inhabited by nearly 50 different residents or families since it was built and is currently run by the National Trust whose programme changes every 18–24 months to present a different era in the building's history. The hall's 18th century wrought-iron railings at the front of the house are a significant feature of the site as they represent some of the finest work of London smiths of the time. Also of note are the Victorian dog-kennels.[Om]

The Trackway (left), The Round House (centre), Rainham Hall (right, image NT/Dennis Gilbert)

Although travel restrictions have made the rest of the world feel much further away, many of us have used the pandemic as a chance to get to know our own neigbourhoods better. The number of people cycling in London boomed during lockdown, as fewer cars on the roads made us feel safer exploring our streets on two wheels. Widened pavements have also made us consider the negotiation of space between walkers, cyclists and drivers, and have renewed calls for more pedestrianised streets across the capital.

The history of London is a history of conflict through different forms of mobility; from horse-and-carts to electric scooters, via trolley cars, railway extensions, wheelchairs, a cable car and many others. This roof finial, complete with globe detail, is a remnant of a particularly fierce conflict of mobilities. It previously stood atop a Victorian terraced house in Wanstead that was occupied by supporters of the Stop the M11 Link campaign in 1994. The protestors sought to prevent the building of a new road through the neighbourhood, and declared the independent states of Leytonstonia and Wanstonia in the process.

Their campaign was ultimately unsuccessful and the road was built, but the legacy of this and other road protests remains. Transport for London is anticipating a tenfold increase in cycling in comparison to pre-Covid-19 levels; perhaps the days of a car-dominated city are numbered.

Redbridge

Roof finial 10 Cambridge Park, Wanstead, anti-road occupation, 1993–94, 240 × 150mm, Museum of London (© Museum of London)

Convivial Spaces
Joy White

As long ago as Charles Booth's 1889 study of poverty in London, the East End has been seen as a foreign land in the shadow of the wealth of the City, populated by communities of poor people and migrants. Situated roughly five miles to the east of the City of London, Newham is now also within blinking distance of Canary Wharf financial district. In that context, the actual achievements and successes of working class multicultural populations in the borough are often considered insignificant to those who would 'regenerate' it.

From the formation of The London Docklands Development Corporation in 1981 onwards, which included Beckton and the Royal Docks (both in the borough), Newham has been subject to large-scale regeneration projects. At the Shanghai Expo in 2010, Newham promoted itself on a global stage as a site of major investment and possibility – an 'Arc of Opportunity'. Newham was also the main site of the 2012 London Olympics. This is a young multicultural borough with a median age of 31.9 and 72% of its population from a Black or ethnic minority background. Its current status as one of the most culturally diverse areas in the UK is in keeping with its history as a location for significant migration from Africa, the Caribbean, South Asia and Europe. Today, Newham continues its process of extensive regeneration and redevelopment. In Stratford, the former Olympic Park has been redeveloped, while the Victoria & Albert museum and University College London will have new sites nearby. Crossrail will have four stations in Newham – Manor Park, Forest Gate, Maryland and Stratford – making the area even more accessible to the few who can afford to buy property. However, by any measure, Newham still faces economic and social challenges. Residents are employed mainly in occupations that are relatively low-paid, such as health, care and retail. At the same time, housing costs are rising.

A strong link exists in Newham between music, place and identity. Making and listening to music can create a sense of belonging, and for the borough's young population, grime, rap and UK drill form a sonic backdrop. Newham was one of the birthplaces of grime. Initially a hyper-localised creative expression, it now attracts a worldwide audience.

As a diasporic cultural form, grime has been nourished by its Black Atlantic connections to the Caribbean, Africa and North America, with all of these influences meeting in Newham where a confluence of people and place created an environment from which this music could emerge. Estates, street corners, youth clubs and schools operated as unofficial creative clusters, where young people would gather to make their own innovative music. Pirate radio stations such as Deja Vu in Stratford and Flava FM in Canning Town provided a training ground for young MCs and DJs to hone their craft. It is unlikely that this sound could have come from a leafy, monocultural suburb – it needed a convivial coming together of music, migration and communities. Inner city teenagers, making music from the limited resources that they had around them, were able to create a Black English aesthetic that pushed back the juggernaut of US hip-hop and rap. Young people who drew on their cultural heritage from the Caribbean or Africa managed to create a sound that spread throughout the world.

It would be reasonable to think that these communities, which had been responsible for so much creativity – and against such odds – would be being celebrated by the borough, and could even be at the heart of how it 'regenerates' itself. On the contrary, as you can see in places such as Forest Gate, regeneration often renders them out of place.

Forest Gate is in the north of the borough. It is bordered at one end by Wanstead Flats – a vast green space which is the southernmost point of Epping Forest. The high street, Woodgrange Road, takes its name from the site of Woodgrange Farm, a 12th century settlement. Some of the streets off Woodgrange Road have large houses with roads named after Queen Victoria's palaces (Balmoral, Claremont, Windsor, Osborne and Hampton). At the junction of Forest Lane and Woodgrange Road there is a drinking fountain for cattle and a clocktower built at the turn of the 20th century. With two railway stations at either end, this environment combines the 'village' feel that tends to appeal to estate agents and middle class incomers with easy access to the City of London and Canary Wharf.

There is a long history of local community buildings here that have carved out creative spaces; originally a Unitarian settlement, Durning Hall Community Centre is located at the junction of Woodgrange Road and Earlham Grove. It was rebuilt after being bombed in the Second World War. The Forest Gate Public Hall was the site of a 'People's Palace' in the late 19th century. It became the Uppercut – a live music spot – in the 1960s featuring artists such as Jimi Hendrix and Stevie Wonder. It continued as an entertainment venue before finally being demolished in 2005 to make way for a Channel Tunnel ventilation shaft. With grime

Baseman × Snizzy – Better Place (Forest Gate) (SBTV)

Newham

E

and rap, meanwhile, artists have often referenced the areas that they came from. When, in 2016, SBTV – the online youth broadcaster – developed a musical series called Better Place, two of these tracks had a Newham focus: Lil Nasty on Plaistow and Baseman × Snizzy on Forest Gate. Both music videos show a tough environment and offer an uncompromising narrative about what it means to grow up in these 'ends' with limited choices. When we listen to the lyrics and absorb the visuals in Baseman × Snizzy's Better Place video there is a sense of deep attachment to place. From the opening shots, we are able to see local reference points in the public realm, such as the park behind the former hospital in Forest Lane, as well as the High Street, Forest Gate Station and the Caribbean take-away. Looking at that video now allows us to see the changes that have occurred in the area, as Forest Gate town centre undergoes a long period of extensive regeneration.

At the junction where the main roads meet is where you will find many of the cultural and social spaces for the new Forest Gate residents – a weekly farmers market, coffee shops and a gastropub. Off Sebert Road, under the railway arches, there is a bar/deli/record store. Further along Woodgrange Rd an organic bulk store allows people to bring their own containers to buy produce such as grains, flour, fruit and vegetables. All of these leisure activities are in keeping with a local development framework within which the 'regeneration of Forest Gate is a key priority for Newham Council'. For Forest Gate, this means the creation of a more genteel night-time economy, with a broader range of pubs, restaurants and cafes. Plans include Forest Gate becoming a site for small-scale business start-ups, as well as creative and cultural workspaces.

The Council wants to maintain the Victorian conservation area in the roads off Woodgrange Road, enhance Forest Gate as a town centre, upgrade the shopping and leisure experience and create a relaxed 'urban village' environment. At the same time, the town planners have identified that the social housing estates in the roads off Woodgrange Road are 'hotspots for crime', deemed to be 'backlands' – less desirable, less spacious, and containing, according to the council, poor quality housing. As in many London boroughs, poverty and wealth sit side by side. Regeneration buried pirate radio station Deja Vu under the Olympic Park, and Flava FM disappeared long before the redevelopment of Rathbone Market in Canning Town. But even in this ever-changing landscape it is possible to see the traces and footprints of Newham's multicultural musical heritage.

Joy White is a Lecturer in Applied Social Studies at the University of Bedfordshire. She is the author of *Urban Music and Entrepreneurship: Beats, Rhymes and Young People's Enterprise* (2016) and *Terraformed: Young Black Lives in The Inner City* (2020)

Thames Barrier Park, Silvertown, Patel Taylor, 1995–1999

A rare good public space in Docklands, and something more poetic than that implies. These sunken spaces, set out to evoke miniature docks, is miles from the functional landscape architecture of granite setts and little pools so familiar in riverside regeneration public spaces. It spurns all that greyness in favour of a *Last Year In Marienbad* architecture of surreal sculpted topiary and formalistic patterning. It is multi-level, with waves of hedges and secret gardens, creating a constant game of hide and seek with the river, the Barrier and the chaotic bustle of luxury flats being built around it. Of these, the Barratt flats immediately overlooking the park are worth a look

too: they have the right sort of scale, with their stepped sections and Red Vienna-style stairwells and flagpoles, though the cheapness of their materials means they already look stained and worn.[OH]

University of East London, North Woolwich, Edward Cullinan, 1996–2000

We have little to show architecturally for the massive expansion of higher education (at a price) embarked upon by the New Labour governments of 1997–2010 – there are isolated gems, yet there is extremely little that betrays any sort of holistic, coherent, thought-out development. But there is this, tucked away between the Royal Docks and City Airport. It might be off-putting at first – the childlike aesthetic is more *Noel's House Party* than Denys Lasdun, and the cheap render and aluminium cries out 'Private Finance Initiative' – but spend a bit of time here, and its deep underlying individuality starts to emerge. The campus, rehous-ing a conglomerate of ex-polys in the East End and metropolitan Essex, is organised around two focal points. One consists of a set of halls of residence in the form of multicoloured drums, a very unusual post-70s example of including student housing in a campus, rather than leaving it to speculators in the area around. The Library and the classroom buildings are in angular, ribbon-windowed white buildings, and in the library, you can watch aeroplanes

take off and touch down. The public spaces between these buildings are clear, obvious and well-used – a dockside promenade, a main square – but they can't make the location feel any less bizarre and implausible, especially as there's no connection with any kind of ordinary residential area around. The result is one of London's most alien landscapes, the unofficial J.G Ballard University.[OH]

Worland Gardens, Stratford, Peter Barber Architects, 2016

If there's good social housing built in London in the 2010s, chances are it's tiny, ingenious, and designed by Peter Barber. Rather a lot of housing has been built in Stratford since it was designated home of the Olympics in 2012, ranging from the Euromodernism of the Olympic Village to the speculative dross foisted upon Stratford High Street. It's quite the indictment that by far the most architecturally interesting new building was a half-terrace of houses down a backstreet. These boast the currently ubiquitous stock brick, arranged into a rhythmic row of houses with archways over the doorways, showing a warmth and friendliness that feels very Arts and Crafts. A monumental tone comes from the triumphal arch, which feels like it ought to be leading you to some grand public garden, but actually just provides a useful place for residents to park their cars. This should be the basis for a district, not half a street.[OH]

Thames Barrier Park (top left) University of East London (bottom left), Worland Gardens (right, image by Peter Barber Architects)

An End and a Beginning
Laura Grace Ford

It's Michaelmas and Tesco Extra is crowded with asters. For weeks gladioli have bunched around the entrance, bending at angles in cellophane sheets, now it's starbursts of daisies, purple and pink like sugared almonds.

The A11, the last scatterings of London.
Edwardian houses, stone cladding, saplings splitting the walls.

We lived above this one. I look up at the window, the faded red curtains, pleats of pale rose where the sun bleached them. The marker pen drawing is still there on the pane, the outline of his hand, a staring eye.
He left marks to guide those coming next, I never imagined that I'd be one of those straggling behind, searching for clues in the walls, deciphering code in whorls of graffiti.
There was a yard at the back with cracked paving stones and roses smelling of sherbert and raspberry sorbet. Next door was Kwik Fit.
We saw them gathering on the forecourt, dozens of them in black salwar and huaraches. He called them psychopomps, caught in the liminal zone between London and Essex. Sometimes they'd be away on jamaat but mostly they'd be here in the oil slicks and black dust.

The River Roding, the North Circular, low rise millennial housing.

There are gaps where there shouldn't be, revenant terraces, mirages over rubble heaps. The September heat brings smells I'd forgotten, red earth and pine needles, mauve shadows under conifers.
The way he directed me is haphazard, a confused cross hatching of scrawls and symbols on a sheet of paper. I scrutinise the lines, the pressure points, the skimming of his hand.

London is contained by the elevated motorway, the pylons and the river.

I follow paths through rusting tangles of buddleia and hawthorn.
Concrete slabs are dumped to hold off travellers, brambles and sycamore break through metal railings. This is an interstitial zone, a nameless place.

I cross buckled tarmac where charcoal and crushed cans of Leck mark old revelries. It's clipped perennials then, red stemmed dogwood in geometric clumps, and a care home, a two-storey slump of ochre brick. Idris is waiting with a cigarette in his hand talking to a nurse in a green uniform. Seeing him is like stepping through a portal, groves of low-rise blocks become radioactive, reanimated as the decades compress.

He pulls me in, smothers me with the catnip of delicious, forgotten names. The nurse shakes my hand and smiles before returning to penumbral rooms of dettol and daytime TV. I told him about the parties Idris says, the power station and that, he's into it. I'd forgotten this, the pied piper gathering of troops.

Desiccated palms in plastic urns, earthenware pots smashed on the gravel. Lavender place. Little Ilford Lane.

We're walking into town to see some old mates. It's strange even to think of them after all this time, I anticipate the visit like a seance or a resurrection.

Shaki and Khalil.

Appliance shops, office blocks, a knot of new towers.

He asks if I remember Pioneer Market.

The shell of art deco arcades, a smell of meat and sawdust, a pie and mash shop maybe. I think about Ilford Sounds where we got rare jungle records, you had to sift through racks, nothing was in alphabetical order. Now the imprint of the market is deep within the foundations of Pioneer Point, twin obelisks dominating the skyline. Idris tells me about property scams, corruption on a massive scale, Nawaz Sharif shuffling money.

The high street is busy, overheated. Someone presses a religious tract into my hand with planets radiating supernatural light.

Idris says Ilford is an important station on a sacred route. For him the town's redevelopment in the 1980s was an attempt to keep everything circulating in an enclosed drum.

Primark. Superdrug. Argos.

I remember that pound shop from before, QuidSaver, a luminous cavern exploding with baubles and tinsel. The woody scents of incense are blue in the air, a smoky drift from the stock cupboard.

We walk round the back to Havelock Street. The pub is still there on the corner. Last time we were on microdots, higher doses than today.

I remember drinking bottles of cold lager watching the glowing outlines of the arched windows. There was a property show on TV with the sound off, I remember bright images of thatched cottages upturned by dark UK garage spilling from the jukebox.

The flat is pressed in between the railway tracks and Harrison Gibson

(Image by Laura Grace Ford)

furniture store, they're demolishing it soon Idris says, turning it into a 30-storey drome. The way he describes the new development is a cold warren, a glacial hive of corridors.

Havelock Road is loading bays and fire escapes, the obverse side of the high street. We stop at a yard with indigo shadows and sharp autumn light, everything razor-edged like a collage. The flat is above the pound shop, you have to climb steel steps to get in, then a caged roof with galaxies of white petalled stars, jasmine broadcasting a druggy sexual fragrance.

Idris shouts through the letter box. The windows are dust caked and barred. There's a temperature drop as we cross the threshold, a cold slap of damp.

Newspapers are spread out across the floor, dishes of food arranged there and I realise they've been waiting for us. The missing years are elastic, cloying stretches of unexplained time. Idris told me he went to see Khalil in detention once. Afghanistan is a scrubbed zone on the map, they're Hazara, an ethnicity the Taliban tried to cleanse. I think of those giant Bamiyan buddhas, cliffs of wreckage there. Now they're working with Idris on this renovation project, houses near the power station.

They have a musical instrument called a tar, I'd never seen one before I met them. It's like an 8, two mulberry bowls stretched with lambskin. They play Farsi folk songs, sounds unfolding in the thick scents of blue-berry kush. Idris calls it bluesy, a buzzing kind of vibe. It's like crystals replicating, the giant's causeway or something.

Conversations unspool in the music. We're discussing new places, the zone round the power station, the tidal shifts of the Thames. There's a new town forming there, and parties in the shells of pubs. They want out of this place, the crazy rent and goggle-eyed landlord. They show me the dustings of mould, the ashy dots from floor to ceiling.

The concrete frame of the furniture store is wrapped in plastic sheeting. A door is propped open, its vast showrooms have become Ilford plaza, a skein of stalls and cabins, plywood tunnels of sepia light.

A heavy Attar fragrance conjures nights in that last house, the roses, the Kwik Fit, the guardians at the gate.

Punjabi film posters, kurtas, embroidered prayer mats. The place is quiet. Idris says it's the first time he's seen it in this state. It feels crepuscular, on the verge of eviction. Then a corner booth with photocopied hands, all the lines labelled – head, heart and life. Idris wants to go in, says it's an entrance to the 'real building, where it's actually happening.'

We push through black baize. There are no lights, just evening sunlight leaching through gaps in boarded windows. The polystyrene ceiling has black gaps like a crossword. I look into the concrete vault above, it's dark and dusty like the backstage of a theatre.
There are empty display units, raised platforms where settees and tables would have nested.

A stairwell is petrol blue like the 70s. At every landing there are padlocked doors. There'a smell of tobacco, and something else, woodsmoke or burnt grasses.

On the 15th floor a nightclub, a carmine shell lined with leather banquettes. I trace patterns in the walls with my fingertips, there are sounds locked in them.
Idris beckons me to a wall of windows. London is there in the distance, serrated jags in a band of hazy violet. The forest is an island chain, a bluish archipelago. I feel its groves, its smoky fragile webs.

I can see the imprint of a roman signalling beacon and Howard's chemical factory, then the iron age hill fort, the care home he drew in blue biro.
I think of the nurse in the green uniform and wonder if we'll ever see him again.

I don't know the time but the sky is indigo like the skin of Japanese plums, the bloom on dark chocolate.

Wanstead Flats, Green Man Roundabout. The protests at Claremont Road. Faces come scuttling back. I think about the end when we were evicted, how Idris was there when it seemed hopeless. Mirrors light up behind an empty bar, I see his face scrambled.

Ibis Budget. Wall End. The salt marshes and container ports.
He points out dusky willow trees, a V formation of geese.

Ilford is a border town, an end and a beginning.

Laura Grace Ford is an artist and writer concerned with architecture, fiction and class. Her work has been widely published and exhibited. She is author of *Savage Messiah* (2011) and is currently a Somerset House Studios resident and a researcher at the Royal College of Art. She is currently working on *Charms over Ashes*, a book of stories.

The Hainault Loop, Charles Holden, 1947–49

Four stations on the Hainault loop, a strange hidden Circle Line near the eastern end of the Central Line, mark the conclusion to the Charles Holden/Frank Pick era of London Underground design. The most famous of these is Gants Hill, which is actually nothing at all on the surface, just a sign leading to an underpass, and below that, the station hall. Here, Holden returned a favour. In the 1930s, he and Pick had advised on the Moscow Metro, whose deep escalators and grand classical spaces were partly modelled on Piccadilly Circus. Gants Hill was Holden borrowing in turn from the fabulous underground vaults of Moscow stations such as Mayakovskaya; the station was even codenamed 'Moscow'. Combined seats and uplighters which make it look even more Muscovite were added in the 1980s. Redbridge and Wanstead are more austere; Redbridge featuring a brick rotunda and Wanstead a stark concrete tower. But the real masterwork in this cross-Essex ensemble isn't by Holden at all, but by the talented eclectic Oliver Hill – the bus shelter designed alongside Newbury Park station. It's a wonderfully simple concrete barrel vault, left open to create a colonnade. The budget was low, but Hill knew exactly what to do with what he had, and created a mini-masterclass in transport architecture – useful, simple, and just beautiful enough to take the edge off the tedium of commuting.[OH]

Fulwell Cross Library and Leisure Centre, Ilford, Frederick Gibberd, 1958–68

These two buildings are very successful examples of Gibberd's attempts to take Renaissance architectural devices and make them a) vaguely modernist and b) cute – you can find very many images of this place on Instagram. The library is a rotunda with a marvellously odd fluted copper and glass roof, something between a big top, and a Persian mosque with a big *Meydan* square in front (like a Persian mosque as imitated by a Soviet architect in 1960s Tashkent). It's definitely a much more architecturally interesting mosque than the actual one Gibberd designed in Regent's Park. An arcade, almost full-scale postmodernism *avant-la-lettre*, leads to the classically disciplined but more obviously modernist leisure centre adjacent, with which it forms a Renaissance-style ensemble of dome and box. Both buildings are similarly fun-filled inside, especially the library, where the circus-like dome's glazing floods a central reading room with light.[OH]

The Cauliflower Hotel, Ilford, 1897

A once spectacular Victorian gin palace, the Cauliflower in Ilford was a hotel, pub and live music venue where bands including the Small Faces and Ian Dury have appeared. It was Grade II listed to protect the battered but spectacular interior, a riot of stained glass, brass rails and carved wood, when it closed in 2013. It reopened under new management in 2018 only to mysteriously fall victim to fire soon after.[PH]

The Barkingside Arch, Assemble, 2013

Among the earliest and least well known of the Turner Prize-winning architecture studio Assemble's permanent projects is the Barkingside Arch. Rough-cast with multi-colored concrete, the arch's constituent blocks are marbled with different textures and pigments turning this humble structure into a pleasing portal at the entrance to Fairlop Waters Country Park.[PH]

Gurdwara Karamsar, Agenda 21 Architects Studio, 2005

A contemporary Sikh temple of sandstone quarried and hand-carved in Rajasthan. The front elevation has heavily profiled carved stonework pilasters, balconies, and Jarookhas – ornately carved stone oriel bay window structures. The front roof terrace is accentuated with small chattris, or viewing shelters, each of which has a small domed roof. The building embodies a transition of cultures, technologies and time, with a largely traditional exterior but a chic white modernistic interior. Two pilasters framing the main entrance were emblazoned with five motifs each representing Punjab and Redbridge respectively.[PH]

Newbury Park bus station (left), Fulwell Cross Library (centre), the Barkingside Arch (top right), Gurdwara Karamsar (bottom right)

Walking Whitechapel High Street
Thomas Aquilina

In the heat of July, I arrive at the large, nondescript junction of Aldgate East station. Except this is not a usual Sunday afternoon. It's the first time I have walked a high street in months. After sheltering-in-place since March, I am feeling attentive to my movements, with heightened senses to the city around me. My feet stride slowly on the street, unnatural for my usual jostling pace; but now there are new rules of navigation and distancing. The solitude of quarantine has made walking a means of escape.

The site of my re-entry to the city is Whitechapel High Street, a densely packed central road shaped by deep histories of migration to east London. The six kilometre stretch extends from Aldgate to Stratford on an east-west axis bisecting the borough of Tower Hamlets. Like a main artery, the high street is a necessary part of the everydayness of the city, yet its features are distinct, with changing spatial patterns at varying increments of scale, from narrow retail spaces and alleyways to substantial public buildings.

I look back from my point of arrival, the view west capturing the distant cluster of iconic London skyscrapers. The buildings around Aldgate East station shrink in their signalling of departure from the nucleus of the city, a more sleek version of the glazed high-rises mirroring each other at this intersection. It is unusually quiet, at this border between the City of London and Tower Hamlets, but the creep of change and increasing gentrification is still visible.

The textile factory turned London Metropolitan University's The Sir John Cass School of Art, Architecture and Design is now tightly veiled in muted grey preparing for its redevelopment into commercial offices. There is no sign of 2015, when students and staff staged a lock-in demonstration against their campus displacement. In its new home, a few blocks away at Calcutta House, controversy has followed. Disaffection from within dethroned its former moniker of Sir John Cass, as they revealed his past as a prominent figure of the Atlantic slave trade. Juxtaposed, across the street, I take in the freshly wheatpasted murals intervening to remind us that Black Lives Matter, in a renewed struggle for racial equality.

At this moment, just the act of walking feels like a subtle protest. The street encourages me to let go of tensions that have built up from being inside. I am disconnected from the digital world and reconnecting with the basic rhythms of breathing. In a borough where over half of residents are from Black and minority ethnic communities, walking the high street provides me with short-term solidarities. The route leads east, towards the less affluent but ethnically and socially diverse part of the street.

To my left, the castellated Whitechapel Gallery is closed, but still adorns the Radical Figures exhibition poster, featuring artist Michael Armitage's Kampala Suburb. The image shows two figures held in an embrace, referencing a faraway city I know but am unsure when I might return to. 'How have people been surviving without touch?' I ask myself and then leave the question hanging in the last stride. A few doors down, just before the entry to Brick Lane, an electronics shop remains decorated with London 2012 Olympics advertisement. It reflects the touristification of this part of east London that has so successfully commodified its culture.

On the other side of the street is Altab Ali Park, which references a different era, named after the 25-year old Bengali tailor murdered there by racists in 1978. His attack mobilised resistance to racism in the area, and the park has since become the site for a Bengali Martyrs Monument, as well as the place of Muslim activism and anti-fascist rallies. Walking through, the park is like an archaeological ruin with a raised terrazzo walkway marking the partial outline of the medieval white chapel, bombed out in The Blitz in 1940. Disposable facemasks litter the edges of the park, alongside hazard tape, marking the contemporary debris of crisis.

The visual carousel of the high street – bodies, buildings, posters, signage and shopfronts – all register the improvisation of this ongoing pandemic. Back on my journey east, I step between spray-painted floor markings that indicate an acceptable distance between strangers. Time is suspended as people wait in long queues to catch a bus or enter a supermarket. Some shops are using lockdown to refurbish, converting their close-quarter businesses into curbside trading. If anything, the high street is a place to learn from people with powerful survival skills. Resilience is, after all, something migrant communities carry and refashion with regularity.

I am now at the corner between the former Whitechapel Bell Foundry and the East London Mosque. The foundry had been making church bells continuously in Whitechapel since the 16th century until as recently as 2017. A few years earlier it designed the Olympic Bell that chimed at the London 2012 Olympic Games opening ceremony. While the manufacturing company retreated, the East London Mosque has incrementally enlarged its complex. This includes turning a carpark into the London Muslim Centre and the opening of the nine-storey Maryam Centre, a community building

Altab Ali Park (all images by Thomas Aquilina)

dedicated to Muslim women. Most recently the conversion of the former Fieldgate Street Great Synagogue into a Muslim charity premises symbolised how immigrant communities have built, reshaped and expanded their claim on an area, from the periphery as outsider to the centre as fully British or East Ender. This mosque campus presses right up to the street edge, obscuring the scale and importance of this religious fixture.

Continuing on the high street, the mosque is now out of sight, but the sound of the call to prayer lingers in the air, played through infamous loudspeakers – they were the first in Europe granted permission to publicly broadcast the *adhan*. From this point, the street takes on a vernacular, with a mix of small units, travel agents, currency exchanges, Asian confectioneries, fast food outlets, mini-bazars, barbershops, shisha stores, language schools, *chai* and vape emporiums and clothes shops selling *abaya*, *saree*, *lehenga*, Haji essentials, perfume and *attar*. This rich array of cultural necessities and global services serve the local population of residents, signalling their Bangladeshi heritage, as well as significant Somali, Caribbean, Chinese, Vietnamese, Indian and Pakistani communities.

This range of backgrounds and diverse ways of being in the city rely on a close proximity to each other. Tower Hamlets is the fourth most densely populated local authority in London. It has an economy worth over £6 billion a year, which is more than the EU nation of Malta. But poverty is present, providing a stark contrast to the amalgamations of plenitude that have grown around Canary Wharf and the fringes of the City of London. The pandemic exacerbates longstanding inequalities, with Black and minority ethnic communities more likely to be exposed, as the disproportionate majority of essential workers.

Suddenly the pavement on the left-hand side widens and distancing is more easily maintained. It also makes space for the historic Whitechapel Market, although only the framed superstructures and empty trolleys suggest the market's presence, open every other of day of the week. In the middle of the street is King Edward VII's memorial drinking fountain, funded by subscriptions from Jewish residents in 1911. Further along the market strip, I pause to see the stonewashed lettering, 'Working Lads' Institute', inscribed onto a tall gabled building. This masculine marker has its female counterpart next door: a public art display of seven portraits, each filling a window and described as the women of TfL. I can't help but think of the ironic poetry in the gradually fading lads.

On the other side of the street are interpretive hoardings, branded with prescriptive histories to obscure the shell of the former Royal London Hospital. This addition is part of a prolonged conversion into a new civic centre. Reading the laminated text, I journey into the past, but my eyes cannot help but catch the back-set and towering new hospital, completed in 2016. Together the site creates a spatial metaphor of broken-ness and repair that aptly speaks to the work carried out in this leading trauma and emergency care centre. The new hospital's blue and green tinted glass panels seem to follow the treatment expressed in the popular Whitechapel Idea Store, facing each other, diagonally rising up from the high street. Except the Idea Store, a mixed-programme public facility, is better sutured into the parochiality of the street, like a home remedy.

From the next interchange, the street further expands with clearly defined tree-lined avenues, and changes its name to Mile End Road, as if to signal a shift in the threshold from high street to domestic thoroughfare. Its promenade is punctuated by busts, a series of colonial reminders. And given the recent toppling of statues, I ask myself 'should William Booth, founder and first general of the Salvation Army, fall?' Behind the trees, laundry lines spill off the balconies to the blocks of social housing, and I can make out that prayer mats are draped in the sunshine. As the traffic thickens and the street tapers, Bow Church splits the way, marking the end to my pedestrian path and the beginning of suburban sprawl. For me, this corridor has offered a glimpse into the substance of the borough, a social barometer recognising the pressures and changes over time and space. The high street has been a way of diagnosing Tower Hamlets and my walk a stethoscope, listening to the pulses of people and place.

Thomas Aquilina is a London-based designer invested in building communities of radical thought and progressive practice. He currently works for Adjaye Associates, tutors for the New Architecture Writers (N.A.W.) programme and is a founding member of Afterparti, a collective focussed on race and space.

Jagonari Centre, Whitechapel, Matrix Feminist Design Co-Operative, 1987

In 1981, the Jagonari group of Asian women intended to develop a site adjacent to the Davenant Community Centre in Whitechapel. The GLC-funded Jagonari Educational Resource Centre was the cooperative's first large-scale project, developed collaboratively via a series of discussions between the two groups. Its distinctive green window grilles and bold entrance were intended to provide security against the violence faced by Whitechapel's Bangladeshi community while also referencing Islamic architectural motifs.[JA]

E. Pellicci, Bethnal Green, Achille Cappocci, 1946

While radical architects huddled around drawings and plans in Bloomsbury trying to work out a new, convivial modernist architecture for the East End – the Festival of Britain's 'People's Detailing' style – this Anglo-Italian cafe in the heart of it all was the East Enders' own modernist style. Rather than looking to Sweden or Finland, it was much more based on Trans-Atlantic glamour, a tiny Empire State Building of brown sunburst marquetry and custard vitrolite. Now a little too packed out and conscious of itself, it should still be seen – once likely considered 'common', it is now almost unique.[OH]

Chalkwell House, Stepney, Alina and Noel Moffett, 1964; Ashington House, Bethnal Green, Alina and Noel Moffett, 1971

These two are interesting miniature experiments in making a small block of flats something more than a housing silo, by an Irish-Polish husband and wife team on commission from the

LCC. Both have a raw, cranky presence that helps them stand out enormously in a context of duller, more linear estates by the LCC's own architects, who were sadly seldom at their most creative in the East End. Chalkwell House is on Commercial Road; it stands next to the pretty decorated shed of the Troxy Cinema, adopting its scale to the street. It meets the pavement with three chunky, corrugated concrete access decks, at an angle to a zig-zag of brown brick flats, and a prow-shaped glass stairwell above; this then leads down Pitsea Street to a mass of brick, with individual flats emphasised by cantilevers, so that each can be picked out clearly by its residents. Ashington House is better known, easily seen by Overground passengers from the Victorian railway viaducts around Bethnal Green station. It resembles a kind of remix of the Stepney building, with its glazed stairwells and cantilevered flats crushed into a spiky, Gothic melange, weirder and smaller than the earlier building but using exactly the same motifs and materials. Punchy, honest architecture.[OH]

Canary Wharf Underground Station

The 300-metre-long station is built within the hollow of the former West India Dock using cut-and-cover construction techniques. At ground level, the station roof is laid out as a landscaped park, creating Canary Wharf's principal recreation space. The only visible elements in Canary Wharf Underground Station are the arching glass canopies that cover its three entrances. Due to the high volume of station traffic, the guiding principles in the design were durability and ease of maintenance.
Contributed by Foster and Partners

Crossrail Place Roof Garden, Foster + Partners and Gillespies, 2015

This lush garden sits atop Crossrail Place, the first building to open for the new Elizabeth Line. Designed to evoke a ship laden with exotic specimens, the roof garden displays plants from across the globe encased beneath a timber and ETFE lattice roof. Directly north of Greenwich, the garden virtually sits

on the Prime Meridian dividing the east and the western hemispheres which inspired the division of the planting into two geographic zones. Crossrail Place also plays host to a selection of shops and restaurants available to visit on both roof garden level and quayside.
Contributed by Canary Wharf

St Paul's Bow Common, Bow, Robert Maguire and Keith Murray, 1958–1960

Much more impressive than the run of post-war churches, built upon a clear principle – a centralised design, around a polygonal glass roof, bringing light into what is otherwise a stark box of engineering brick. Unlike many modernist churches, it's not an 'exercise', and you don't feel that the architects would much rather be designing something else. Everything is motivated by a passionate, if restrained religiosity, all organised around the alternation of darkness and light. No cliches – the exterior features neither spire nor campanile, but does carry the words, pressed into concrete, 'THIS IS THE GATE OF HEAVEN'.[OH]

Jagonari Centre (left), Crossrail Place Roof Garden (top right), St Paul's Bow Common (bottom right)

This is a wild silkworm cocoon imported though the East India Docks, likely from India in the early-20th century. Initially imported for use in handicrafts, the cocoon and the docks are both artefacts of the historic violence of the British Empire in India, Africa, the Caribbean and elsewhere.

In the late-18th century, what is today the Bengal region of South Asia was a global powerhouse in textile manufacturing. Cotton textiles and silk products from the Indian subcontinent were hugely popular in Europe. The arrival of the East India Company in the late-17th century, however, begun a long process of plunder and deindustrialisation in the region, for the direct benefit of British importers and manufacturers.

Similarly violent histories are contained within the tea, textiles, tobacco and other commodities that enriched the British Empire. Yet these histories have traditionally been obscured by racist narratives of economic or societal progress and hidden behind statues of traders or opulent cityscapes paid for by the spoils of colonialism. Today, the stories behind these statues and monuments, re-purposed docks and institutions built on colonial wealth are being revisited in contemporary struggles for racial justice, through Black Lives Matter protests and more.

Tower Hamlets

Wild cocoon, 1900–1935, 43 × 30mm, Museum of London (© Museum of London)

Trees were Important
Eli Davies

I remember learning to write my address as a child. It trips off my tongue now like a memorised line of poetry or part of a times table, the last line particularly: 'Chingford, London, E4 6QR'. My relationship with London had layers: I knew that I lived somewhere in the city, as per this postal address that I wrote for handwriting practice and on letters to pen friends, but I also knew it as somewhere not quite in immediate reach. This London was where we 'went up to'. To 'go up to London' was a treat – usually in the form of a trip shopping or to see the Christmas lights, maybe a show – and it generally meant the areas around Oxford Street, Leicester Square, Piccadilly or occasionally, a visit to my dad's office in Marylebone. (I still love this old-fashioned idea of 'town' – a place of spectacle, occasion, somewhere you go for a bit of razzle-dazzle and you make an effort for). These excursions involved some combination of bus, train and tube, or sometimes the car. However we got there, though, *this* London was a place I was very much at the edge of.

When I went to university, and people asked me where I was from, I'd answer London because, well, what else was I going to say? It seemed to me, though, that in the environs of Sussex University in the late 1990s, to be from the capital meant to be from Hampstead, Islington, Muswell Hill, Camden, Brixton, maybe Streatham or Clapham, and didn't really encompass my part of the world. I negotiated many exchanges familiar to anyone from Chingford – namely that when you say you're from London people will tell you that actually, you're from Essex. It can be hard to respond to this without colluding in some subtle way with a kind of loathsome anti-Essex snobbery, while at the same time doing justice to the very real historical and spiritual connections that Chingford has with the county. (It *was* in Essex until 1965.) One response, though, is to point out that it's in the London Borough of Waltham Forest. And so it is, at the very north of this borough on the outer edges of north-east London.

Waltham Forest, created in 1965, comprises Chingford, Walthamstow, Leyton and Leytonstone, all of which had formed their own municipal districts before this (Leytonstone was part of Leyton). It's a very long borough, and growing up E4 did feel different to these other areas.

We had no tube station, a source of fury to me as a teen, and our main transport hub was Chingford rail station. The biggest, most uninterrupted sprawl of Epping Forest begins here, where Waltham Forest bleeds into Epping, London becomes Essex. Chingford has always got a large part of its notoriety over the years from its solid Tory pedigree, with Norman Tebbit MP for the area between 1970 and 1992, followed by the current one, Iain Duncan Smith. The name of Winston Churchill, once MP for Epping which then comprised Chingford, was frequently invoked. But further local notoriety can be found up here at the edges of the forest, in the form of the Queen Elizabeth Hunting Lodge, built for Henry VIII in 1543 to watch deer chases and later renovated by Queen Elizabeth I; all of this seems to sit comfortably, somehow, alongside this macho Tory lineage and the seemingly unshakeable Conservative-voting character of a large section of the place. (I've also often wondered whether this historical association may partly explain the proliferation of mock Tudor architecture in Chingford which so fascinated me when I was a child.)

It was all very foresty in my childhood, then, beginning with the area around our semi-detached house and radiating outwards from there: our back garden had several fruit trees, one of which was blown over in the famous storm of 1987, and a wooded lane ran along the end of it. Trees were important – to climb up, clamber over and sometimes, as in the case of the hollow oak tree at Warren Pond up by the station, crawl into. This was all great fun as a child, but as a teenager it became a huge bore. I was no longer interested in walks through the forest peering at tadpoles and collecting conkers, and became typically absorbed in the inner life of the adolescent; I'd smoke cigarettes out of my bedroom window and look out over the indistinct mass of trees on the horizon, imagining in some indistinct way all the experiences *somewhere else* that this leafy zone 5 existence kept me from.

This was deep suburbia. To get further into the city we had to travel to Walthamstow, either via the train from the station or the 97 bus. Walthamstow's sources of fame – its bustling market (adverts on the side of local buses proclaimed it the longest street market in Europe), the dog track with its striking neon-lit art deco frontage – felt more urban than Chingford's. I think of the 97 route, now, as my passageway out, slowly bringing me closer to London's surface, from the Ridgeway, through Chingford Mount, across the Crooked Billet roundabout, down Chingford Road and Hoe Street. The route not only takes in both the market and the dogs – the latter, predictably, now turned into flats, though its gorgeous frontage has been preserved – but it was also dotted with various significant childhood and teenage venues. These included Walthamstow Pool and Track (now site of larger leisure facility Waltham Forest Feel Good

The illuminated signage at Walthamstow Stadium in 2016 and a dog race in progress, 1994

Centre), creepily time-worn school outfitters Henry Taylor's (no longer there), and site of my first Saturday job, the Top Shop in Selbourne Walk (now called The Mall). Not quite on the route, but not far off it, is Lloyd Park, behind the William Morris Gallery, where I learned to ride my bike, and a few minutes down Forest Road stands the dazzling municipal grandeur of Walthamstow Town Hall, which bestowed a sense of occasion every December when we went to see my dad sing carols with the Forest Choir in the Assembly Hall next door.

My relationship with Leyton, further in still, and where the 97 terminated back then (it now goes on to Stratford) has always been more patchy, despite being where my mum grew up and where the family on her side goes back several generations. As a kid, uninterested in family history, my main experience of E10 was provided by Leyton Orient, where I was taken every few weeks to muck about in the stands or on the terraces. My attendance dwindled as I got older, in spite of its firm status as the family club for. I now go to a match once every few seasons, at a generous estimate.

But while Leyton and Walthamstow felt less suburban to me, Epping Forest is crucial to these areas too, with significant portions of it dotted throughout the borough. Sitting alongside main roads, bus stops and other amenities, these patches need no special excursion, and can be cut through or easily popped over to in the middle of doing something else. We could go for a walk or take a boat out at Hollow Ponds after a hospital appointment at Whipps Cross (birthplace of David Beckham, Harry Kane and myself, among others). If getting the bus to my grandparents' house in Walthamstow after school, I'd cut through a small area of the forest at the top of their street to get to their house from the bus stop. My granddad Terry, a Leyton native who was always involved in the local politics of the area, often took us tramping through this stretch, encased by Forest Rise and Woodford New Road. Terry had adored the forest his whole life and was something of an expert on it; as we walked alongside him he would cheerfully tell us the names of trees and plants and identify birds by their song.

I don't live in London anymore – I haven't actually lived in Waltham Forest since I was 19 – and these days, when non-Londoners ask me which part of the city I'm from, I often just say 'near Walthamstow', because it is less likely to require explanation. For those of a certain age, Walthamstow was put on the popular culture map by rough diamond boy band East 17, and around the early 2010s achieved fame of a more 21st century – and much less fun – variety, when Waltham Forest became one of the 'Olympic boroughs' and E17 became, not unrelatedly, the subject of various 'where shall we move to' type articles in newspaper lifestyle sections. It was around this time that certain friends and family were priced out of the area and homelessness began to rise.

That's a typical kind of London story these days, one of 'placemaking' and unaffordability. Last time I visited Walthamstow in late 2019, for my niece's 8th birthday party at the Feel Good Centre, I waited for the 97 at the bottom of Hoe Street and thought of that story as I looked over at the 'creative hub' of Central Parade with its artist studio space, sourdough bakery and coffee shop. Terry died in 1995 and I wonder what he would make of the borough now, the language used to describe it by estate agents and lifestyle writers no doubt rendering the place unrecognisable to him, and I can imagine him riffing off it humorously. But while the forces of hollow branding and gentrification can often feel depressingly powerful, that is only one tiny strand of what Waltham Forest is. What Terry embodied about this part of the world – civic responsibility, a certain everyday creativity, and enthusiasm for the forest and its wildlife – is still very much part of the borough's, and London's, story.

Eli Davies is a Belfast-based writer and academic researcher. She has written on literature, music and politics for *The Irish Times*, the *Guardian*, *Tribune*, *The Tangerine* and *The New Statesman*. She is the co-editor of *Under My Thumb: Songs that Hate Women and the Women Who Love Them* (2017), and is currently working on a collection of essays about everyday life and loss, for which she received funding from the Arts Council of Northern Ireland.

Waltham Forest Town Hall and Assembly Halls, Walthamstow, Philip Dalton Hepworth, 1932–1941

Thankfully still serving its original function, this is the best of the clutch of halfway-house moderne/classical town halls in east London, more monumental than the smaller Hackney Town Hall and more architecturally coherent than the Dutch/Georgian cross-breed of Barking Town Hall. Its commanding scale, at the centre of a large site, most likely derives from Walthamstow's independence of the London County Council, a self-governing working class suburb.

It is dominated by an elongated stripped classical portico of four tall columns, surmounted by a copper tower cribbed from the Town Hall in Ostrava, Czechoslovakia, which stands at the centre of a long Portland Stone enfilade of offices, symmetrically arranged. Flanking it on the right are the Assembly Halls, the cultural adjunct to the big (local) government, whose municipal largesse is expressed through a lofty public anteroom. A stiff and conservative design in many ways, but a space of public splendour nonetheless.[OH]

Central Parade, Walthamstow, F.G Southgate, 1954–1958

The Festival of Britain style's modernist/nostalgic mashup at its most gleeful, full of great little bits and bobs and decorative fripperies to irk the purists. This is a block of council flats, with shops on the ground floor (many of them reworked recently into an industrial-chic co-working space), under a wavy concrete canopy, currently painted a fetching yellow. The flats have deep balconies and look like they'd be great places to live. The central tower, which faces the junction of the High Street and Hoe Street, is where the Borough Architect F.G. Southgate has really let himself go, with a decorative pattern evoking the Festival Hall carpets, a clock, a belltower, and a load of coats of arms cast in tiles, all with flats inset into it. The sort of festive, cheerful populist modernism that makes you wonder if the Brutalists might sometimes just have been puritan bores.[OH]

Rose & Crown, Walthamstow

The Rose & Crown is a proud corner building on Hoe Street. The build date is not well known but it was first licensed in 1890. A true community asset, it holds curious tales of the licensing having been objected to by the neighbouring landlady, who actually turned out to be dead. Along with ghost stories and the like, it maintains many traditional features.[ZC]

The Leyton Technical, John Johnson, 1895

Leyton's Italianate former Town Hall sits just the right side of gaudy with its main facade comprising a striped base of white stone and red brick banding beneath three blind arcades with inset stone niches. It is eclectic and vicacious, only ceasing to be a centre of local government when the municipality of Leyton was subsumed into the larger London borough of Waltham Forest in 1965. The Leyton Technical pub, now operating occupying extensive rooms within the former Town Hall, was established during the 2012 London Olympics as a pop-up boozer, but has managed to put down roots and, pandemic aside, is still thriving.[PH]

Walthamstow Wetlands Visitors Centre (formerly Ferry Lane Pumping Station), 1894, refurbished, Witherford Watson Mann, 2017

Walthamstow Wetlands is a 200-hectare nature reserve surrounding a chain of reservoirs running down the Lea Valley. Marking its western entrance is a new visitor centre occupying the extensively refurbished carcass of a defunct 1894 pumping station. Architects Witherford Watson Mann, working with Kinnear Landscape Architects, have opened up the wetlands inserting a series of paths and bridges into this beguiling post-industrial landscape. The sturdy brick pumphouse has been gently repaired, with new steel gantries threaded through. A new brick tower housing swift boxes and bat roosts has been built on the existing chimney plinth with the words 'Wetlands' picked out in glazed brick.[PH]

Walthamstow and Chingford Almshouse, 1527–2018

Walthamstow Village retains an unusally high number of historic and contemporary almshouses. A charity, amalgamated from a number of smaller organisations established by philanthropic benefactors, now operates 62 apartments across five buildings reserved for local over-55s. The almshouses range from historic listed terraces such as the George Monoux and Mary Squires Almshouses to a newbuild block of 20 units completed in 2018 by Pollard Thomas Edwards architects.[PH]

Town Hall (top), Walthamstow Wetlands (bottom, image by Iain Green)

Bexley, Bromley, Croydon, Greenwich, Lewisham, Southwark

SOUTH-EAST

A Poem for Living In
josie sparrow

'...the art of house-building begins it all: if we did not know how to dye or to weave; if we had neither gold, nor silver, nor silk; and no pigments to paint with but half-a-dozen ochres and umbers, we might yet frame a worthy art that would lead to everything, if we had but timber, stone, and lime, and a few cutting tools to make these common things not only shelter us from wind and weather, but also express the thoughts and aspirations that stir in us.'
—William Morris, *The Beauty of Life*

We dwell in our doing, and our doing makes the places that we dwell. Our inhabiting creates what is habitual; likewise, our habits unfold within and around the places we inhabit. Everything is situated, everything is relational, everything is in process – and so there can be no absolute beginnings, only points of departure. These points are accretions of moments, of memories; they are places that shelter and nourish. They are sites of folding-in that make unfolding possible.

We might call them homes.

In 1859, William Morris – aged 25 and newly-married – set out to build a home. Purchasing a plot of land in Upton, a small hamlet in what was then rural Kent, he and his friend, the architect Philip Webb, created what would become Red House almost from first principles. Another friend, Dante Gabriel Rossetti, is said to have described it as 'more a poem than a house'. I would want to say that it was both; I might say, too, that it was Morris's first political statement. What better or more succinct expression of his commitments and hopes than to insist that a house can be a poem, and that poetry can be a thing we can inhabit?

Built from the materials available locally, with none of the excessive ornamentation characteristic of mainstream Victorian design, Red House was intended to house not just the Morris family, but their friends and comrades too. As such, its design prefigures Morris's later insistence that 'the arrangement of our houses ought surely to express the kind of life we lead, or desire to lead'. Its furniture was constructed according to Morris's exacting specifications; its walls and ceilings were hand-painted and hung with Jane Morris's own embroideries. The garden, too, was carefully composed, with separate 'rooms' enclosed by trellises and planted with carefully-chosen, free-growing flowers. Every detail, down to the angle of the sunlight on the hand-carved wooden staircase, was first dreamt, and then made real. A poem for living in; a poem written by the process of living. A home.

To make a home is to dream of a future. Even if we might want to trouble the notions of permanence, of eternity, I think we can say that to commit to a place, to say *here I will live*, suggests an unfolding that happens spatially and temporally. (These two things are intertwined.) The *unfinishedness* of Red House bears witness to this situated dreaming. The planned extension was never built; a series of Chaucer-themed tapestries, stitched by Jane and her sister Bessie, was left uncompleted. This doesn't matter. It was the making, the doing, the *living* that counted. The 'purpose' of a building – of any kind of structure – is to render possible certain kinds of dreaming, making, and being. It isn't just that the means are more important than the end; it's that those means will determine what the end might be. It may be that the end we have in mind slips and shifts; perhaps it changes shape, or colour; perhaps it seems somehow to be fixed to the horizon, always within sight but never quite within reach. That's okay. The means are transformational in and of themselves. They change us, they teach us, they encourage us. They make it possible for us to soften, to open, to enter into good relation with every thing with which we live. Red House, then, is a means rather than an end. It makes solid this dialectical, reciprocal relationship between *habit* and *habitation* – the ways in which the places we inhabit co-create our habits of living, just as our habits of living co-create the places we inhabit, in a perpetual process of (ex)change.

This attentiveness to context and interconnection is profoundly eco-logical. So, too, is Morris's lifelong concern with what he called 'making socialists', as distinct from the more orthodox approach of 'building socialism'. His was not a practice towards some rigid institutional form, later to be imposed upon others, who would soon learn to live according to its contours. He saw that all that was required for things to open up was a moment, an encounter – however brief, however flickering – that might suggest, subtly, another way to live. Another way to live, with and for others: birds, humans, trees. For Morris, the task – perhaps the duty – of those of us who had already experienced this moment of transfor-mation was to create spaces within which others might do so, too. And, once transformed, he said, '*they* will find out what action is necessary for putting their principles in practice'. This trust in everything that lives – this certainty that, whoever and wherever we are, *we* are the experts on

Design for Trellis wallpaper, William Morris and Philip Webb, 1862 (© William Morris Gallery)

our lives, our needs, our hopes – is characteristic of Morris's ecological socialism. There is much to learn from this approach.

It is not just *what* we learn that matters, but *how*. It's strange, perhaps, to compare the architecture of Morris to that of Le Corbusier; but the two had certain similar preoccupations. Both felt that buildings could be 'moral' and 'healthy'; both were concerned with the everyday; both felt that their work had something important to communicate about what it means (or doesn't mean) to be human. Where Morris's architecture is pedagogical, however, Le Corbusier's is didactic. Where Morris is open-ended and trusting, Le Corbusier is determinate, almost repressive. Morris cares deeply about means; Le Corbusier is all about the ends – the finished object, which will transform people, yes, but not towards liberation. So committed was he to the rationalisation and disciplining of the body that, in an astounding bit of fascist phrenological crankery, he designed his buildings according to 'the Modulor' – a system of measurement based on what he considered to be the 'average' human body, which he later revealed to be based on 'the good-looking policemen in English detective novels'. The range of possible bodies excluded by this 'system' is as astonishing as it is enraging.

For all their stark beauty, Le Corbusier's villas are teleological: they put an end to dreams. Their intent is to enforce a rationalised, impersonal, rigid sort of modernity: a perfection to which our bodies must aspire, towards which we must be disciplined. Things cannot be permitted to be what they are. The architect knows best. He dominates.

How different this is from the freedom and trust we find in Morris. To plant flowers and know that they will grow in their own way, and to welcome this lack of control. To make a home and let the process of living in it determine how it develops. To know that we are not atomised, machinic individuals, but part of multiple ecologies, which unfold themselves across time, through space, through our relationships, through our words, our dreams.

I have never been to Red House. For me, it is an imagined place; a place no less real, no less possible, for the fact that I have never seen it. Would Morris have wanted me to go there? I'm not sure. Red House was a home; the point was to live in it. It cannot be lived in now, nor can it live. There are thousands of people waiting for a home in Bexley; meanwhile, Red House stands empty. It is a heritage property, preserved in as much of its 'original' state as possible. The National Trust, its current owners, are undertaking a project of restoration in the gardens, tearing down the trees that have made their homes there in the 160 years since Morris planted his roses and honeysuckle. Perhaps we'd rather this than the alternative – a City hedge fund manager adding a grotesque extension to accommodate his home gym – but the fact remains that Red House is not, should never be, a shrine. 'The remedy,' as Morris observed in his own polemic against restoration, 'lies not in standing still.' A place that is frozen in time is a place without a future. A place from where we cannot dream, cannot unfold.

But we can imagine Red House as it was: a poem for living in, written by people, and which inscribed itself upon them, too. We can think about questions of construction; we can consider what, and how, and where we want to build. We can practice tenderness and tending and attention; we can open ourselves, flower-like, to people and their needs – to 'making socialists' – rather than subjugating all to some rulebound system. We can dream, imagine, build together.

I'm imaging a house, a home. A place without domination, without force; a place from where every living thing can unfold itself as it will. A place for us to dream. Always open, always in process, always unfinished.

josie sparrow is a writer, an artist and a philosopher. Her interests coalesce around the intersection of the poetic and the political, with a particular emphasis on process, relationality, socialism, ethics, ecologies, words and flowers. Her future plans include dismantling capitalism and co-creating a more beautiful world, with and for others.

Thamesmead, Greater London Council Architects Department, 1968–1986

One of the most extensive and photo-genic of the modernist schemes of the 1960s has been subjected to various drastic forms of surgery, to remove the taint of 'the old ultraviolence' from it, but much still remains. The best way to see Thamesmead is to start at Lesnes Abbey, a set of ruins in front of a conserved woodland, a short stroll from Abbey Wood railway station. A walkway leads directly from the abbey through the estate, a continuous elevated route that passes the raked, stepped-section concrete panel low-rise maisonettes (with neat, legible public squares between) that dominate the estate, past grazing horses and overgrown grassland. You will eventually arrive at Southmere Lake. From behind the (disused) pub and community centre, a smart pedestrian bridge over the Eastern Way leads to Phase 2, a relatively conventional series of long interlinked grey Brutalist blocks sheltering some elegant red brick maisonettes, and Phase 3, where Thamesmead went postmodernist, with fussy retro details and a transplanted Victorian clocktower to replace the promised future, all along canals to the Thames. Ignoring the informal Phase 4 of retail parks and Barratt Homes and the seemingly random patches of demolition, there is still a great deal here to admire, an intelligent if overambitious attempt at creating an entire new London in microcosm.[OH]

Erith Pier, designer unknown, 1957

Erith Pier is an impressive concrete structure that launches out into the Thames from the town centre. Originally constructed from wood in 1842, the industriousness of the working pier was offset by the pleasure gardens along the river bank. From then on there has been a long lineage of wooden piers, but finally, in 1957, concrete came to Erith Pier and remains in the structure standing today. Such a change in material upped the ante of the industrial activity that the pier could host, which came to include train tracks, a turntable, a series of large cranes and a deep wharf to accommodate large ships. By the early 1990s, with the demise of manufacturing and industry, it was left abandoned and derelict. As part of a regeneration project, the pier has now had a lick of paint and enjoyed a new lease of life with pop-up restaurants, art installations and festivals, reconnecting Erithians with the Thames.[ZC]

Erith Playhouse, designer unknown, 1973

Erith Playhouse, originally the Oxford Cinema, opened in 1913. Described then as 'just a brick box', it screened films onto a whitewashed wall. The brick box was adapted during the war and was utilised by amateaur dramatics groups to keep the flow of entertainment going, gradually converting from cinema to theatre. The theatre was altered in a major 1970s refurbishment which changed most aspects of the building (save the auditorium) including the creation of its current asymmetrical bauhaus-like brick frontage.[ZC]

Gothic Bathhouse to the rear of number 112 North Cray Road, *c.*1766

One of Kent's oddest monuments can be found hidden in the garden of an ordinary semi-detached house in Bexley. Here, at the end of its garden, sits a unique garden ornament: a Gothic bath house. Built circa 1766, originally in the grounds of Vale Mascal, this cold plunge bath house is fed from the River Cray. Flint with brick edging with pairs of cinquefoiled windows to the north and south.[PH]

The King's Head, Bexley, 17th century

A pub on this site has been traced back to as early as 1662. Today, The Kings Head is timber-framed listed pub with a form that suggests it was once a hall-house. Hall-houses were a type of vernacular building indigenous to the British Isles, built by an untrained amateur whose design would have been shaped by local understandings, norms and techniques. The pub is now clad in white horizontal boarding.[ZC]

De Luci Fish Sculpture, Erith, Gary Drostle, 2006

Commissioned by the local authority, this seven and a half metre-high mosaic-covered sculpture depicting three writhing fish sits in the middle of a roundabout on the A206. It is known locally simply as 'Fish Roundabout' and in 2008 won the Best Architectural Mosaic award at the Mosaic Arts International festival in Miami, Florida.[PH]

Thamesmead (left), Erith Pier (centre), Gothic bathhouse (right)

People in the Suburbs were Existentialist
Hanif Kureishi

A few weeks ago, I was writing about a writer called E. R. Braithwaite, for whom I've recently adapted to *To Sir, With Love* for the BBC. I read these lines: 'I didn't know I was coloured until I went to school.'

My experience of the suburbs was my father coming from India, marrying a white woman, and being a mixed-race kid in an almost entirely white, homogeneous, post-war, bombed down wasteland. For me, my hatred for the suburbs was really to do with race, and to do with trying to work out why everybody else asked me throughout my childhood where I came from. People in the suburbs were existentialist. They would say to you all the time: 'Where do you come from?' And I would say, 'Well I come from that house, over there, and there's my mum, in her slippers.' And they would say: 'Yeah, but where do you really come from?' And then I would say: 'Well, I really come from that house over there, and there's my mum in her slippers.' And then it would go on and on and I began to think I was going mad. So I spent most of my childhood trying to work out who I was in relation to what other people said about me. They'd say things like 'is it too cold here for you?' And then in those days, the schools were really Dickensian. I mean they were violent and rough, teachers hit you. I remember the first day of being at secondary school, and the teacher put two sticks on his desk and he said: 'this is big Willy, and this is little Willy. And you'll be seeing a lot of these'.

It was bombed out then, even then, bombed-out and sort of broken. And you began to realise there's probably most of the grown-ups around you have been traumatised by the war. I knew a lot of East Enders in Bromley who escaped from where they were bombed and would then come down our way. So there was a real sense that something really terrible had happened. And it was the end of the empire. Britain has sort of collapsed and was withdrawing and all of that. So I spent years and am still trying to figure out what went on and how you fit in to all that. And I guess *The Buddha of Suburbia*, which was the book that I'd been writing throughout my teenage years, was sort of trying to find out how you could be a hippie and a paki at the same time, in south London, in the 70s.

London was out there, just a train ride away. And you'd walk through the fields and there were cows and sheep and you'd go and hide in haystacks and loaf around. In those days of course, people didn't care for their children in the same way. You know, your mum would give you some money in the morning and she didn't expect to see you till 6 o'clock. And she didn't phone you up or didn't know where you were. You weren't tracked by anybody and you were just completely free, you would just fuck off and disappear, and have adventures. When you went across the river, by Battersea Bridge, you would cheer. I mean, your heart would lift, you were out. You'd go to Notting Hill and so on and you'd see Black, Asian people and there'd be other foods and so on. And you really felt then, that you weren't picked on, that you weren't stared at. When you walked around Bromley, and particularly for my father, who was always being chased, people were always giving you the eye. They'd always look at you, you'd always feel like you're in danger, that someone would have a go, that someone would say 'fuck off, Paki'.

My father had come to England to live, he'd given up on India and he married my mother, and he made a life here and he wanted to be here. He wanted me to be English. He said 'just pass, just pretend to be English', and then he said 'you should change your name'. He said, 'you know, why don't you change your name to Paul or Richard or something? And then no one will notice you?' As though that could change the colour of your skin. So my dad thought we could just disappear into England, that you'd become white and then you wouldn't be chased.

The only contact with outside world we had as kids really was through music. You'd listen to John Peel, and there was a group of kids called The Bromley Contingent, who I was at school with who later became Siouxsie and the Banshees, and a little boy who became Billy Idol, who went to Bromley Grammar. So it was affluent, there were garages and you could go there and play music in people's garages, and listen to the Velvet Underground, and then you could paint your bedroom and you could make a group. And in Bromley Tech, the college I went to, there were a lot of bands and you'd see Pink Fairies and all those semi-kind-of-early punk bands. Influenced by the MC5, would come down and thrash around in Bromley, it wasn't very far for people to come down. I remember being very, very impressed one day when Roger McGough came down with Brian Patten and gave a reading and then they went back to London in their van and then I thought, 'That's glamour.' 'That's what I want to do.'

It was a quiet place. It's a decent place to live, people had a reasonable standard of living, they had nice houses. But they were mostly concerned with their furniture. You know, I remember people saying 'I want a G-plan' and it was really aspirational in that sense. It was materialistic. What they wanted was better furniture. They didn't want more culture or better words or books or any of that stuff. They wanted a higher standard of living because most people, in most of their houses, had furniture from before the war. And most of the houses were still pretty rough. So the idea was that you would get G-plan and you'd spend – we'd spend all weekend with our dad, looking at carpets.

I so much wanted to get away from all of that, that I really left it behind and those friendships behind as well. Because I couldn't have, with people that I was at school with, the conversations that I wanted to have. I was a kid, I was reading Baudelaire and Rimbaud and Dostoyevsky and all of that stuff that you'd get in the library, in the days when they had libraries. And they had really good libraries in Bromley. So every day after school I'd got to one of three or four local libraries and I'd sit down and read. And you know, you could just sit down and read *Crime and Punishment*, it's incredible that you could do that for free. So I thought 'where are the most interesting people? Where are they? Where are those people?' And I'm going to get on a train and sit with them and join them. And I went to the Royal Court when I was 18 and the first afternoon I was at the Royal Court, I met Samuel Beckett, who was rehearsing a play called *Footfalls* with Billie Whitelaw. And I was sat at the back and I thought 'this morning I was in Bromley and now I'm sitting here with Samuel Beckett' and I thought 'this is the life for me, I know which one I prefer'. And so, just finding interesting people, who would extend you, who would say things to you that you've never heard before – that was what I was drawn to.

I never thought that if I came to New York I would become a better writer. I'd probably have a higher standard of living and the parties would be better, but I always thought of myself as an English writer. And as an English realist writer I want to write about what I see when I walk down my street, what people are wearing, why are there Somalians sitting in the park, why are they there, what's their journey. When I was in Los Angeles I thought, well, I can't write about this, I can't work out why these people are here. I can work that out in Bromley and in Shepherd's Bush. I wouldn't understand that anywhere else. In London, the way people dress, the way people speak, every nuance in relation to them tells you who they are and where they're from.

My mum left Bromley three months ago. I went to the house. I was in Bromley three months ago and I went to the house and I walked out and I thought 'this is the last time I ever come here and walk down.' Saying goodbye and that was that. All the shops are Indian now. You know, you walk around all the old shops where you worked as a paper boy and you knew this person and that person and that is actually all Indians and Chinese restaurants now, so it's become, as they say, as multicultural as everywhere else. But I haven't come here to talk up Bromley. Of all the things I wanted to do with my life, I never thought for a moment that would be one of them.

Adapted from a talk at the Architecture Foundation with Will Self, October 2015.

Hanif Kureishi is a screenwriter, playwright and novelist. His work includes the screen-plays *My Beautiful Laundrette* (1984), *My Son The Fanatic* (1998), *The Mother* (2003) and *Venus* (2006), the novels *The Buddha of Suburbia* (1990) and *The Black Album* (1995), and *Something to Tell You* (2008), and a memoir, *My Ear at His Heart* (2004). He has been awarded the Chevalier de l'Ordre des Arts des Lettres and a CBE for services to literature. His work has been translated into thirty-six languages.

National Sports Centre, Crystal Palace, London County Council Architects Department, 1964

Crystal Palace Park is the most surreal public park in Britain, centred around an absence – Joseph Paxton's enormous glass exhibition building, that was relocated to this green in suburban Sydenham from the 1851 Great Exhibition in Hyde Park – famously, its pioneering prefabricated design meant it could just be disassembled and put up somewhere else. It burned down in the 1930s, but the space where the Palace used to sit is still defined by the sculptural sequence of Orientalist figures, sphinxes and stairways that originally led to it. Opposite is this, the largest LCC non-housing project, at least after the Festival of Britain that was the Great Exhibition's purported successor – a giant sports centre with several swimming pools, sports halls, and outside, an athletics track, all in one overarching structure. Reached by a long walkway across the park, it is symmetrical, unusually for a Brutalist building, with everything in the design subordinated to holding up the vast central space that serves the various different functions. The concrete columns are like thickets, creating a Cathedral-like effect of organic openness. Unlike the Crystal Palace and its High-Tech successors, which aimed at being intangible, coldly logical and extendable, this is a singularly conceived one-off, weighty and grimly exciting.The difference is encapsulated outside in the absurd bust of Paxton on top of a squat square plinth of engineering brick.[OH]

Chiselhurst Caves, architect unknown, 1232–1830

Chislehurst Caves is a 35 kilometre network of tunnels which were carved out by hand between the 13th to early 19th centuries. Originally exploited as a source of flint and lime-burning chalk, the labyrinth was later repurposed as an ammunition storage dump for the Royal Arsenal at Woolwich before being used to grow mushrooms during the 1930s. The caves were briefly fitted out with electric lighting, toilets and washing facilities to serve as overnight air-raid shelter accommodation for around 15,000 people at the height of the Blitz. In the decades following the war, this mysterious subterranean space took on a new life as a conveniently sound-proofed nightclub – playing host to major acts such as David Bowie, Pink Floyd, Jimi Hendrix, The Yardbirds, Eric Burdon and The Animals. Today the caves are run as a museum with guided tours allowing safe exploration. Highlights include an imaginative and humorous wall carving by artist Sandy Brown which weaves together the cave's history and mythology – featuring a tree of life, skeletons, the River Thames, spiderman and the skyline of Canary Wharf.[MF]

Apex Close, Beckenham, Derek Sharp Associates, 1966

Apex Close is a modern housing development quietly nestled within the leafy suburban landscape of Beckenham. The close featured in the Architectural Review's landmark 1970s Manplan series and is locally listed by Bromley Council in recognition of its extraordinary appearance. The complex was built at the same time Derek Sharp Associates was creating a series of eight modernist pavilions in Frimley, Surrey for the same client, Apex Drive. Both projects reflect enigmatic visual themes seen in the works of internationally acclaimed architects such as Ricardo Bofill and Robert Venturi, and demonstrate the expressive work taking place in unexpected corners of the capital by lesser known architects during a time of exuberant house building infused with optimism for the future.[MF]

Crystal Palace Subway, Charles Barry Junior, 1865

A fan vaulted chamber made of red and cream brick built as part of the relocation of the Crystal Palace following the Great Exhibition. First class passengers visiting on the dedicated railway line were able to walk directly from the new station into the Crystal Palace through the ornate vaults illuminated by gaslight in ornamental globe fittings. Following the destruction of the Crystal Palace by fire in 1936 the subway had a chequered history. It was used during the Second World War as an air-raid shelter. The music video for the Chemical Brothers' 1996 number one single *Setting Sun* was partly shot in the subway. The subway was reopened in 2013 for Open House festival by the Friends of Crystal Palace Subway but has since been closed again for restoration.[Om]

National Sports Centre pool (left), Chiselhurst Caves (centre, image by Christine Matthews), Crystal Palace subway (right, image by James Balston)

Public Spaces, Private Land
Katrina Navickas

At the end of Surrey Street, where the steps go up to High Street, is a plaque that reads:

> THIS TABLET
> COMMEMORATES THE WIDENING OF
> HIGH STREET CROYDON
> FROM A WIDTH OF 29 FEET
> TO ITS PRESENT WIDTH OF 50 FEET
> A.D. MDCCCXCVI
> FREDERICK THOMAS EDRIDGE J.P. MAYOR

A couple of years ago, *Londonist* dubbed this 'the dullest plaque in London'.

OK, it is a boring plaque. But yes, it is significant for what it represents about public space and urban regeneration in Croydon. The road widening in the 1890s was part of a comprehensive scheme to improve shopping and transport facilities and erect new civic buildings, notably its superbly confident town hall, designed in 1896 by Charles Henman. Out of all London boroughs, Croydon has been reimagined from scratch the most number of times, with grand plans for the future, whether that future was the 1890s, the 1960s, 1993 (a fantastical architecture competition called 'Croydon: the Future'), 2005 ('Croydon Gateway'), or now ('Croydon Vision: 2020').

Croydon has multiple identities. It is medieval and Victorian and a post-war 'space age town'. It is an 'edge city' between the central metropolis and the Green Belt. It has been a London borough since 1965 and unsuccessfully applied for city status several times, but still remains a slice of Surrey commuter suburbia. An article bemoaning the 'rise of the suburbs' in the *Contemporary Review* in 1891 predicted, 'not one but a dozen Croydons will form a circle of detached forts around the central stronghold'. Croydon has its own 'detached forts' of residential estates on its own outskirts, notably New Addington, built between the 1930s and 1970s, but only properly connected to the town centre when the tram was reintroduced in 2000.

The thrill of Open House is in getting into the usually inaccessible, the private. We don't do Open House specifically to look at public spaces

High Street, 1977, London Metropolitan Archives, City of London (COLLAGE: the London Picture Archive ref 161010)

that we go past every day. But how many of us actually look closely at those spaces, and investigate their histories? And how much of public space is truly public? What we think of as public space, where people have gathered for leisure, sport, shopping or protest, has often been privately owned. After the 20th century high point of public ownership, it is again increasingly private. The lockdown restrictions underlined the vital importance of public space, its distance from one's home, and inequalities of access to it. But there's no legal definition of public space, or our right to it. We all experience public space differently, dependent on what part of the borough we live in, and our class, gender and ethnic identities.

There's no large paved square or open area in Croydon. The pedestrianised North End is the main place for busking, preaching and protesting, but it is a shopping more than a civic space. An obvious site for protest would be outside the town hall, but there's not much room there either; Croydonians might take their lunch break in the day and do less legal activities at night in the sunken Queen's Gardens, over the road. If there's a need for a demonstration, it will be on the pavement outside, dodging the buses and construction lorries. The other side of the busy dual carriageway is College Green, currently being relandscaped by MICA Architects as part of the refurbishment of the Fairfield Halls, but, for now, it's hardly used for everyday leisure, except perhaps at lunchtime by the students of Croydon College opposite. It's an awkward L-shape, mostly carpark and bus stops, any conversation drowned out by the traffic.

The closest Croydon has to a town square is not in the centre but in Thornton Heath. The forecourt of Ambassador House (another 1960s office block, itself claimed as a public space by squatters) underwent an 'urban regreening', though with a piecemeal implementation in 2019. It was an obvious place to gather for a Black Lives Matter demonstration in June 2020. As for High Street – NB to non-Croydonians, it's not the high street (that's North End) – it was pedestrianised in 2017 as part of the council's 'placemaking' strategy and so-called 'parklet' wooden raised beds were dropped awkwardly alongside the pavement as seating. Marked with 'do not climb' signs, these quickly became useless as street furniture.

Surrey Street is the oldest urban public space in Croydon. It is reputedly the oldest market in Greater London, receiving its charter in 1276. Guy Fawkes' night was traditionally celebrated there – Victorian local authorities moved from tolerance of the 5th November drunkenness to seeing it as a public disorder problem. Attempts to suppress it led to crowds battling with the police throughout the 1870s. In 1877 the council arranged an official fireworks display on Duppas Hill, but this did not stop the revelry in the town centre and the conflict continued for a few years. A similar fate happened to the annual fair on Fairfield in 1868. The site was used as railway sidings and a gravel pit until the construction of Fairfield Halls (Robert Atkinson & Partners, 1962). Periodic attempts at regeneration have focused on Surrey Street, including an installation of contemporary art, but the market thankfully retains its purpose and character.

The lack of open civic space in Croydon is mainly a legacy of the 'property boom' of the 1960s. By the mid-1950s, the imperious leader of the council, Sir James Marshall, pushed for autonomy from government interference in planning with a private piece of parliamentary legislation, the Croydon Corporation Act 1956. The Act gave the council far-reaching powers to compulsorily purchase two acres in the town centre, extend the road system and lease off the rest to businesses. The London County Council plan to combat congestion in central London of 1957, decentralising office accommodation to the outer areas, was taken up with aplomb. By 1971, there were 40 new office blocks in the centre. Croydon writer John Grindrod sagely notes that while post-war reconstruction plans 'represented a socialist urge to bring great swathes of land back under central ownership and set them to work for the good of the people', by contrast, 'the Croydon Corporation Act was an expression of pure capitalism, designed to encourage the vigorous commercial exploitation of land that was currently occupied by inconvenient schools and houses'.

You can see the problem easily: the road system cuts up the central public spaces. As with many postwar reconstructions, the dominance of the car and the van held sway, determining the need for flyovers, underpasses and carparks. Retrofitted pedestrianisation isn't always the answer. However much planners seek to determine the location of civic areas, people don't always use these in the way intended. That's either a problem or an opportunity – these tensions are what makes public space public.

When people ask where I live, their usual response is 'all that concrete brutalism'. I respond with 'we have loads of lovely parks and we're close to the North Downs'. Croydon is green, although the south has better access to open space than the north, a reflection of social class as much as topography. The Victorians laid out parks as a solution to urban overcrowding, crime, pollution and disease. It's no coincidence that the council tried to sanitise and control Bonfire Night festivities by moving it to Duppas Hill. Public Health legislation enabled the council to purchase sites such as Addington Hills in 1874, Park Hill in 1887, and Addiscombe

Park Street, Croydon, 1972, London Metropolitan Archives, City of London (COLLAGE: the London Picture Archive ref 162003)

Recreation Ground in 1905. The rise of a countryside preservation movement also fuelled pressure on local authorities and charities to buy up open spaces. The council purchased Croham Hurst from the Whitgift Foundation (still a major landowner today) after a popular campaign to save it in 1901. The decline of aristocratic estates in the early 20th century also enabled more land to be publicly owned or managed. Lloyd Park, part of the Coombe Estate belonging to newspaper proprietor Frank Lloyd, was given to the Corporation in 1927. Haling Grove was given to the Playing Fields Association in 1933, and Heathfield, a 19th century house and gardens, were bequeathed to the council in 1964 by the art collector Raymond Francis Riesco.

'Emparkment' of land was a form of enclosure, and created more spaces of control. Croydon Corporation required political groups to ask permission to hold rallies, but there was less conflict over their use of parks. Duppas Hill park became the main site after Fairfield became inaccessible. The Women's Social and Political Union held a suffragette demonstration there on 8 October 1910, attracting over 1,500 people. The Independent Labour Party held meetings there too. In 1936, the British Union of Fascists held meetings to which the council had 'no objection but subject to the usual condition that no literature is distributed, no collection is made and there are no speech amplifiers'.

Wandle Park was dedicated in 1890, and was the site of the May Day gatherings by the Labour Party in the 1930s. Near East Croydon station, Park Hill has been an area of leafy villas built for wealthy commuters since it was leased out by the Ecclesiastical Commissioners in the early 19th century, and redeveloped by Wates in 1964 and 1970 – the highlight of Open House for me is usually the Atelier 5-designed St Bernard's Estate. Over 1,000 people attended an anti-war demonstration in Park Hill park on 8 July 1936. During the Second World War, the park was used by the local branches of the Anglo-Soviet Unity Committee and Russia Today society. More recently, it was the site of the Black Lives Matter demonstration in June 2020. The legacy of the massive acquisition and preservation of open space was threatened with being rolled back in the Croydon Local Plan, in development since 2012. In 2017, the government planning inspector recommended removing development protection from over 70 parks and recreation grounds. The council sought to solve the issue with a designation of 'Local Green Space', which is still under review.

So where are the newest public spaces in Croydon? In the summer of 2018, every TV bulletin on the World Cup seemed to repeat footage of the exuberant crowd inside the BoxPark, showering themselves in beer as they leapt to their feet in celebration of each goal scored by England. The foodcourt enclosed by shipping containers (a 2016 temporary structure as part of 'Croydon Vision 2020') felt, at least at that moment, like an alternative town square. But it is private, controlled and locked up by security guards.

Squares are back. The major developers all deliberately use the term 'town square' to describe the open space accompanying their mega-storey towers filling up the gaps in Croydon's 'mini Manhattan' skyline. The connotations of a civic arena that they suggest are yet to be fulfilled. The somewhat windswept Saffron Square (Berkeley Homes, 2016) off Wellesley Road, and Ruskin Square (Stanhope and Schroders, 2014–ongoing) don't currently feel like a truly public amenity. Croydonians have repeatedly shown the agency to create their own public spaces, but they will more likely than not be on private land.

Katrina Navickas is a historian and university lecturer. She is currently working on her third book, a history of public space in England, 1700–2000. A Croydon resident since 2012, she tweets from @ruralmodernism and @modernistsocCRO.

NLA Tower, Croydon, Richard Seifert, 1970

Despite the intensity of building activity in sixties and seventies Croydon – the once famous 'Mini-Manhattan' of speculative office towers, a clunkier precursor to Canary Wharf whose story is told with considerable wit in John Grindrod's *Concretopia* – not all of the actual buildings are memorable. Most are a matter of undistinguished corporate modernism on the cheap, by journeymen British firms, impressive from a distance, occasionally interesting as an *Alphaville* streetscape, but not worth much up close (though real enthusiasts should find at least something in the soon-to-be-demolished Nestle headquarters and in the recently renovated Fairfield Halls). The big exception, Croydon's seventies 'icon', is the NLA Tower, or as it's also known, the '50p building' due to its intersecting, heptagonal plan. The way that this arbitrary shape is twisted and turned into a logical and sculptural volume is typical of Seifert in its combination of science fiction pulpiness and structural ingenuity. Like a New Labour-era 'landmark building', it tells you where you are, it makes lots of money, and it doesn't do much else – but there should always be a place for cheap thrills in architecture, and the twists and turns of the NLA Tower have that in spades.[OH]

St Bernard's Houses, Croydon, Atelier 5, 1969–1972

As a set of buildings, this quiet, low-rise housing estate is the antithesis of the high-rise Croydon. Similarly, we're not dealing with state planning, but the activities of mass-market developers – in this case, the volume housebuilders Wates. Unusually, they decided to hire the cult Swiss firm Atelier 5, whose high-density, low-rise Siedlung Halen, which fit lush gardens and tightly packed terraces into a hilltop site, was the basis in many ways for later experiments in Camden, Lambeth, Mitcham, Cambridge and Sheffield. This Croydon scheme is less ambitious, but it's well worth the challenge of finding this sheltered pair of elegant, low terraces, almost closed off from the street. It's very dense, secluded by trees, detailed in wood and stock brick to a very un-British standard of precision. When they were built, the developers marketed these as a 'New Swiss Concept In Living', but it's more interesting how the ensemble incarnates traditional suburban values of privacy, seclusion and hierarchy in a very different way from most of the sprawl where London meets Surrey.[OH]

Fairfield Halls, Robert Atkinson & Partners, 1962, refurbishment MICA, 2019

Intended as a scaled-down version of the LCC Architects Department's 1951 Royal Festival Hall and sharing the same acoustic consultant, Fairfield Halls was created at a time when London's outer suburbs were reinventing themselves as epicentres of contemporary youth culture. As a legendary venue, the halls hosted musical acts such as King Crimson, The Nice, David Bowie, Kraftwerk, the Beatles, Pink Floyd and Canned Heat along with comedy acts such Morecambe and Wise. The halls closed in 2016 for a major restoration and light-touch upgrade by MICA which has brought technical facilities up to standard while respecting the original experience – particularly the first floor sun lounge which is now an excellent base for a spot of Croydon skyline gazing. The latest facilities, which include the renewed theatre and concert hall along with a new community hub cafe, two studio theatres and a gig venue demonstrate the potential of Croydon's wider town centre area to welcome greater audiences in appreciation of its unique charms. A consortium led by MICA (including Charles Holland, whose chapter on Hillingdon Civic Centre can be found elsewhere in these pages) recently won an international design contest for a new plaza reconnecting the halls to nearby East Croydon station, drawing on the rich architectural heritage of the area which was once Croydon's ancient fairground. A visitor to Fairfield Halls is immediately aware of Croydon's ongoing transformation where a legacy of car-focussed postwar development is now making way for greater pedestrian priority.[MF]

NLA Tower (left), St Bernard's Houses (top right)

Each For All And All For Each
Rosamund Lily West

The Royal Borough of Greenwich, made up of the old metropolitan boroughs of Greenwich and Woolwich, is a borough characterised by its proximity to the river, as well as beautiful green spaces. Plain old Borough of Greenwich became the Royal Borough of Greenwich in 2012 to mark the Golden Jubilee of Queen Elizabeth II. It is a borough that is no stranger to visitors and tourists, being home to the Old Royal Naval College, the Cutty Sark, the National Maritime Museum, the Royal Observatory and the Queen's House in the heart of Greenwich town centre, as well as the art deco treasure that is Eltham Palace. However, step away from the Christopher Wren, the Inigo Jones and the glamorous Courtaulds, and the borough is home to many ordinary sights, far more interesting than the domain of naval officers, monarchs and socialites: the footprint of ordinary people. It is to these we can look and see the remarkable in the everyday and how we used to value the housing – and quality of life – of ordinary people. This Greenwich is for the lesser-known parts of the borough, deserving of more attention: Eltham SE9, Woolwich SE18 and Abbey Wood, SE2.

A visitor to Woolwich cannot but notice the enormous Tesco that now dominates General Gordon Square. Indeed, the building won architecture website Building Design's 2014 prize for an 'unforgivably bad' building, known as the Carbuncle Cup. But, it is to quite a different retail giant that Woolwich owes a debt of gratitude: one that has left a rather more subtle architectural legacy across the borough, and continues to house thousands of residents. Forget Tesco, it was the Royal Arsenal Co-operative Society (RACS), founded in 1868 by a group of engineers from the Woolwich Arsenal, that was the retail force that shaped the borough, particularly its east side. The aim of the RACS was to sell reasonably priced, unadulterated food to the local working population. The RACS was always one of the more political of the cooperative societies, becoming involved with the growing independent labour movement in Woolwich from 1892. Its reach extended beyond food retail and into other areas such as education, with the RACS Education Committee and a Woolwich Reading Room both established in 1878. Before 1900, the RACS held lectures, weekly concerts, members' outings, children's teas and flower shows. In terms of housing,

Engraving of the Royal Arsenal Co-op Society buildings in Powis Street, 1884

the RACS was involved in the Bostall Estate in Abbey Wood and the Progress Estate in Eltham: the Bostall Estate was built on RACS farmland and the RACS bought the Progress Estate off the government in 1925.

First, to Abbey Wood: a mile or two east of the military might of Woolwich and south of its more boisterous architectural neighbour, Thamesmead. The Bostall Estate in Abbey Wood sits on low-lying ground, a reminder that, although you cannot see the river from the estate, the low-lying marshy ground reminds you of your proximity to it. This estate, known locally as the Co-op estate, was built by the RACS between 1900 and 1914 on RACS farmland. The street names echo the ideals of the Co-operative Commonwealth and the convictions of Robert Owen and the Rochdale Pioneers in Commonwealth Way, Owenite Street and Rochdale Road, to name a few. The backbone of the estate is mainly made up of two parallel roads, Abbey Wood Road and McLeod Road (named after Alexander McLeod, RACS secretary), with terrace streets running between the two, all sloping upwards towards Bostall Hill. The houses are typical London terraces, modest in size, of London stock brick and with front and back gardens: I used to live in one, on Owenite Street. McLeod Road has slightly grander houses and also has the Abbey Wood branch of the Co-op. At first glance, this is an uninteresting one-storey corner building not more than a few decades old on the corner of McLeod Road and Bostall Lane. However, turn into Bostall Lane and you will see the plaque on its side, obviously relocated from an earlier (and probably more attractive) Co-op building. The plaque, too large and majestic on the side of this most uninteresting building, gives the RACS motto, 'each for all and all for each' as well as describing its purpose, 'to commemorate the commencement of building on Bostall Estate October 17th AD 1900'.

The RACS bought the estate at Well Hall in Eltham off the government for £375,000 in 1925, renaming it the Progress Estate. It had been built at impressive speed by His Majesty's Office of Works, started in February 1915 and finished by that December to house munitions workers from the Arsenal at Woolwich as locally-housed workers were desperately needed to manufacture munitions. The speed of construction meant that the site worked with the contours of the land and the pre-existing trees, making navigating the estate today all the more pleasant as the roads curve and meander gently. Once off the busy roads that intersect the estate, Rochester Way and Well Hall Road, walking around the Progress Estate feels like walking around a quiet, rural town in Kent. The estate is very pedestrian friendly, having wide walkways and cut-throughs meaning walking away from the traffic is easy: a pleasant reminder of early lockdown days when people were leaving their cars at home. As with the Bostall Estate, the road names at the Progress Estate have a theme: Arsenal Road and Shrapnel Road being the more obvious.

The presence of the RACS can also be felt on Powis Street, Woolwich's main shopping thoroughfare. The older of the remaining RACS head-quarters, rebuilt in 1903 by F. Bethell, has a statue of Alexander McLeod over the main door, as well as the Society's motto – 'each for all and all for each' – on the façade. Sadly like much of this end of Powis Street, the building is looking slightly tatty on the upper storeys where much of the RACS detail is to be found. Such a shame, as it's a short walk away from the mass redevelopment of the Royal Arsenal, attracting a wealthier resident than Woolwich has been used to. The presence of Poundland and similar establishments on Powis Street, compared to the Marks & Spencer food shop and gastro pubs inside the Arsenal development, would suggest these wealthier Woolwich residents do not yet seem to be spending their pounds here. The Arsenal wall, though lowered since its munitions days, still provides a boundary in Woolwich. According to its Grade II listing description, the style of the 1903 RACS building imitated the façade of Harrods – a poignant reminder that for much of the 20th century Woolwich was enough of a shopping destination that East Enders would cross the river on the ferry to visit the department stores of Woolwich.

Across the road, the second RACS building on Powis Street also gives hints to the past grandeur of Woolwich's shops. The stylish 1938 building, now being marketed as Wick Tower, with its elegant curved balconies, lay derelict for years since its closure in 1999 and has now been converted into flats currently on the market for north of £400,000. The development was converted by Lawray Architects and comprises seventy-three one- and two-bedroom apartments. A type of accommodation clearly in dire need in Woolwich: as of January 2020, 32.61% of all of applicants for housing in the borough have been waiting between five and ten years for a home.

Against the backdrop of gentrification and the redevelopment of parts of the borough such as 'Royal Arsenal Riverside' by Berkeley Homes, perhaps it is time to remember the local, and the community, and how a large organisation supported both. While we have been forced to look to our immediate locale during our allocated exercise time and shunning of public transport, perhaps we can remember such local endeavours as the RACS and particularly their motto.

Rosamund Lily West is a curator and urban historian with an interest in public sculpture, London's communities and housing. She works as the Paul Mellon Research Curator at the Royal Society of Sculptors as well as a Documentary Curator at London Transport Museum, a role that involves documenting modern London. She is also writing up her PhD with Kingston University, *The 'concrete citizens' of the London County Council's housing schemes, 1943 to 1965*. Rosamund was born and brought up in the Royal Borough of Greenwich.

St Saviour's Church, Eltham, Cachemaille-Day, Welch and Lander, 1933

An incredible brick eruption in a bland bit of suburban Eltham, one of a group of interwar churches by Nugent Francis Cachemaille-Day that are small in size, enormous in presence, with others in Gipton and Wythenshawe. Thin, dark brown bricks, selected with an obsessive eye, piled up into a mountain of brute form, a Gothic tower reduced to the essentials of huge mass and roaring upwards motion. The brick is shaped into spiky corners and turrets, and otherwise relieved only by dark-looking, tall windows. To find the Church of England doing something so extreme in the interwar years is highly unexpected, making this a sharply discordant presence in these vague parkways. Unlike a lot of harsh churches, the darkness doesn't come across as meanly Protestant, but as some sort of horrible revelation, ascension through agony. Inside, the spacious structure gives some kind of uplift, but the main relief from the brown brick and brown concrete is the windows which, narrow on the outside, reveal themselves to be pulsating slivers of blue light, the way out just about in reach. A free leaflet in the church will tell you about the building, and about how its forbidding concrete exterior conceals a lovely brick interior, which is exactly the wrong way round – but it captures well the game of inside/outside Cachemaille-Day was playing.[OH]

85–91 Genesta Road, Plumstead, Lubetkin and Pilchowski, 1934

A remarkable private scheme by the hardline left wing modernists at Tecton, using the exact same repertoire they would use for a 'vertical garden city' at Highpoint in Highgate for the purposes of a terrace in a very ordinary suburb of Woolwich. What is so interesting about these is how the layout uses high modernist ideas for totally domestic, terraced-house purposes, rather than for a *Ville Radieuse* of flats and public open space. Although it is totally different in appearance from the high Victorian bay-windowed houses all around, the boxed-out ribbon-windows on these

houses play a similar role on the street – you immediately know that these are the living rooms, even though they're on the first floor, with the entrances below. The large, black-framed bedroom windows, glittering rendered concrete surfaces and the gentle curved kink in the balconies, meanwhile, are exactly the same as in Highpoint. In showing that modernism could be adapted to the historic street without losing any of its integrity, these houses are unusual for the 1930s, but point the way to the experiments in Camden, Milton Keynes and elsewhere in the 1970s.[OH]

Greenwich Town Hall, Clifford Culpin, 1939

A public building of great decency and monumentality, and, as Pevsner pointed out, one of the few 1930s town halls to have been built 'in the style of our time', which in this case means the style of Wilhelm Marinus Dudok, with Dutch-style brickwork and a compromise between the rectilinear geometries of Piet Mondrian and the extension of craft traditions in the Amsterdam School. In practice this means beautifully laid bricks without ornament in an asymmetrical composition, including several distinct public functions, all of them clearly visible as separate components, in one coherent structure. The two most important sections are the Borough

Hall, an essay in Anglicised modernism that anticipates some aspects of the Royal Festival Hall, and the clocktower, intended solely as an accessible campanile for the workaday, non-Royal bit of Greenwich where it edges into Deptford and Blackheath, which has sadly been closed to the public for decades.[OH]

Vanbrugh Park Estate, Blackheath, Chamberlin, Powell and Bon, 1962

Unlike most of their contemporaries, Chamberlin, Powell and Bon never did the same thing twice, so at first you might be surprised that this small estate on the north side of the heath is the work of the designers of the Barbican, Golden Lane and the University of Leeds. It comprises a series of terraced houses around asphalted squares, with surprisingly little greenery (presumably, the acres of it on the heath was considered quite enough), around a single tower block. If you're approaching from the heath, the entrance is indicated by two otherwise purposeless brick towers, working as heraldic turrets. Then you find yourself in a grid of breeze-block houses with first-floor ribbon windows, neat little drip mouldings and space-age kitchen windows on the ground floors. The tower is particularly excellent – two symmetrical volumes of spacious council flats with commanding views, linked by a dramatic open stair tower.[OH]

St Saviour's Church (top, image by John East), Greenwich Town Hall (bottom)

TELEGRAPH CONSTRUCTION & MAINTENANCE COMP.Y LIMITED

ATLANTIC SHORE END

Our communication infrastructures have never felt as vital as they have in this pandemic, allowing us to stay connected to our colleagues and loved ones as travel restrictions and lockdowns keep us apart. As intangible as it may often seem, the history of London's communications infrastructure is as rooted in real places as our sewers or our roads. This hefty object is a shore end section of a transatlantic submarine telegraph cable, manufactured in Greenwich by the Telegraph Construction and Maintenance Company in 1865.

The icon of communication infrastructure in London is, of course, the BT Tower (Cleveland Street, W1). Officially opened in 1965, full public access to the tower was prohibited in 1981 and today it can only be visited during Open House weekend.

The landmarks of our contemporary communication infrastructure – the internet – are somewhat more subtle. In the former Docklands, on the opposite bank from Greenwich, you can find architectural manifestations of the network in Global Switch 1, one of the largest purpose-built data centres in Europe, and Telehouse Docklands, the main hub of the internet in the UK, neither of which is quite so dramatic as the BT Tower. Spare a thought for one lost internet landmark; between 1994–2004 Whitfield Street (W1) was home to Cyberia, London's first internet cafe. Initially intended as a women-only space, the popularity of the cafe made this impossible and early internet explorers from across the city, David Bowie among them, flocked to Cyberia to discover the new information superhighways.

Greenwich

Telegraph cable, 1865, 77 × 65mm, Museum of London (© BT Heritage)

An interview with Nicholas Taylor
Magnus Wills

A Lewisham resident for 55 years and Labour councillor for 31, Nicholas Taylor became chair of the Lewisham Council Planning Committee in the 1970s and of the Housing Committee in the 80s; he worked with like-minded councillors Ron Pepper, Alan Pegg and Ron Stockbridge to develop the borough's housing programme into one of the most important and experimental in London. It is now best known for the self-build clusters, designed in Walter Segal's system, at Brockley Park and Honor Oak Park, but this was only part of an overall approach uniting modern design with traditional domesticity.

Now 79, Nicholas Taylor took tea with Pevsner when he was 17, having written to him with corrections to *The Buildings of England*, the product of countless cycle rides. His career has spanned architectural journalism, lecturing, housing association work in Lambeth, and 12 years at Camden Council Housing Department. In 1973, he published *The Village in the City*. Described by Ian Nairn as, 'a brilliant defence of those suburbs which everybody has looked down on for so long', it was also critical of much of the high-rise and high-density housing that was being built at the time. I met him for a socially distanced interview in June 2020.

What made you want to write *The Village in the City*?

During the mid-60s, when I was assistant editor of the *Architectural Review* (AR), I was gradually asked to lecture more and more on the state of architecture at the time – on one occasion being heckled by George Finch in front of his own students, when he was star assistant architect at Lambeth. The AR's editor, J.M. Richards, declared that high-rise developments, even system building, were perfectly acceptable for housing, provided they were designed by a 'good architect'. I was not convinced that this was the case – Basil Spence's Gorbals flats in Glasgow, for instance, I felt were worse than most system-built housing, and arrogant with it. I had meanwhile been teaching classes for the Workers Education Association (WEA), which involved taking middle class and middle-aged 'workers' from Upminster and Potters Bar on tours of estates in Peckham, such as Elmington and Brandon. My adult students had bemused reactions to such buildings; and when I was asked to edit a special issue of the AR on Housing in November 1967, my keynote article entitled 'The Failure of 'Housing'' brought into the open my own true feelings. Then Paul Barker, editor of the much-missed weekly *New Society*, approached me with his publisher Maurice Temple Smith, and I poured out the essence of my lectures on paper.

Did Lewisham as a place have much effect on the ideas in *The Village in the City*?

Lewisham may not be fashionable, but for me it was my education for life. I had been brought up in a military enclave (Sandhurst) and educated in a boarding school on the Sussex Downs, so I knew little at first-hand about ordinary life, apart from exploring the back streets of Brighton. In the summer of 1965 my first wife and I decided – she in her first term of teaching, myself on journalist's minimum pay – that south of the Thames was cheaper than north and that south-east was cheaper than south-west; and that is how we came to buy a small unimproved terraced house in Quentin Road, SE13. It may be worth a million to someone now, but for us it cost £3,800 with a council mortgage. Beginning with our neighbours, I then began my own crash course in observing the lives of the ordinary, working class, residents of Lewisham, particularly during my many hours of canvassing for the Labour Party – thus making friends for life. It soon confirmed me in the belief that low-rise 'cottages' were vastly superior as places to live than high-rise blocks. In 1971 I was elected as a Labour councillor for Ladywell Ward.

What were your proudest achievements in your time at Lewisham Council?

I remember feeling excited the moment I walked through the doors of Lewisham Town Hall. As a councillor I turned from a nervous depressive to someone who was politically fluent to an almost precocious degree and was able to work with others to achieve a rapid revolution in Lewisham's architecture, and particularly in housing design. This was initially in the teeth of opposition from older councillors and officers. The retirement of the then Borough Architect and the promotion (elsewhere) of the Borough Planning Officer allowed us to start again. Julian Tayler (no relation) was the new Borough Architect and understood exactly what we wanted, which was not only low-rise architecture that fitted in to the suburban context and could still provide small, well-lit private spaces, but also to develop each scheme in a manner sensitive to its surroundings, a community approach which tied in with our widespread designation of conservation areas. (As an architectural historian, I had been a very active member of the Victorian Society's committee in the 60s.) But we also gave great freedom to the project architects, both functionally and aesthetically. Have a look at Warwickshire Path or Ludwick Mews in Deptford, or Hurren Close in what used to be Blackheath Station Goods Yard, or the little courtyards on the corner of Chinbrook Road in Grove Park. We used an awful lot of a cheerful 'multi' red brick from Ockley in the Weald.

Julian organised the Architects Department into studios of 5–6 staff, each under the control of an Assistant Borough Architect, and we had a

Housing Plans sub-committee of councillors who met frequently to approve each scheme after a Q&A session similar to an architecture school 'crit'. The whole idea was not to have 'star' or iconic schemes. Unobtrusiveness was the essence of it. Not flagship tower blocks but quiet little buildings that would fit into the existing townscape. Nonetheless we sponsored some extremely attractive architecture, such as the Brockley Park estate, built between 1978 and 1980 and designed in-house by Geoff Wigfall, which was (and remains) an experiment in cross-generational living, providing 'pods' intended to be granny flats at the front of the house with timber cladding and grass roofs. The houses were grouped closely round a 'village green' of shared space for children's play. The high quality facing bricks 'came off the back of a lorry', as the council got them at a huge discount from a private development which had gone bust. I was also proud of schemes where we were able to combine new development with the retention and refurbishment of existing buildings, such as Eliot Lodge in Kirkdale, where a Victorian villa was bought and renovated by the council with new housing in two-storey terraces as a necklace around it.

What do you think we can learn from those ideas of the 1970s and 1980s today?

These ideas are not of the 70s and 80s but for all time! The principles go back centuries into vernacular architectural history. There is nothing new about these ideas, although a great deal is new in terms of the layouts and functionality of our houses today. But issues of privacy, protected space and comfortable areas to sit, both inside and out, remain constant, although always open to reinterpretation. The fundamental issues are always those of human scale and human relationships rather than architectural style. Intimacy of scale is very important, and the avoidance of unrelieved expanses of a single surface material.

The self-build schemes in Honor Oak Park and Brockley Park that you commissioned Walter Segal to work on are now quite a cult in architecture circles. What about them would you do differently if you could do them today?

I don't know that I would do them today! The success of the Lewisham scheme, although driven by Walter Segal himself, was very largely due to an Assistant Borough Architect Brian Richardson, an anarchist who spent much of his spare time supporting travellers in Kent. Brian knew that Walter had done a number of very interesting self-build schemes for individuals and asked if I thought it possible for him to do group schemes for families on Lewisham's housing list. Fortunately we had a number of unstable sites that could only be used economically with Walter's lightweight timber frames.

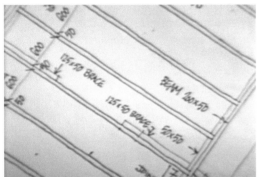

Stills from a film of Walter's Way under construction

Brian's enthusiasm infected a whole group of council officers who did the complex administration required to facilitate the project. The problem with self-build is that it is labour intensive, and not just for the builders; it can also be impossibly demanding for the professional staff supporting them. Each scheme is normally run as a little co-op, with meetings, meetings, meetings – every smallest detail being decided democratically. Walter Segal was a very libertarian individual and had endless patience – except for the issue of pitched roofs. He was a child of the 1930s, a modernist, and he insisted on flat roofs! Self-build schemes with intense tenant involvement can create huge satisfaction, but are a very slow method of producing houses and are only really viable as an outrider alongside a much bigger programme of more conventional social housing.

In *The Village in the City* you observe that Maxwell Fry and Jane Drew's 1948 Passfield Estate on Bromley Road was the most 'in demand' with Lewisham Council tenants in 1970. Do you know if it is still popular, and would you still recommend it for a discreet, socially distanced Open House visit?

Yes, I think it is still a successful scheme, well worth visiting. It may seem simple, but it is really clever: the slightly higher block at the back of the site has a subtle enclosing curve. I was responsible for adding the private gardens to the ground floor flats in 1982, not only because of a lack of private external space, but also to help protect the fabric of the building. We were lucky to have Sue Sulis as a landscape architect during my time as Chair of Housing; she and her colleagues carried out an amazing amount of inexpensive improvement by trellises and planting.

When I look at the situation of housing in London today, my primary emotion is one of anger. We have gone backwards for forty years, resulting in gross shortages for young adults and for the elderly, and we are seeing a revival of slum conditions in private renting (even 'beds in sheds'). We older people just don't seem to care enough. To achieve the change we require in housing, we need political change and massive new investment based on taxation (and not be afraid to demand it). But we need to persuade people by talking 'with' them, not 'at' them ; and first we need to observe how they actually live, and want to live.

Magnus Wills is an architect and Lewisham resident. He is currently leading the competition-winning design team for The Fair Field Landscape project in Croydon, having recently delivered the refurbishment of the adjacent Fairfield Halls, both for MICA Architects. He has previously worked at FAT, BDP and Panter Hudspith.

St Dunstan's College Dining Hall, Catford, Verner Rees, Laurence and Mitchell, 1961–63

A great bit of silliness, a dramatic hyperbolic paraboloid dining hall for the pupils of this Gothick public school in Catford, linked by a glass walkway but making zero concessions to context or being 'in keeping'. It is quite the surprise to find this from the top deck of a bus in SE6, a joke at the expense of public school pomposity – although the joke's on us, given that so many of the equally interesting state schools of the same era in the same city have been demolished and replaced with PFI tat, while this one has been preserved as well as the turreted pile next to it. *They* know what's good for them.[OH]

Charlotte Turner Gardens, LCC Architects Department and Lewisham Council Architects Department, 1930s and 1970s

An accidental-looking public space carved in the 70s out of the industrial interzones of this most characterful of London's riverside districts. These slightly scrubby, wild gardens stand inbetween two distinct moments in housing architecture. To the east, a monumental 1930s neo-Georgian/Red Viennese housing estate with grand arches, Hanseatic balconies and decks with clothes drying in the summer, an image of slightly regimented collectivity and urbane noise and clangour. To the west, a series of 1970s mews and terraces that feel like an Anglicised version of the suburbs of Oslo: black stained wood, tiles, good bright red brickwork and cobbles, intimate but not cutesy. In an area that always seems to be permanently damp, these houses feel appropriately sheltered and warm. These two very different approaches

to council housing are well linked by the gardens, two equally viable ways of living in the inner city.[OH]

Laban Centre, Deptford, Herzog and De Meuron, 2001–2003; Stephen Lawrence Centre, Deptford, David Adjaye, 2004–2007

These two small public buildings at different ends of Deptford Creek are roughly on the same scale, both low-rise and almost windowless structures which present decorative screens to the street, and try to create their own landscape rather than 'engage' with it in the currently popular sense. The Laban dance school is the more famous, a Stirling Prize winner and, for once, justly so – it's a limpid and perverse building. Surrounded by its own world of specially created grass escarpments, a translucent, synthetic cladding is shaded sky blue and punkish pink as it embraces the muddy trickle of the Creek. Inside, the sombre and claustrophobic interior of black-painted rough concrete is not at all what you'd expect.

At the other end of Deptford High Street, the Stephen Lawrence Centre does something more serious – named after the young student and aspiring architect who was stabbed to death in a racist attack in nearby Eltham in 1993, it houses the Trust set up in his name, which runs community programmes (architectural included) largely aimed at young people. Adjaye's design is accordingly harsher, perhaps too harsh, as a justified fear of vandalism and attacks has led to an elaborate security system, with none of the easily accessed public areas and cafes of the Laban. Adjaye's cladding screens are not translucent, but protective, jagged;

the garden is smaller, and though public, is much more for the users of the building than for stray visitors. Both are interesting and intelligent buildings in their own way, these are also two poles of inner city London – a lavish outward-aiming spectacle for the tourists and the arty types, and a more austerely financed, inward-facing parallel infrastructure for actual Londoners.[OH]

The Deptford Lounge, Pollard Thomas Edwards, 2011

This remarkable project mixing a school, library, community hub and 38 flats should be more widely studied. Its blingy copper-clad facade is deceptively monolithic but conceals multiple functions including a rooftop sports pitch. The academy's north and south wings are separated by an undulating playground closer to what pupils generally enjoy in Denmark than the flat puritanial yards most British schools provide. The Deptford Lounge is a persuasive example of what can be accomplished when cash-strapped institutions share resources and architecture.[PH]

St Dunstan's (top left), Laban Centre (centre, image by Martin Jordan), Stephen Lawrence Centre (top right), The Deptford Lounge (bottom right)

This leather cash bag was used by a chimney sweep or nightman in the mid-19th century. As with many of those performing the dirty work to keep London running, their labour went largely unseen as they removed sewage from cesspools during the night when the rest of the city slept.

Cleaners and other maintenance workers still go largely unseen and under-appreciated in the city. Today, this essential workforce is predominantly made up of women and migrants who often experience precarious working conditions and the same highly unsociable hours as the nightmen. A few recent developments signal some changes in this regard. As we clapped for key workers, the cleaner was reframed as a pandemic hero alongside nurses and doctors. Pre-pandemic, campaigns to improve working conditions for cleaning staff at the Ministry of Justice and London universities including the London School of Economics and the School of Oriental and African Studies achieved major successes.

What's more, as the climate crisis continues to run its course the importance of maintaining buildings – rather than demolishing and rebuilding them – will take on a renewed significance and our relationship with waste and recycling will continue to change; an increasingly popular spot for visitors to Open House London is the Southwark Integrated Waste Management Facility (Devon Street, SE15).

Southwark

Chimney sweep's cash bag, 1848–60, 99 × 70mm, Museum of London (© Museum of London)

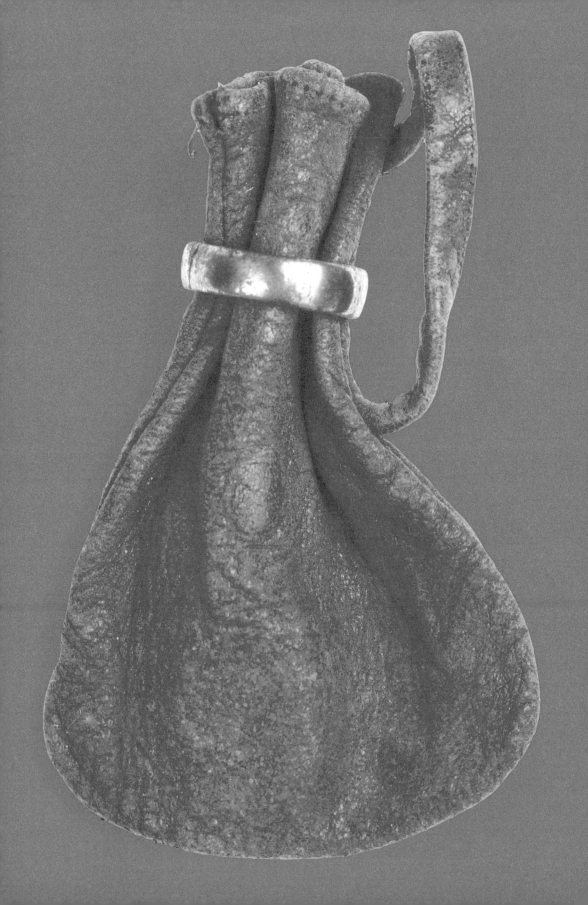

Romance in Rotherhithe
Johny Pitts

During an especially rainy April in 2012, I embarked upon a photographic commission in response to an essay by the novelist Caryl Phillips, written for Artangel. He'd spent four nights in a boat designed by David Kohn Architects after the Roi des Belges in Joseph Conrad's *Heart of Darkness*, perched awkwardly atop the Royal Festival Hall, as though a great tsunami had washed it up there. The iconic view before him – a north bank lined with St Paul's Cathedral, the Savoy hotel and the Palace of Westminster – began, he wrote, to irritate him. This vista suggested an antiquated idea of Britain that no longer chimed with the reality of the peopled streets below. Phillips set me the challenge of heading East along the Thames, with the idea that I should bring back a document to challenge the reductive, imperial iconography most usually associated with the Thames. A portrait of 'another' London.

When I set out a young single man with bicycle and camera, and boarded a Thames Clipper at the start of this month-long creative voyage, I had no idea, then, that in a sense I would never return. I found another London, alright; landscapes you won't often find in tourist brochures or the myth-making of British national identity. A London of Irish traveller ponies wandering freely among the maze of GLC's brutalist Thamesmead Estate, West African families making their first tentative steps in Britain with 'tobacco stained teeth' (to quote one journalist); the faded futurism of the Morris Walk Estate. I met with the Bangladeshi community living in the Smithsons' Robin Hood Gardens before the bulk of it was torn down, cycled along a graffiti 'wall of fame' fragranced with Daz detergent – it backed onto the Proctor and Gamble plant near Rainham Marshes. I ventured all the way down to Gravesend, where Pocahontas is buried next to a Wilko's, and finished my journey across the river at Tilbury Docks where, in 1948, the Empire Windrush famously docked, carrying 1,027 passengers and two stowaways from Jamaica.

What Caryl and my commissioners didn't know during that period, was how adrift I was in my personal life, and how much the project gave me something to anchor myself to. I'd just broken up with my long term girlfriend, Natasha, was back living at my Mom's, unable to afford

London rent, and was trying to reinvent myself after a series of ill-advised odd jobs in a stuttering TV career. To be able to afford to carry out my work for the project, I'd need to stay in hostels, that much was certain, and the only place I could find in my budget was a bunk in a Seaman's Mission in the curve of the Rotherhithe Peninsula.

Before the Thames project, I'd avoided this part of London. Being someone with brown skin, an internal, imaginative map of the capital had been downloaded; in the south-east, Brixton, Peckham and Lewisham were safe, but Rotherhithe belonged to a no-go stretch that included The Den, home of Millwall football club, famous for its racist fans, Deptford, the stomping ground of the National Front in the 1970s, and at its fringes Eltham, where Stephen Lawrence was murdered. Indeed, throughout my Thames trip I noticed far-right graffiti daubed on walls all along the south-east banks of the River Thames. Rotherhithe itself divides sharply into two tribes – there are the city workers in the financial sector who lock themselves behind gated and anti-social new builds or converted riverside factories, and then, an East End white working class community who are hanging on for dear life in the surrounding social housing blocks. Michael Caine was born in Rotherhithe and it remains one of the few surviving Cockney enclaves in zones 1 and 2. And in the middle of all this: my digs for the next few weeks, on Albion Street, opposite a charity shop for local churches and a derelict pub inhabited by squatters.

However, as soon as I entered the Finnish Church, which stands above the polluted Rotherhithe tunnel, I felt I'd found an oasis of Scandinavian calm; an undersubscribed hub in an oversubscribed city and the definition of what some call a 'safe space'. For twenty pounds per night I'd get a simple breakfast, use of a sauna and a bed in a six bunk room, which I often had all to myself.

There was something special about this building; it held a tranquil ambience – not religiously zealous but rather contemplative, designed for low-key spiritual communion. The Church of the Finnish Seamen's Mission was designed by Finnish architect Cyrill Sjöström Mardall of the firm Yorke, Rosenberg and Mardall, and was erected in 1958. Sjöström belonged to that influential generation of Finnish modernists who were youths when the Russian revolution took place and was succeeded by Finnish independence. If there was a whiff of Finnish nationalism, it was charged with making tangible a Finnish identity that was moderate, egalitarian, in harmony with nature, modern and built to what Alvar Aalto – an inspiration of Sjöström's – called 'a human scale'. It was this vision of Finland that I felt powerfully in the Finnish church and hostel. Perhaps the building was so important to me because it seemed that British nationalism was heading in the opposite direction of what the space in the Finnish church suggested – growingly unequal, unaffordable, unsocial, ostentatious, and looking backwards rather than forwards.

Woolwich (left) and Rotherhithe (right), images originally commissioned for Artangel for
The Space (all by Johny Pitts)

In Sjöström's Finnish Church I'd found a middle way, imbued with what in Finland is known as *Kohtuus*; although untranslatable to English, it might loosely be compared to the Swedish term *Lagom*, which suggests moderation. That April I was slowly bewitched not just by the Finnish Church, but also by Rotherhithe. Now that I'd found an affordable place to put my head down in London, in future I could travel in from Sheffield, keeping one foot in the marketplace of the capital.

Then, in January 2013, my ex Natasha got in touch. She was one of the lucky ones on London's social housing list, and had been offered a studio flat in Rotherhithe, of all places, and wondered if I'd accompany her to the viewing, as I knew the area. The flat was in one of the most impressive pieces of social housing in all of London; the Civic Trust award winning Thames Tunnel Mills, one of the first factories to be converted for residential use, and not for city workers but key workers. We entered the building, a former cereal mill, with its lofty atrium, flooded with natural daylight, visited the roof terrace and cactus garden, tended by residents, and, finally, entered a tiny, empty third floor riverside flat. As we stood in the middle of this 25 metre-squared nest, listening to the waves lapping at the base of the building, we knew we were going to get back together, and it was going to have to be all or nothing. That month, Natasha asked if I wanted to move in with her, the next year she fell pregnant, and the year after that gave birth to our daughter Célia, right where we were stood looking at each other on that first viewing.

Over the years we jokingly began to talk of ourselves as 'river folk', tuning out of the city at large and into the peculiarities of the Thames; speed boats with screaming tourists speeding along every other hour to the themes of James Bond or *Baywatch*.

We'd mudlark at low tide, to find things to decorate our home with; shells, stones and a washed-up money plant which still survives. We alternated babysitting duties every Tuesday night to nip over the road and spend an evening with the Sands Films Cinema Club (for a donation at your discretion, with a complimentary cup of tea), hosted by the effervescent Rotherhithe treasure Olivier Stockman. If we wanted to entertain, we'd do it at the Mayflower pub next door, from which the pilgrims set sail for America.

We lived among a cast of characters that included drug dealers and pimps, artists, hipsters and homeless people (one resident had given up his flat to live on the streets, but still had a key to get into the building, so would spend a night on the roof every now and then), Danny, a Nigerian who lived on the ground floor and served as unofficial security guard when he wasn't chatting up the single ladies of the building, and José, a gay Brazilian man who put on an annual exhibition of resident's

The Finnish Church designed in 1958 by Cyrill Sjöström Mardall

art for Open House. If Danny was the brawn of the building and José the heart, we had Jenny the brain, who had worked in housing and helped us battle the landlord's crippling bureaucracy.* I speak of these people as caricatures, but they wore these identities proudly and loudly, and while our landlords were peevish and draconian, a community persisted, held together by our efforts, and encouraged by the original design of the building. Residents would joke that the ample negative space – excessively wide corridors, open atrium, ground floor common room, outside deck, and huge roof terrace – was much more spacious than the areas dedicated to private habitation.

In some ways the building was too communal, which meant that as my daughter grew into a toddler and I signed my first book deal, I had nowhere to write because of constant interruptions. I wrote in a few local cafes but had to rotate between them, because once I became a fixture in a social scene writing was impossible. But there again was the Seaman's church. Staff knew me well by now; I'd been going there for years, first as a hostel resident, then to take my daughter to the small play area every other day, and treat her to a Moomins lolly from the little Finnish convenience store. Because the staff were friendly in a Finnish way, comfortable with being quiet, I could exchange pleasantries and work peacefully in this place of worship. I wrote a full book there and began another one, which became the initial sketches of my book *Afropean: Notes from Black Europe*. Though I'm not religious, it struck me that Sjöstrom's church was functioning as a place of religion should do; as local amenity, community centre, space for contemplation, and, yes, philanthropic service to struggling writers.

As our daughter grew, we knew there was no future in our bonny little box on the river, and thus no future in Rotherhithe. But like the sailors the area had once embraced, Rotherhithe – a working class enclave not long for this world – took us in, gave us our start, and offered us sanctuary and friendship in the face of an indifferent city.

*pseudonyms used to respect privacy

Johny Pitts is a writer, photographer and broadcast journalist. He has received various awards for his work exploring African-European identity, including a Decibel Penguin Prize, an ENAR (European Network Against Racism) award and a Society of Authors Travelling Grant. He is the curator of the online journal Afropean.com, and has contributed words and images for the *Guardian*, the *New Statesman* and *The New York Times*.

Dining and Assembly Hall, Brunswick Park Primary School, Camberwell, Stirling and Gowan, 1961

The site of this building is about as spacious and eerie as you could get within inner London, occupying the space between school buildings in the interzone where Camberwell, Peckham and Walworth meet, an area made up of various estates of varying quality, all poorly connected to each other. Responding to that disjointed space, Stirling and Gowan created this tiny monument as a circus around which it can revolve; a circular mound has, just set slightly into it, a building divided like a piece of origami into four parts: three monopitch halls for school activities, plus a small playground with a stark wall connecting it to the main facade. It looks more than a little knackered now, and like practically everything Stirling designed it is much smaller in real life than in the architectural history books. Even so, it is the best building to display the way that overeducated Brutalist architects derived ideas from the ideal plans of the Renaissance, via the art historian Rudolf Wittkower; so here, everything you see derives from an extremely clever diagrammatic plan, translated into a strange miniature landscape, a vision of celestial geometry in cheap stock brick and standard glazing.[OH]

The Aylesbury Estate, Hans Peter Trenton, 1963–1977

The largest housing estate in Europe at the time of its completion and the site of Tony Blair's first public speech as Prime Minister, the Aylesbury Estate comprises a dwindling grid of substantial residential blocks, interspersed with green spaces, pubs and community facilities. Dwindling, because the estate is gradually being demolished to make way for new development in line with a controversial regeneration masterplan. Nonetheless, the remaining portions of the Aylesbury, though suffering from poor maintenance, are impressive in their generosity with sweeping spiral ramps and broad external walkways raised above traffic. This raised access allowed Trenton to flip the conventional flat plan in medium rise blocks so that residents enter at bedroom level and either descend down to a garden kitchen in the case of lower flats or, for upper flats, climb to a living room with panoramic views over Southwark.[PH]

Walter Segal, 1986, refurbished PUP Architects, 2020

Loomed over by Canary Wharf's high-rise cluster across the river, Surrey Docks Farm is a quiet presence on the Thames, providing space for rearing animals alongside community and education facilities on a small site. The main building – a black-painted three-storey tower newly topped by a weathervane in the shape of a golden pig – was designed by Walter Segal. Recently refurbished by PUP Architects, the site has gained civic character in embracing the riverfront it had previously turned its back on, with a new glazed river room sporting a sawtooth roof looking out over the water.[RM]

Ivy House, Nunhead, EA Sewell, 1930

This Grade II listed pub was designed for Truman's Brewery. Still boasting its original curved bar and timber panel walls, it was a key site in the pub rock movement of the 1970s.[Om]

Bellenden School, Peckham, Cottrell and Vermeulen, 2018

Bellenden School is a stand-out exception to the depressing recent run of school-building. It is in an alleyway, between deck-access council flats and mundane but recently lucrative Victorian terraced houses. A curved brown brick wall with portholes satisfies the stringent current security regulations without feeling aggressive or obnoxious – quite some achievement. Then you come to an opening for a nursery, with yellow pitched-roofed pavilions poking their heads above the wall. Follow the curved wall a little further, and you find a row of classrooms on pilotis, in a fifties retro language of sans serif signage and a mix of coloured vitreous panels and stock brick. The curved path then arrives at the playground, where those classrooms on pilotis are raised partly above the play areas. This is exactly what building in a residential area in a big city should be like, and usually isn't – making walking a pleasure, and doing something imaginative and strange with the odd in between spaces rather than shoving a slab or an icon into them. The school should also be a great place to be in as a child, when what you want is secrets, adventure, surprise, not big dumb things you can understand right away. If only there were more like it.[OH]

Siobhan Davies Dance Studio, Sarah Wigglesworth Architects, 2005

Abutting the neighbouring listed Victorian School, this redundant school annexe had gone largely unappreciated until its conversion into a bespoke set of dance studios. By replacing the old roof structure with new asymmetrical vaults, the dance studio can span the length of the building, its ceiling undulating in a rhythm that mimics the movements of its users.[NM]

Surrey Docks Farm (centre), Bellenden School (right)

Kingston upon Thames, Lambeth, Merton, Richmond upon Thames, Sutton, Wandsworth

SOUTH-WEST

An Astounding Flatness: The Tolworth Tower
Joanne Murray

Due to its peripheral position, Tolworth and its environs may not immediately seem like a destination on the architectural tourist trail for the passing driver, local resident or intrepid rambler. Indeed, its position next to the A3 might also initially deter exploration on foot – amusingly, one friendly yet concerned lady in a stationary car presumed I was lost in my most recent walk around the area. But Tolworth has some interesting lesser known architectural and historical points of interest that are worthy of closer inspection, particularly the iconic Tolworth Tower, designed by George Marsh of R. Seifert & Partners and opened in 1964.

The Tolworth Tower has loomed large in my psyche for some time now. I first set eyes on it when visiting the Kingston University on an open day in the late 1990s as a prospective student. Driving up the A3 from the south coast with my Dad, the rolling fields of Surrey either side of the dual carriageway suddenly gave way to a monolithic slab of a building that seemed to boldly announce the liminal zone of suburbia; a forthright punctuation mark on the arterial corridor into central London. The Tolworth Tower continued to gain momentum in my mind as a student, along with nearby Surbiton station, an art deco Grade II listed building designed by James Robb Scott. Nights out at university tended to begin at the station as we journeyed into central London, and frequently culminated at the Tolworth Tower after falling asleep on the N77 night bus. Further personal Tolworth connections were forged when I heard rumours that David Bowie had performed his inaugural gig as Ziggy Stardust in 1972 at the Toby Jug pub (demolished 2000) that used to sit opposite the Tolworth Tower. Recent homage was paid to Bowie's alter ego in the form of a Ziggy inspired lightning bolt emblazoned on the south elevation of the Tolworth Tower, which highlights the importance of this piece of cultural history to the suburb, but also the significance of the tower as a local landmark.

The practice behind the design of the Tolworth Tower, R. Seifert & Partners, is more readily known for their Grade II listed work such as Centre Point (1966) and Space House (1968) in central London. Richard Seifert (1910–2001) was prolific in the post-war period, designing hundreds of commercial office buildings that would transform the skyline of many UK cities, and the 22-storey Tolworth Tower is no exception. Unlike Seifert's sister towers in central London, however, the Tolworth Tower erupts from an astounding flatness. It is literally the *only* tower for what seems like miles around (the more diminutive CI and Apex Towers in New Malden are probably the closest and only visible from Tolworth when at height). When standing on the roof of the tower looking up the A3 towards central London, the skylines of central London and the City are visible. The Tolworth Tower seems to almost face its more familiar counterparts, along with other landmarks and towns visible from up top, such as the Wembley arches, the Queen Mary Reservoir, Windsor, the Surrey Hills and Croydon.

The Tolworth Tower exudes a sense that it has landed here, or is about to take-off, initially through the sheer magnitude of scale in comparison to the surrounding architectural vernacular, but also through some of the building's design features. John Grindrod suggests that 'the concrete gables at either end of the building [are] in the shape of a thrusting arrow pointing upwards, like the smoke trail of a rocket', and he goes on to ponder why the Tolworth Tower was not given a more cosmological name, like some of Seifert's other more well-known buildings: 'Rocket House would have suited it perfectly'. The tower furthers its spacecraft-like status through the visual lightness of the curtain wall façade (perhaps it *could* take off?), and the economy of materials used in construction. The tower is engineered with a slender concrete frame and pot and beam flooring, making it surprisingly lightweight for a building of such monolithic stature.

There is a striking repetition of elements found throughout the Tolworth Tower complex that creates an overall sense of visual coherence. The vertical aluminium fins mirror the visible internal columns of the tower, for example, and these pronounced vertical elements are also reiterated in the raw concrete slabs of the mural mounted on the lower level podium wall. Photographs from 1964 show a long-gone water feature (now a car park) that comprised an overlapping square and rectangular pools with vertical and horizontal planks, further reflecting the rhythmical repetitions found in the curtain wall façade. An additional mural was also once located on the south elevation of the tower, and consisted of more raw concrete panels (similar to those used in the enduring mural) with vertical detailing, traversed by a horizontal steel beam and a series of L-shaped steel sections welded together to form overlapping squares. This exhibition of raw concrete and the internal structural components of a building chimes with the approach to materials found in the New Brutalism. These sculptural and landscape elements act as a further cue for the onlooker to think about the interconnection of these forms with the building itself, both structurally, but also in plan, where the various blocks of the complex also overlap and interlock.

Tolworth Tower, 1964 (all images RIBA / Taylor Woodrow Group)

Closer inspection of the Tolworth Tower, however, highlights subtle tensions that take place between its overtly repetitive rectilinear geometries and slightly more off-kilter quirks. It has been noted that buildings by Seifert & Partners (particularly those designed by George Marsh) often eschewed the right angle, but here this characteristic seems to be deployed as a point of contrast. The gable ends of the tower taper as they reach the top, with the window spans inversely proportional, and the pilotis, when viewed from the side, demonstrate a comparable playfulness in form. The structural uprights supporting the roof of the stairwell entrance on top of the level 2 car park concourse resemble the pilotis turned on their heads, and the angled roof looks like a playful inversion of a mid-century Palm Springs butterfly roof. In contrast to the rectangular tiling used on this stairwell and elsewhere in the complex, the mosaic tiling on the pilotis is eccentrically trapezoidal, which is a detail that can only really be seen up close. Another peculiar aesthetic twist are the expressed spandrel panels that splay out around the core (referred to as 'bottle openers' by the architects working on its proposed redevelopment). Acting as a visual break to the curtain walling on the north elevation of the tower, the panels extrude at a bizarre angle, which, along with the pilotis, disrupts the rectilinear geometry of this elevation.

At the time of writing in summer 2020, construction work on the Tolworth Tower is imminent, and the architect's proposals aim to 'celebrate and enhance' Seifert's design. This sensitivity certainly seems to be reflected through the amount of research and work that has been undertaken by the design team behind the scheme, particularly in relation to the appearance of the façade of the tower. The eventual fate of the existing mural and stairwell entrance is yet to be decided, however, as phase 2 proposals will include the construction of two additional towers and the mural might have to move out of necessity (if it can be moved), possibly to be reused in the new concierge area. As it stands, the final form the two new towers might take is yet to be decided. If they do get built, then the Tolworth Tower may have some equally statuesque neighbours to keep it company in the outskirts. On the one hand, the existence of further towers might detract from the Tolworth Tower's monolithic presence, but it might also further emphasise the vast contrast in scale between the tower and the surrounding sea of suburban semis.

The plans for the refurbishment of the Tolworth Tower into a build-to-rent scheme promises a residential utopia reminiscent of J.G. Ballard's *High-Rise* (1974), with on-site gym, cinema, meeting spaces, lounges and flexible workspace. J.G. Ballard was no stranger to Kingston, loosely basing his 2006 novel *Kingdom Come* on the nearby Bentall Centre. Certainly the Tolworth Tower, perched on the edge of the A3, seems to

inhabit a Ballardian landscape of motorways and concrete islands. For an unexpected point of contrast though, it is worth heading on foot to the meadows in Tolworth Court Farm Fields, just the other side of the A3, where views of the tower are framed by ancient oaks and wildflowers. No matter where the tower is viewed from, however, it is instantly impactful and unforgettable. Seifert's island of hyper-modernity demands more than a cursory glance in the rear-view mirror.

Joanne Murray is a garden designer with a particular interest in mid-century design. Her doctoral research explored the links between New Brutalism and the fiction of J.G. Ballard. Joanne has lived in and around Kingston upon Thames (apart from the odd spell away) for the past 21 years.

The author thanks Project Manager Rory O'Dwyer for giving an impromptu tour of the tower and Charlie Whitaker and Graham Hickson-Smith at 3DReid for their insights into the history and forthcoming redevelopment of the tower. Thanks also to Dominic Bradbury for an insightful email exchange.

Cambridge Gardens, Norbiton, Sydney Clough, Son and Partners, 1949

The Royal Borough of Kingston upon Thames is not the sort of place you expect to find monumental Red Vienna style public housing schemes; but leave Norbiton station to find what appears like a huge red fortress towering over the usual semis and villas, and a direct route to the estate's grand archway, where you'll find paired columns and two plaques, one to celebrate its opening, the other to celebrate its renovation fifty years later. The effect of power and pride is lessened a little at the main frontage facing the busy high street, where the inability of this axial, pomp-driven style to deal with slopes and asymmetries becomes uncomfortably clear, and the fortress-like effect is lessened by some straggly planning – but the finishes, in Dutch brick with curved decks and streamlined glass stairwells, are still impressive. So too is the comparison with the 1960s system-built estate over the road.[OH]

The Tony Leitch Townscape Awards

Every year, the Kingston upon Thames Society present the prestigious Tony Leitch Townscape Awards to the places that have done most to enhance the environment in the borough. Recent award-winners include the Alexandra pub, in Park Road, north Kingston, which was beautifully restored by architect Matt Allchurch as six flats. Meanwhile, the Church Hall at Christ Church New Malden, designed by Roger Molyneux, is unapologetically modern, though the use of timber brick and rendering sit well with the old hall.

On Richmond Road, Kingston, was the old Penny School, a simple honest Georgian building, which the Society fought to have preserved but failed. However the replacement, Kingston College Creative Industries Centre, designed by Hugh Bennett, is a thoroughly worthwhile building which enhances its site. At 117 London Road, a showroom for Topps Tiles, with flats above, architect Andrew Simpson IDP has broken up the wall surface using panels of knapped flint, reflecting the nearby Lovekyn Chapel, the oldest complete building in Kingston. This building has a quiet elegant modesty which is a delight to behold.
Contributed by the Kingston Society and Royal Borough of Kingston upon Thames

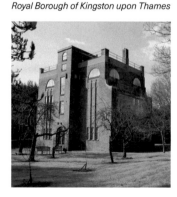

Dorich House, Kingston Vale, Dora Gordine, 1936

The distinctive Dorich House on the edge of Richmond Park was designed and built by the Russian sculptor, artist and designer Dora Gordine and her husband, intended to create a space for Gordine to produce and display her art. After Gordine's death in 1991, the home was restored before reopening as a museum in 1996. The design of Dorich House draws on a variety of international sources: the architecture of the Estonian capital, Tallinn, where Gordine had lived as a young woman; her experience of Parisian studio houses, including elements drawn from Auguste Perret's design for Gordine's own home in the city; and references to the architectural and interior design of south-east Asia.[Om]

Kingston Centre, Kingston upon Thames, Owen Luder Partnership, 1974–76

A suburban megastructure, a towering, asymmetrical multi-storey edifice looming over all around it, shoving car parks, offices and retail into one mass. However, it's located in a genteel part of outer south London, and so treated rather differently than Luder's mangled Eros House in Catford – its future is assured as a hotel, which has meant a smooth paint job that, while not as destructive as the cladding of Eros House, is obviously at variance with Luder's rough-arsed approach to Brutalism. As with the latter building, it's a regular grid interrupted and flanked with melodramatic service towers, sculpturally modelled. Seeing it across the large park nearby, what the paint can't hide is the flamboyantly profiled stair-tower, whose presence and force still bursts through.[OH]

Cambridge Gardens (top), Dorich House (centre, image by Ellie Laycock), Kingston Centre (right)

Pilgrimage on the P5 Bus
Jason Okundaye

When Martin Linton was the Labour Member of Parliament for Battersea from 1997 to 2010, he introduced the P5 bus route which runs from the periphery of the borough of Wandsworth, the Patmore Estate in Battersea, where I still live, through to the borough of Lambeth, via Brixton, and terminates at Elephant & Castle Station. As a child I resented taking this bus. Being a single-decker bus it was frequently overcrowded, delayed, and would stop every two minutes. Years later, my appreciation of the P5 has changed – not that these 'problems' have disappeared, but I've come to understand how bus routes born from grassroots-level, democratic, and local consultation provide the best mechanisms for residents of community estates to explore, and to live. Avoiding main roads, the P5 stalks the more serene backstreets of inner London, stopping past the building complexes and amenities which define community housing structures. For African and Caribbean residents of the Patmore and other neighbouring estates, the P5 bus is primarily the vehicle we used to easily access Brixton market. Its conception was, after all, not as much a simple formulation of new transport opportunities as it was a matter of public health – allowing, in particular, disabled and elderly residents to access fresh produce, seasonings and cultural foods from Brixton market, only requiring a short walk from their doorsteps to the bus stop, rather than to bus stops outside of the estates or to Stockwell station.

Locally-determined innovative uses of transport and transport infra-structure have, in this way, come to represent the community-mindedness which has enabled migrant communities to bloom in concrete. It is for this reason that I have always been fascinated by how Windrush migrants occupied the Brixton railway arches – an architectural feature which has long caught my attention when loading off at the market on those P5 trips. Brixton was built as a middle class suburb for white Britons in the 19th century, and following the bombing campaigns of the Luftwaffe during the Second World War, Brixtonians began to leave for pastures new in overspill towns. In their absence, Windrush migrants began to revitalise the vacant homes and commercial sites they had abandoned. But the very presence of these migrants accelerated the process of counter-urbanisation, more specifically through the ideology of 'white flight' in which white Britons retreated from inner London, repulsed by the apparent social decline and risk of miscegenation which Black people supposedly carried with them. Black migrants were not a colonising force displacing white middle class Brixtonians. Rather, the reimagining of architectural infrastructure like the Brixton arches into commercial sites by working class Black Caribbean populations showed the innovation required to overcome the hostile and infertile spaces that had been left behind for them. And of course beyond the arches, Brixton market itself, stretching through from Electric Avenue to Brixton Village, has been feeding the African and Caribbean populations of south London through cafes, fishmongers, butchers and grocers providing, at times when these could not be found in supermarket chains, Dunn's River seasonings, plantain, fried dumplings, cuts of oxtail and scotch bonnet peppers – all staples of our cuisines.

Railway tracks have always been considered visual markers of an 'urban' territorialisation of space – from the graffiti lining bridges and tunnels, to the Black hair and beauty shops which fill the arches. Migrants did not seek permission to transform these railway arches which had typically been used as light industrial units or storage – instead, they pioneered a new way for making use of transportation infrastructure. And it is for these reasons that Brixton has not only been seen as a British epicentre for Black African and Caribbean cuisine and culture, but for why the arches remain both a symbolic structure and the most contested frontier against the imperial forces of gentrification which threaten Black and migrant life in Brixton.

In 2018, the Save Brixton Arches Campaign lost their three year struggle against Network Rail's refurbishment plans. The campaign stated that they simply desired the kind of democratic, locally-driven consultation with tenants and traders to ensure that the businesses they had built from scratch, and which had serviced both Brixtonians and non-Brixtonian frequent visitors like myself, weren't simply forced into surrender. Network Rail terminated leases and enabled a 300% rent increase, forcing, according to the campaign, 'small family businesses from their premises and essentially ending their livelihoods.' Years later, many are still furious. Amidst the closure of businesses during the Covid-19 pandemic, Lambeth Council released a statement about the Grade II listed gay entertainment venue, the Royal Vauxhall Tavern, claiming: 'We musn't lose those places and organisations that make Lambeth, Lambeth.' It is my right as a Black gay man to ask why queer venues, mostly frequented by the white LGBTQ+ population of Vauxhall, are viewed as more integral to the social fabric of Lambeth, whilst the Black, brown and migrant families who traded carpets and synthetic wigs under the Arches for generations were not.

Nour Cash & Carry (image by Save Nour, Save Brixton)

Recently observing the arches when walking along the underpass on Brixton Station Road has shown that redevelopment, like many other ambitious regeneration projects which have jarred the landscape of inner London for the past decade, is slow. My last memory of witnessing the arches was when I caught the P5 and jumped off at Brixton market to grab some Jamaican beef patties from First Choice Bakery, which is on a corner of Atlantic Road. Though some shops along the arches remain open, on estimate over three-quarters are boarded up – providing a canvas for local amateur artists to decorate with graffiti. There is the typical bubble graffiti, often painted as a romantic declaration, or statement of allegiance to local postcodes, which quite charmingly complements the ultramarine blue of the railway bridge which structures the arches – but there are also quite explicit messages, including a very colourful 'fuck u bourgeois scum'. The sturdiness of the arches, the railway bridge's pillars, its vibrant blue paint, and the expressions of local rage it is passionately vandalised with, have also come to symbolise the strength and endurance of Brixton's Black, migrant and working class communities. It is con-tentious, sure, but perhaps no other area of London has been so fiercely resistant to the occupying forces of gentrification. Even if when trailing Brixton I bump into gentrifying peers from university who originate from the home counties, or if another Pret opens within a two minute walk of the Pret already to the right of the tube station, the community has never, to me, lost its character.

Even as the area has been forced to adapt to the demands of develop-ers and super-gentrifiers at the expense of local economies, the endurance of the community's soul in Brixton has perhaps been determined by a number of sociological and architectural factors. Quite simply Brixton's architecture is dominant and it anchors its social demographics; the out-skirts of its centre are domineered by large housing estates such as Angell House, Stockwell Park, and Somerleyton, home to the Brutalist 'Barrier Block' which provide very physical frontiers against gentrification's waves. Perhaps no physical structure in Brixton represents its endurance better than the Brixton Recreation Centre which, after threat of closure, was successfully listed at Grade II in 2016 due to its 'cultural importance' and 'sculptural concrete forms.' Like the Arches, these are structures which Brixton's communities have fought tooth and nail to defend. The very emotional and symbolic importance of Brixton as a historic site of the post-war Windrush settlement, and how these migrants built Brixton from the neglected ruins of war, means that the very dignity of Black British communities feels dependent on its survival.

Organising and riotous protest, as is the just and democratic right of our communities, have helped to protect both these architectural giants, and the bustling Brixton Market. And one recent victory has made me more hopeful for the future and endurance of Brixton against the aggressive occupying forces of gentrification – that is, of course, the victory of campaigners to save Nour Cash & Carry. Nour had been provided with a Section 25 notice to vacate its site by 22nd July 2020, but a tireless campaign predominantly facilitated through social media due to the social distancing requirements of the Covid-19 pandemic, meant that Nour had been able to secure a stable, long-term lease with genuinely affordable rent. My mother, like many other migrants, had frequented Nour as a shop which provided cheap, fresh produce and groceries and ultimately vital nutrition. As I've said, access to these stores are a matter of public health for immigrant communities – and so campaigns against their closure must be anchored to narratives of health and nutrition, alongside community.

But equally, Brixton itself, as the spiritual and geographical epicentre of Black British life, must be defended as a vital emblem of Black British history. And shops like Nour cannot simply rely on community-organising, but require long-term, permanent and sustainable solutions to protect them from eviction. Southwark campaigners evoked the Public Sector Equality Duty, which compels public authorities to consider how their policies and decisions affect those who are protected under the Equality Act 2010, as a legal basis to defend the bowling alley and Palace Bingo of the Elephant & Castle shopping centre. Lambeth Council could, rather than twirling for developers, recognise their obligations under this duty and as such appeal for Electric Avenue, the market and, of course, the Brixton arches, to be declared as sites of Black cultural heritage which must be protected accordingly. After all, even though Linton lost his seat in 2010 and the constituency of Battersea has since changed political hands between successive elections, the P5 bus has still endured, as it is sacrament for local residents. Similarly, for Black Britons, Brixton itself is a regular site of pilgrimage – it too requires a permanent solution to ensure its survival.

Jason Okundaye was born to Nigerian parents in south London in 1997. He writes mainly on LGBT issues and racism for publications such as the *Guardian*, the *London Review of Books*, *Dazed*, *Vice*, *GQ*, *The Independent*, and *i-D*. He is also a political columnist at *Tribune*. He holds a first class degree in Human, Social and Political Science from Pembroke College, University of Cambridge. He is working on a non-fiction book about Black British gay men.

Lambeth Towers, Lambeth, George Finch for Lambeth Borough Architects Department, 1965

On an inner city site opposite the Imperial War Museum, this sparky cluster of towers was designed by George Finch under Lambeth's Borough Architect Ted Hollamby. Like Sidney Cook in Camden, Hollamby assembled a tight-knit team of designers who created, for the most part, unique designs for specific sites. Unlike in Camden, this often meant high-rise, and George Finch had a terrific eye for skylines, rivalled in London only by his life partner and architect at the neighbouring borough of Southwark, Kate Macintosh. Here, what initially looks like several towers bunched together is actually just one, twisting and turning its way upwards, with neat boxed-out flats, around a cylindrical glass stairwell; a lot of excitement packed into a very small space, scaled so that it's not remotely overbearing. Shops and a doctor's surgery are built into the ground floor – a model of the currently fashionable 'inner city mixed-use building'.[OH]

Central Hill Estate, Gipsy Hill, Rosemary Sjernstedt for Lambeth Borough Architects Department, 1967–1974

If Lambeth Towers displays Ted Hollamby's team mastering concrete urbanity, Central Hill is a perfect modernist suburb, the finest of its kind south of the river. Designed by Rosemary Sjernstedt, one of the original team at Alton East, it's built across a large swathe the otherwise nondescript Gipsy Hill, with two distinct faces. Abutting the Victorian and Edwardian villas all around are grey-black weatherboarded houses, a familiar Anglicisation of Alvar Aalto's Finnish rural modernism, with slightly rustic tiled paths leading you into, as it were, the 'central hill'. Mounting the slope, into which space for sports has been unfussily fitted, are stepped-section concrete and pale brick maisonettes, with nice big balconies and panoramic perspectives; the way these blocks step down and then rise up the hill, shadowed by trees, shows a rare command of the integration between townscape and public gardens. Its intimate domestic spaces gently lead to sweeping panoramas with a hide-and-seek lightness; suburban, for sure, but not at all parochial or pinched. Only the poor upkeep and the deciduous trees tell you that Central Hill is not in some affluent Swiss modernist hill village. Currently, Central Hill is slated to be demolished and then 'densified', though it uses its space much more effectively than the suburban villas all around – except these can't be just sold off en masse by local government in the way this can. One of the great tragedies of social housing in London is how the instruments that built it are now being used to destroy it.[OH]

Newport Street Gallery, Vauxhall, Caruso St John, 2015

It is good to find, for once, a London building that is the poor relation of similar buildings for similar functions by the same architects beyond the metropolis. Newport Street, a private gallery owned by Damien Hirst, can't compare with the ingenuity and discovery of Caruso St John's other galleries in Walsall or Nottingham. Perhaps the architects had less interest in housing Hirst's art collection and his theme restaurant, than they did in creating what were effectively new town centres in those two Midland cities. For what it is, though, the Newport Street Gallery is more than decent. It resembles a luxury engineering workshop, a light industrial sawtooth joining onto some genuine industrial remnants along the Waterloo-Southampton viaduct. Inside are airy galleries and a sensuous concrete staircase. Along with their refurbishment of Tate Britain over the river around the same time, it marks Caruso St John out as the most remarkable staircase designers in British architecture since Lubetkin; a grey swirl through a brick vault, a glamorous dungeon. All of this careful balance tips into unfortunate bathos in the restaurant, Pharmacy. Hirst originally designed this himself in the 1990s, and so the architects have tried to replicate it, relenting their firm, reliable grip. The space's wall-to-wall collection of medicine packets and pills is one not very funny joke repeated a thousand times, much like the man's art.[OH]

Lambeth Towers (left), Central Hill Estate (centre), Newport Street Gallery (right)

At Open House we love an urban myth, even the odd conspiracy theory. Heard the one about Elephant & Castle roundabout? The glimmering metal box in the middle has puzzled passers-by ever since it was erected in 1961. Is it a power station? Public art? A memorial to a local chemist? Or the home of electronic musician Aphex Twin? You'll have to visit to find out.

Just down the road, Keystone House inspired similar suspicions. The brutalist complex, which stood in Vauxhall from 1975 to 2016 was officially an international and inland telephone exchange (and home to this NTU 6B/2 signalling card), although it was also rumoured to be an MI6 building complete with underground tunnels and access to Westminster.

Speaking of tunnels, what do you know about the Mole Man of Hackney? Formally known as William Lyttle, a former civil engineer, the mole man lived in a De Beauvoir town house for forty years, during which he gradually dug away a network of caverns beneath the Hackney streets, reportedly spreading up to 20 metres in every direction from his house. Lyttle was eventually evicted in 2006 and 33 tones of soil and debris were removed from the house, which was eventually refurbished by David Adjaye (Mortimer Road, N1). The tunnels, and the Mole Man himself, are sadly no longer still with us.

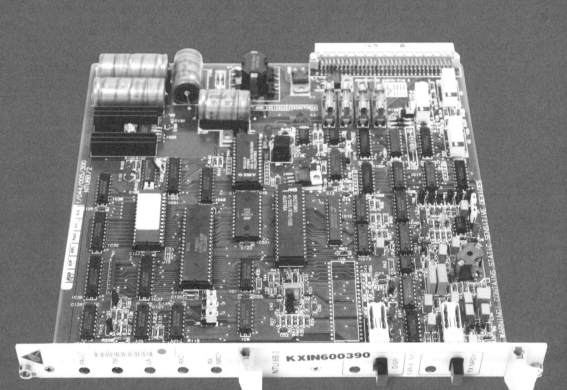

The Low-Rise High-Density Housing of 1970s Merton

John Boughton

Before Camden, there was Merton. The borough's pioneering low-rise, high-density council housing of the late-1960s and 1970s was celebrated; lauded in the architectural press, a subject of study for architectural students and innovators. But, while many will know Camden's show-pieces, relatively few now remember Merton or visit its ground-breaking estates set in the south London suburbs.

The catastrophic partial collapse in May 1968 of the system-built Ronan Point tower block in east London is conventionally taken as marking the end of the fashion for high-rise that characterised the later-1950s and 1960s. In fact, suitably modified high-rise construction continued into the 1970s. Moreover, the backlash against high-rise had deeper roots. While some critics were already decrying its allegedly antisocial nature, practically, it was the expense of multi-storey construction and a growing realisation that it didn't guarantee higher housing density that were the tipping points. In this lay the origins of the low-rise, high-density architecture that influenced and graced council housing design in what became its swansong before 1979.

Housing density was in those pre-metric days a relatively straight-forward calculation of people per acre. The open space required by tower blocks to prevent overlooking and overshadowing allowed a fairly common-sense realisation that they weren't necessarily housing greater numbers than the tight terraces they typically replaced. There was no desire to replicate previously overcrowded conditions but increasingly architects and planners were exploring forms and layouts that could deliver greater density in attractive surrounds. The Centre for Land Use and Built Form Studies in the University of Cambridge, founded in 1967, led by Lionel March and Leslie Martin, would be at the forefront of such efforts. March was a mathematician, architect and digital artist; Leslie Martin had been Chief Architect at the London County Council before becoming an influential academic.

The theoretical models devised by March and Martin proved that low-rise housing, appropriately planned, could provide densities at least equivalent to those of tower blocks. Two principal templates were suggested: 'courtyard housing' arranged, as the name implies, around a series of public and private courts, and 'perimeter housing', arranged – you've guessed it – around the edge of a shared open space. It was one of their students at Cambridge, Richard MacCormac, who turned the latter into reality in Merton.

The new London Borough of Merton had been created in 1965, a merger of two urban district councils – Mitcham and Wimbledon and Merton and Morden – in an area of Surrey by then recognised as forming part of Greater London. It was – and is – a Conservative-Labour marginal, under Conservative control for most of the period under review here, so there is no obviously political explanation for what Bridget Cherry described as its 'brief golden age of experiment'. We'll give credit to Borough Architect Philip J. Whittle, a low-profile figure but one credited as having a 'keen eye to spot people with architectural gifts and enthusiasm' and a willingness to throw them in at the deep end.

Whittle commissioned MacCormac and some colleagues from Cambridge to design council housing in Merton. The outcome was Pollards Hill in Mitcham, at the extreme south-eastern corner of the borough, officially opened in January 1970. This was, in bare terms, a development of 562 houses and 288 flats on a 41-acre site previously occupied by temporary post-war prefabs which had long outlived their designated ten-year lifespan. The new estate's genius lay in its layout – the first executed example of perimeter planning. At Pollards Hill, this is usually described as a 'Greek-key meander' but, if that reference escapes you, you can think of it as a series of inverted Ps – short cul-de-sacs hanging from a semi-circular service road bordered by an almost continuous line of housing and fronting onto a large area of green open space. The design enabled a density of 116 persons per acre, with most homes boasting an integral garage, small private backyard and views of shared open space. MacCormac himself added that the scheme was 'effectively Radburn', a more established design principle of the day which sought to separate pedestrians and traffic. Visually, the estate presented a stark modernist appearance – flat-roofed, with dark wooden window frames, and clad with gleaming white stove-enamel panels concealing its prefabricated concrete construction.

The estate would feature in at least five articles in the contemporary architectural press and in 1972 received the South East Region Award of the Royal Institute of British Architects. Bernard Ward, who had succeeded Whittle as Borough Architect in 1970, thought the award reflected a recognition that:

Pollards Hill houses a large number of families without the architects having to resort to high-rise blocks to do it. Those who have visited the estate since it was completed have been surprised at the spacious surroundings in which so many people can be accommodated.

The local press praised the Council which 'had managed to house hundreds of families while adding to the quality of the environment'. But it wasn't all plain sailing: rents averaging £9 a week were judged unaffordable by many who needed the new housing most, and protests marked its official opening.

MacCormac left Merton in 1972 to go into private practice. A distinguished career, major commissions and a knighthood followed, but in 1972 he was the lead architect for the recently completed Eastfields estate in central Mitcham. In its essentials, it replicated the Pollards Hill template – 466 three-storey houses (no flats this time) of similar style in a perimeter layout. On this smaller, seven-acre site, the housing was arranged in an enclosed court format, providing what MacCormac described as an 'intermediary between court and street, having geometric advantages of the former while admitting vehicles'.

Merton's final foray into perimeter planning, credited to R. Hodge and A. Bews of the Borough Architect's Department, followed at Watermeads, completed in 1977 in an idyllic setting next to the River Wandle. That site, prone to flooding, imposed its own constraints in terms of land set aside for water capture and a lower housing density, but the retention of mature trees and a bucolic outlook to the rear make it the most successful of the three estates.

There was also a deliberate learning of lessons, formalised in a survey of Pollards Hill residents that was critical, amongst other things, of the estate's monotony. Watermeads was, in any case, a smaller scheme – a 50:50 mix of 186 three-bed houses and one-bed flats – and it retains a far more intimate feel. That softening is seen also in what Bridget Cherry described in *The Buildings of England* as its 'looser and less dogmatic arrangement'; a less angular form with splayed corners and more sensitive landscaping. One small humanising intervention which took into account the houses' upstairs living rooms was noted by a resident who moved into the newly opened estate: there was 'a tea-making facility in a cupboard – apparently people didn't want to go downstairs to make a cup of tea in the evening!'

In other respects, the established model of three-storey, white-clad housing and integral garages was followed. In 1979 the estate won a Good Design in Housing award from the Secretary of the State for the Environment. As importantly, it remains popular with residents both past and present – a diverse community and 'a great place to live' according to the current chair of the residents' association. The homes themselves, built to Parker Morris standards, are described as spacious, light and airy.

Eastfields Estate (top, image by Sydney Newberry, © Merton Photo Archive); Rawlensea House on the Watermeads Estate (bottom, © Merton Photo Archive)

Children playing in front of Rawlensea House on the Watermeads Estate, *c.*1980
(© Merton Photo Archive)

History has been less kind to Pollards Hill and Eastfields. The former, transferred to the Moat housing association in 1998, is now undergoing a major regeneration which, apart from necessary upgrades to existing homes, will see 24 homes demolished, 90 built, and a significant increase in parking spaces. As a visitor, one of the most noticeable and unfortunate aspects of all three estates is the sheer number of cars parked, cluttering the open space that was once an attractive feature. At Eastfields, presently unregenerated, and Pollards Hill, the cladding looks tired and faded, though whether architectural aesthetes will think the colour-coded panelling being introduced at Pollards Hill an improvement remains a moot point.

MacCormac, writing in 1976, claimed attitudes towards housing had 'changed fundamentally over the last decade or so' – 'the presumption that architects should provide people with what they ought to have has given way to investigating what they want'. It's ironic therefore that developers Moat's own more recent planning statement on Pollards Hill is critical of the 'largely experimental and untested architectural principles…derived from a vision of how the designers envisaged how people might live in the future' that allegedly underpinned its design. 'Many of these theories and principles', it continued, 'have over time proved to be misplaced or unworkable'. That's a harsh and self-serving judgement which takes little account of how unforeseeable social shifts and unavoidable obsolescence have undermined past ideals – but it reminds us to be humble.

Despite that condescension, the three estates deserve far greater recognition and remain an essential reference point for anyone interested in the evolution of housing design in recent decades. In the event, with the single exception of the large Duffryn Estate designed by MacCormac for Newport Borough Council in 1978, Merton's pioneering perimeter planning efforts left little legacy – not least through Margaret Thatcher's assault on council housing in the 1980s. Merton itself disbanded its Borough Architect's Department in 1980. Camden's low-rise, high-density housing of the 1970s remains 'iconic'; it seems 'sexier' somehow – a judgement fairly reflecting its undeniably more striking aesthetic, but also perhaps denoting a certain architectural disdain for suburban south London. I hope this chapter will put Merton back on the map.

John Boughton is a social historian whose book *Municipal Dreams: the Rise and Fall of Council Housing* was published by Verso in April 2018. He has published in the *Historian* and *Labor History* and gives talks on housing to a range of audiences. He is involved in a number of housing campaigns and lives in London. He blogs at municipaldreams. wordpress.com.

Buddhapadipa Temple, Wimbledon, Sidney Kaye Firmin Partnership, 1980

Situated in a quiet residential area, Wat Buddhapadipa is one of Europe's most important Buddhist training centres and thought to be one of only two 'architecturally perfect' Thai Buddhist temples built outside of Asia. The community moved to the present site on Calonne Road in 1975 after ten years in a house in East Sheen when, with support from the Thai government, they were able to purchase four acres of land on which to build a temple of their own. A contemplative walk through the garden takes visitors over a bridge crossing an ornamental lake, past a flower garden and grove, and into an orchard. The gilded exterior of the temple itself opens up to reveal an interior featuring vibrant floor-to-ceiling murals evocative of both Buddhist myth interspersed with some western public figures including Charlie Chaplin and Margaret Thatcher.[RM]

Northern Line Extension, Charles Holden, 1926

A clear brand, between Clapham and Morden: white stone corner buildings, angular, wide glass surfaces, decorated with the London Underground roundel. Underneath, the design of the relatively spacious stations, with their bronze uplighters and their strange undercurrent of the sacral, highly influential on the Moscow Metro. Created before the mythic trip to the continent when Charles Holden and Frank Pick found something a little more radical than Portland stone stripped classicism, these tube stations are nonetheless very impressive little structures, both in the way they casually slip into the streetscape, immediately marking themselves as public buildings and as portals to the underworld (not to mention their prescient factoring in of possible air rights – so Morden has a dull 60s block on top of it, and Clapham South a good block of 30s streamline moderne flats). The best is Tooting Broadway, where the integration of the symmetrical station with a Victorian civic square made an appropriately municipal socialist backdrop to the intro of *Citizen Smith*. The buildings show an open-minded neoclassical architect trying to think his way out of the cliches and restraints of the style with some success.[OH]

Rogers House, Wimbledon, Team 4 (Richard and Su Rogers), 1967–1969

One of the first examples of High-Tech architecture, by the famous team that united the future Lords Rogers and Foster. Unlike Team 4's slightly earlier Murray Mews in Camden, this is pure High-Tech, one of the first places you could see that something new was happening among technophile London architects – a combination of Californian supervillain private modernism and a nerdy love for exposed mechanics. Here this is expressed through two glass bungalows in yellow-painted steel frame, with shelving and doors and everything else in curved perspex – spacious, refined and alien. The first Rogers building – it is generally considered to be largely his design – to be really enjoyable on its own merits rather than as first steps on the way to something else.[OH]

Tooting Police Station, Gilbert Mackenzie Trench, 1939

Possibly one of the capital's most overlooked 20th century buildings, Tooting Police Station sits on the boundary of Wandsworth and Merton on what had once been the edge of Greater London. The cruciform-plan structure – just a few minutes walk from the unmissable Grade I listed Tooting Granada – sits behind a landscaped civic plaza and appears like a tollbooth or checkpoint demarcating an invisible line between the metropolitan and once rural. Highlights include the vehicle ramp gates, stylistically monogrammed 'MP' for Metropolitan Police which are visible from Mitcham Road, and the curved ocean liner-style annex facing Ascot Road. It is one of six police stations across London earmarked for disposal and potential redevelopment.[OM]

Buddhapadipa Temple (top), Tooting Police Station (bottom)

Sketches of Curvilinear Hothouses
Douglas Murphy

Richmond upon Thames is barely urban. Of all London boroughs it is the least densely built up, consisting mostly of a series of open spaces. Richmond Park, Kew Gardens, Bushy Park, they blend together, sweeping into the city from the south-west – an intrusion of Surrey on Thames. The settlements surrounded by such swards have the character of villages, cricket pitches, quaint houses of all different shapes and sizes, arranged all higgledy-piggledy, catnip for a certain English taste. But at the same time Richmond is home to some radical spatial experiments, whose remnants and traces are still present today, where our very ability to see the landscape was first aestheticised, then fully alienated from itself. Richmond's easiness on the eye is the result of revolutions in the understanding of landscape and nature.

It is a fantastic place for a walk, of course, amongst the deer on Richmond Park, or viewing the prospect from Richmond Hill, barely changed since it was painted by Turner two centuries ago. Follow Douglas Footpath onto – I kid you not – Melancholy Walk to see Ham House, or pile the family out to Hampton Court to see Tudor cosplay enacted in a predominantly Baroque setting. It is, of course, a largely conservative landscape; indeed, a landscape that has paradoxically been a source of much innovation in the practice of conservation. For example, that view from Richmond Hill, surveying a set of villas hugging a sweeping bend of the Thames, was protected by an act of parliament in 1902, setting a precedent for a statutory instrument that continues to constrain London's development elsewhere to this day.

But being sparsely built and consisting of parkland does not mean that Richmond is in some sense more 'natural' than the rest of London. As is often pointed out, the English landscape is a manufactured one: born of agricultural development, enclosure, and the tensions of town and country. There is almost no part of the landscape that hasn't been for centuries an open-air factory worked by organic machines. Yet despite this, a commonsense aesthetic appreciation of a highly specific landscape as somehow 'timeless' or 'natural' is one of the hallmarks of the English mind. In Richmond upon Thames, lakes shimmer, trees sway and deer roam, but nothing here has come about through chance. The straightened formalism of the modern age can be seen in radiating vistas at Ham House and Hampton Court, while the insouciantly rolling parkland of Richmond Park was enclosed and manufactured deliberately for the deer-hunting pleasures of Charles I.

There is something strange and uncanny about this desire to unsee the effect of humans on a landscape. The English landscape, as the one first subjected to industrialisation, suffers acutely from this. Nestled within suburban Twickenham, Horace Walpole's house Strawberry Hill is often assigned as the moment where, in the middle of the 18th century, the gothic revival begins. It suggests a shifting sensibility, whereby mankind's control over nature, the clockwork cosmos amenable to mastery, became increasingly unhinged. The growing influence of romanticism on the English mind, the questioning of reason and the appreciation of the terrors of sublimity, mark a turning point – unprecedented scientific manipulation was a domesticating force but at the same time revealed nature increasingly as contingent, vast yet fragile, a dangerous unruly spirit.

Kew Gardens was, like so much else in Richmond, forged from the grounds of royal residences. Established by Princess Augusta as a small physic garden in 1759, and merging soon after with George II's neighbouring estate, it was soon established as an early example of the botanic garden. In a flurry of scientific development and interest, its walled enclosure became part-park, part-laboratory, tied up together with the blossoming of scientific taxonomy and mapping, and networks of global trade and shipping. Imperial plunder abroad brought seeds back to the UK, and with the introduction of the Wardian case in the 1840s, living plants could be transported successfully across the globe. Kew filled with exotic plants and trees, a living encyclopedia of the world's natural systems, and became a demonstration of British dominion, exporting plants throughout the empire and remaking agricultural economies across the world.

The aestheticised English landscape itself was partially created at Kew, with William Chambers, Capability Brown and William Kent among the garden designers who worked there, helping to give root to the image of the rolling English countryside, nature itself 'improved', extractively terraforming the colonies while simultaneously transforming the home landscape into something more resembling paintings. The English garden, compared to the French, was not a omniscient vision of order but something designed to be experienced in sequence, subjectivity enhanced by revelations and contrasts.

At the same time, new material developments in the foundries of the north were making new spatial forms possible. Greenhouse technology was developed at the end of the 18th century, creating a new typology

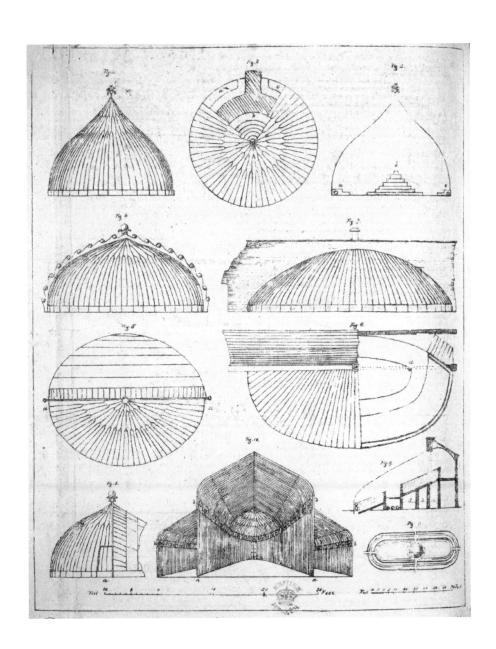

Illustration from *Sketches of Curvilinear Hothouses*, J. C. Loudon, 1818 (British Library)

Gardeners in front of the Palm House in 1915 (top); a daguerreotype of the Palm House under construction, 1847 (bottom, image by Antoine F. J. Claudet) (both images © Royal Botanic Gardens, Kew)

which took the microclimatic effects of the walled garden into a new dimension, using iron frames and plate glass to create transparent interiors capable of sustaining entirely different atmospheres. Attached to country houses and mansions, the beginning of the 19th century saw the construction of greenhouses across Britain, bringing orchids, bananas and other exotic plants into an inhospitable climate.

When Sir William Hooker became director of Kew in 1841, he took full advantage of these new technical opportunities. The architect Decimus Burton, most known for his neoclassicism, was architect for the Royal Botanical Gardens at Kew, and had previously worked at Chatsworth House, signing off on Joseph Paxton's 1838 design for the 'Great Stove', one of the most impressive early greenhouse structures. Hooker commissioned the construction of what at that point was the largest greenhouse yet constructed, to house palms from distant equatorial habitats.

Burton had been studying J. C. Loudon's 1818 work *Sketches of Curvilinear Hothouses*, which recommended vaulted and domed greenhouses as a way of optimising solar radiation. So had Richard Turner, who owned foundries and had recently built a large greenhouse for botanic gardens in Belfast. They came to collaborate on the Palm House at Kew, which brought together many of these influences, but exceeded them all in turn. Built from 1841 to 1848, the Palm House is over 100 meters long, with a large double vaulted main hall and two single vaulted wings which stretch out beyond it. Every surface of the exterior is curved, held in place by a lacy filigree of skeletal white structure.

The Palm House arrived at a cusp of a fever for iron and glass – three years later Paxton would create the Crystal Palace for the Great Exhibition of 1851, and until the end of the century thousands of these vast structures were built across the world in a flurry of technological excitement, from railway stations to exhibition halls, although the majority have long since disappeared. Burton and Turner collaborated on another Kew glasshouse, the Temperate House, recently refurbished and the largest surviving example of a 19th century greenhouse in the world.

A most serendipitous factor was that at the time, structures like these were not considered to be architecture. Iron structures lacked historic precedent, and they lacked the solidity, gravitas and sense of workmanship that came from masonry buildings – John Ruskin was typical, if hyperbolic, in arguing that an architecture made of cast-iron was impossible. But this exemption from aesthetic rules was a blessing to creativity. Released from the need to follow conventional proportions or forms, fantasy could take root. In the Palm House, Burton gave the slender cast-iron columns strange foliate details that mimic the fronds of the plants within, looking forward to the tendril-like forms of Art Nouveau a half century later.

The apparent fragility of a greenhouse is something that struck visitors at the time, and is still remarkable to this day. Set axially across a pond, to look straight on at the Palm House is to see diaphanously through it – its curved form appears almost as a bubble traced around the trees that are mistily visible within. Inside, this slenderness is a ghostly mimic of the forms of the plants and trees themselves, and the hot wet air within makes the ironwork clammy, giving forth rust and growing lichens as if itself were somehow alive.

Victorians, trained in the aesthetics of the supernatural, were quick to spot important characteristics of the new greenhouses. They were dreamlike, fairy-like, fata morgana, or, quintessentially, 'phantasmagorical'. One could express delight at the delicate fantasy of the delirious hot-house while also admiring the scientific nous that allowed them to exist. Architects gradually caught up, however, and only when mechanisation's command was irrefutable, and the search was on for a new architecture, were the intrinsic architectural qualities of the iron and glass age rendered visible to eyes that had previously not been able to see.

Revolutionaries saw in this new form of space a vision of a new human society, modernists saw a new aesthetic based on efficient structure and efficiency. Philosophers and critics have noted not only the melancholy qualities of their paradoxical techno-romanticism, but also their uneasy symbolic relationship with colonialism and extraction. Indeed, today they offer not only an appealingly utopian vision of industrial society fruitfully harmonised with natural systems, but also serve as a warning of the air-conditioned dystopia of an altered climate. There's something for everyone.

Douglas Murphy is a writer, teacher, and architect. He is the author of *The Architecture of Failure* (2012), *Last Futures – Nature, Technology and the End of Architecture* (2016) and *Nincompoopolis: The Follies of Boris Johnson* (2017)

Strawberry Hill House, Walpole, 1717–1797

A whimsical ode to exuberance, designed by avid collector and 18th century arbiter of taste Horace Walpole, Strawberry Hill House could claim to be a starting point of the Gothic Revival. Conceived of as a family castle, the design was driven by a desire to instill the newly built project with a sense of immediate history. This was achieved with heavy reference to the architectural pattern book. Rooms in the house are faithfully modelled after aspects of St Paul's Cathedral, Westminster Abbey and Windsor Castle amongst many more – the latter so accurately that it was used as a template for restoration when the original Queen's Dressing Room was lost in a 1992 fire. Whilst the Grade II listed garden is bucolic and joyful, the interior assemblage takes the visitor on an emotive journey between 'gloomth' and light, atmospheric darkness contrasted with brilliant colour to create a backdrop for an extensive collection of objects that attracted tourists in Walpole's lifetime and beyond. The house and garden were reopened to the public in 2010 following extensive restoration.[RM]

Parkleys, Eric Lyons and Span, 1956; Langham House Close, Stirling and Gowan, 1958

Two famous places doing the same thing – providing speculative housing for middle class professionals between Richmond Park and Ham Common, a spacious Georgian green that feels like something out of a 1960s Joseph Losey film. Parkleys, which joins onto a dull Georgian shopping parade, is the first and best of Eric Lyons' private estates for his development company Span. It introduces what would become the biggest cliches of post-war private housing – the zig-zags of weather boarding, the flat roofs, the neatly trimmed lawns, the northern trees and evergreens – but here, they all still feel fresh. The landscape has a rare sense of flow – each terrace and block of flats, each with its wonderful (and intact) typographical and spatial touches to the stairwells, entrances and signs, is placed in a sequence of gardens, with a delicacy and poise that is more Mies van der Rohe than Bovis. Best of all, unlike at Lyons' estates in Blackheath, there are no signs telling you that you shouldn't be there – presumably this is because in Ham, there's no Lewisham or Woolwich nearby to worry the owners.

Langham House Close has none of this ease of interlocking, abstract space – you can see it from the Common as a set of flats crammed awkwardly into an alleyway behind a Georgian townhouse. It's much more 'important' for architectural history, because here Stirling and Gowan took the heavy brick and concrete materials of Le Corbusier's Maisons Jaoul and fused them with the precise geometries of De Stijl, and created the New Brutalism in the process. The blocks now look elegant rather than violent, particularly the low-rise 'pavilions', which are usually credited to Gowan alone. It still feels, all these decades later, oddly cranky compared with Parkleys – narrow, personal. In this it's like a reversal of Alton; there, the Brutalists are responsible for the sublime and the epic, and the 'Empiricists' for intimacy and irrationality. At Ham, the Empiricist Lyons is in confident command of what Ian Nairn described as '20th century space', while Stirling and Gowan are doing murky things behind the bikesheds. Another important difference is that Lyons's blocks have had to be strictly maintained for them to look this good, but Langham House Close looks better the mouldier it gets, right down to the reddish-yellow mildew on the emphasised concrete drip-mouldings.[OH]

Richmond and Hillcroft Adult Community College, Morris + Company, 2015

The consolidation of the college's two campuses onto one site required modification and additions to an existing collection of imposing Edwardian buildings. Morris + Company's interventions form a trio of cubic blocks behind the historic terrace extending, linking and reconfiguring the site's access and layout. Organised around a central courtyard, cloistered away from traffic-filled Twickenham Road, the solid, brick-skinned, orthogonal forms are topped by folded metal 'lanterns' which bring light and height to the interiors within.[RM]

Strawberry Hill House (left, image by Justin Coe), Richmond and Hillcroft Adult Community College (right, image by Mark Hadden)

When did you last wash your hands? Public hygiene has not been such a constant, day-to-day concern since the early-20th century, when public washhouses, leisure centres and new council housing were designed, among other reasons, to improve the health of London's citizens. The legacy of this moment remains visible through much of the city; Goldsmiths Centre for Contemporary Art (St James's, SE14), renovated by Assemble in 2018, is a former Victorian bathhouse, and the Finsbury Health Centre (Pine Street, EC1R), designed in the 1930s by Berthold Lubetkin, remains a keystone of local health infrastructure in its locale.

This bar of soap provided by the London County Council, the elected assembly that ran inner London from 1889 to 1965, demonstrates the intimate involvement the administrative body had in the hygiene of its constituents at the time. The bars were used on council premises and in schools. It's hard to imagine the London boroughs providing branded toothpaste or tampons in their facilities today, although the public accessibility of hand-sanitiser has made pandemic life a little easier. Speaking of which, isn't it time to wash your hands again?

Wandsworth

Soap, 1930–1960, 52 × 71 × 44mm, Museum of London (© Museum of London)

A Monument to Missed Chances
Michael Badu

Although I no longer live on the Purley Way where I grew up, and even though there is now a tram that will take you from IKEA to Mitcham – as close to the subject of this piece as any form of public transport would get you in one hop – it felt right to take the 264 bus from Croydon Town Centre. It takes in Lombard roundabout (where the electronics factory my dad worked for used to be, before it moved to China), Croydon Cemetery (where my little sister is buried), and south London's version of the Moors, Mitcham Common. With due apologies to those for whom Sutton mainly means Cheam, I took the straight and wide Croydon Road to the southern part of the borough, where BedZED, designed by Bill Dunster's ZED Factory in the late 1990s, is located.

Croydon Road is a green corridor of big trees, wild brush and stinging nettles that is to some degree walkable, absolutely cycleable, but over-whelmingly drivable. If you want to understand the topography (and demography) of this part of London, all you gave to do is take note of the dearth of tube stations. The boroughs forming London's southern border were mostly late additions to the city, long before overpriced living accommodation in the E's, N's, and SW's made doughnuts cool. And if character means anything, this whole outer belt is really one continuous 'borough' of its own. That belt is made up of ring roads and dual carriage-ways, commons and greens, the phantasmagoric 'nature' of electricity substations, pylons, water treatment works and out-buildings too big for anything but industry – somehow not derelict, despite the sweeping away of manufacturing by shopping that is encountered everywhere out here.

Still, if you live in south London and have ever missed a delivery from Yodel, you'll know what those big buildings are for (and even if you *really believe* London's doughnut is cool, the Mitcham Road is unlikely to ever form part of your mental map. Just straight facts dude). It's easy to dismiss this part of London as being nothing but Tory pubs, greasy spoon caffs, builder's yards and places where you can learn to ride a quad or enduro-bike from the age of 12. However, there is more here than that for the architectural connoisseur. The 264 'air-drop' to Mitcham lands you among a crop of older buildings, which includes a couple of pubs, an interwar fire station and a fine almshouse. There's the cricket ground of course, attached to the nearby club and (for all you LCC Festival of Britain maniacs you) even a good example of a 1960s police station. Those of you who like real vegetables will be glad to know that there is now a well-established Polish presence in the area. It's easy to see that this place could very well be the 'next Croydon' in terms of the rebranding exercises that seem to constitute planning nowadays. That said, those pesky pylons with their attendant signs reading 'DANGER: 132,000 volts' just won't go away.

This isn't an area of 'inner city' council estates, but nobody really chooses to grow up in a semi around here either, where your garden and upstairs bedrooms come at the cost of possible increased cancer risk from diesel engines. Getting stung by nettles beside palisade fencing – invariably guarding something large and scary, which hummed – I always felt like Truman sailing his ship into the stage-set. I remember first seeing the 'danger 132,000 V' sign, and feeling as if I could literally touch the web of physical relationships that enabled both my dad's profession and the cartoons I watched on TV. Later in life, this memory helped me to almost physically relate to concepts such as transmission losses in the vast national energy grids and consequently, the inherent common-sense of localised power production, and what this meant for sustainability in conurbations all over the world.

So it's strange, but also fitting, that BedZED (standing for Beddington Zero-carbon Energy Development) should have been built in this area. About half an hour's walk from the cricket green and the almshouse, the walk takes in a bit of everything described above and more. The busy roads, traversed by cars accustomed to giving pedestrians absolutely no quarter, almost feel like they could be in the countryside. I saw people fishing in what turns out to be a tributary of the River Wandle, and although this area is very definitely about tattoos and bacon butties, I saw an Indian family and a woman in a sari calmly enjoying a pint in the beer garden that I passed.

The housing is generally poor, almost all of it low rise and pitched-roofed, giving rise to big skies. The way the car dominates (there is *one* bus route that serves this road) makes it all feel sort of American, which I think is the general aspiration around here. BedZED lies at the southern edge of this cultural milieu. Beyond it you'll find the altogether leafier, greener, summer-fete-enjoying pastures of Wallington and Carshalton, where you'll also find a constructivist conversion of a village hall done by Ted Cullinan in the late 80s (the subject of my undergraduate dissertation).

That BedZED flies in the face of all this can be very clearly seen from the sort of aerial photographs and coloured sections that attended its initial publication in architectural journals. While the pitched roofs and faux-half timbering of surrounding housing seek to distract the gaze from the semi-industrial context, BedZED gratefully receives the permission all this gives for its custom-designed heat-recovery wind-cowls and the unashamed galvanised steel of its stairs and balconies. I remember BedZED as being the vanguard of a new kind of architecture, one which was to end the style wars once and for all, as the urgency of the climate and energy crises meant that architects had to leave all that childishness behind. But, of course, we didn't, and approaching it today on foot, it seems a forlorn reminder of a brief but bygone age when the will and the wherewithal to make serious inroads into the saving of the planet seemed within our grasp. In 2002 when it was just completed, I was graduating, having specialised in sustainable architecture. Everything was so urgent, my tutors adamant that we were the generation that was going to fix things. We *had* to fix things.

BedZED is a self-contained neighbourhood comprising 82 homes, which range from one to four bedrooms in size and incorporate some live/work spaces. The neighbourhood had its own CHP biomass wood-chip plant that was meant to enable it to be completely self-sufficient in terms of energy, but this has never really worked. If architects were ever going to abandon their stylistic fetishes and adopt the 'way of the Dunster', the numbers would have had to have been really impressive, and they just weren't. The energy consumption of a typical BedZED resident is a rather uninspiring 89% of the average. However, it was always clear that the architecture of BedZED was never meant to do the work on its own. Living at BedZED requires that you change your way of life; that you don't use energy as if it were an infinite resource. It's horrifying to think just how much more electricity we use on average today (with our smart-phones, laptops and gaming consoles, not to mention the vast servers from which we now stream our entertainment) as compared to the turn of the millennium when construction on BedZED began. The development is isolated, geographically, politically and philosophically. This, in conjunction with the guide price for a 3-bed maisonette (only £415,000!) confirms its failure as the leaven that would infect the housing market that Dunster intended it to be.

It might have fared better (and been more lucrative) had it been built in one of those N, E, or SW postcodes, but in its current location it is certainly still seen as 'barmy' – one guy who saw me taking pictures of it mentioned the Teletubbies. A vote-loser, and thus, a one off. Had it been given a chance, BedZED Mk II would certainly have improved on those energy consumption figures and as a pioneer, Bill Dunster – who moved his ZED Factory into one of the estate's work units, and after whom one of its streets is named – could have become one of the most influential

Sutton pylons (top, image by Michael Badu), BedZED (bottom, image by Bill Dunster)

architects in Europe and perhaps the world, as a turn to a sustainable architecture took hold and his expertise was increasingly sought after.

Upon returning to BedZED, I had expected to find a relic to a less sophisticated period of recent history. Instead, I found a monument to missed chances, an island of optimism against all odds, and a time-warp to a period when we still didn't do things by halves. The wind cowls and quirky forms are what tended to grab the headlines, but what is most impressive about BedZED is its urban contribution. The little alleys, mews, pathways and streets, along with the large communal garden and the way these spaces work perfectly with building heights to make a variety of semi-public spaces and outdoor rooms, is both a delight and a testament to just how much thought went into its design. BedZED's failure to spread outside of the unsympathetic area in which it is located is emblematic of our inability to face the reality of contemporary life in this country, and the inconvenient fact that human-life must radically change if the earth is going to be able to continue to support it.

Michael Badu is an architect and writer teaching at Kingston University.

Sutton Life Centre, Curl La Tourelle Architecture, 2010

The Sutton Life Centre is a useful reminder of the years immediately following the financial crash before the UK shifted political gears to embrace austerity, when new multi-purpose community buildings by ambitious contemporary architects were expected to play a leading role in mitigating the worst of the crisis. The £8.15 million Sutton Life Centre combines a district library, youth activities, media lab, meeting rooms, external sports facilities, eco-activity garden and the immersive 'Life Skills Tours'. The latter is a series of interactive sensory environments constructed with dynamic sound and lighting offering helpful guidance on road safety, healthy living and how to play a positive community role in mitigating global climate change.[MF]

Maggie's Centre for the Royal Marsden, Ab Rogers Design, 2009

Since 1996, Maggie's has been creating humane and uplifting environments for cancer patients and their families at hospitals throughout the UK. The Maggie's Centre for the Royal Marsden cancer treatment hospital features four inter-connected volumes with large fronts glazed in red terracotta, curved at the cornice evoking a gregarious industrial shed. The centre is surrounded by a garden designed by the acclaimed Piet Oudolf who played a key role in the creation of New York City's High Line linear park. An interior heavy with gaudy block colours can feel institutional at many hospitals, but in Ab Rogers hands, aided by plush rugs and soft furnishings, the centre's vibrant rooms feel reassuring and upbeat.[MF]

Whitehall Historic House, architect unknown

Whitehall is one of the few surviving Tudor timber framed buildings in Greater London. Its origins are mysterious. It does not seem to have been built as a house and its original purpose is unclear. It was, however, converted into a house which was occupied by the Killick family from the mid-18th to the 20th century. The building was modified and restored over the centuries and is now a fascinating structure full of period details. Inside, exhibitions include permanent displays about the history of Whitehall, Cheam and the surrounding area.
Contributed by Sutton Council

Honeywood Museum, architect unknown, 1650

Honeywood stands in a distinctive location at the western end of Carshalton Ponds which is an area rich in historic buildings. Originally a small structure of flint and chalk chequer work erected around 1690, the building was modified and extended leaving a rich legacy of period details. Major extensions in 1898 and 1902 turned it into a substantial upper middle class house including a purpose-built billiards room.
Contributed by Sutton Council

Little Holland House, Frank Dickinson, 1902

Little Holland House is a modest detached Arts and Crafts-style house which was self-built by Frank Dickinson in 1904. He and his wife Florence handmade almost all the furniture, paintings, metalwork and other decorations giving the house a unique and very personal character. Little Holland House is therefore not an example of the Arts and Crafts consumer lifestyle drawn from fashionable shops or expensively commissioned from bespoke designers, but instead the work of an artist living the movement's all-encompassing ideals and creating a unique home for him and his family. Their unique collection of decorative details and furnishings remain in the house today.
Contributed by Sutton Council

Charles Cryer Theatre, Edward Cullinan Architects, 1991

The Charles Cryer Theatre is a remarkable conversion of a former 1874 village hall originally created for the Surrey village of Carshalton. Formerly used as an ice rink and then a cinema, the building was given a new breath of life in 1991 when it received a new roof and imaginative facade featuring a pair of audacious tiled eaves extending outwards to create a welcoming cloister on the otherwise busy, and sometimes unwelcoming, road between Sutton and Croydon. The redevelopment delivered a 200-capacity studio theatre, workshop and ground floor restaurant and is a happy reminder of both the humane warmth and architectural idiosyncrasy of the architect Edward Cullinan, who died in 2019. Tapping into the long-running local enthusiasm for environmentalism, Cullinan's conversion included an innovative ground source cooling system which uses water drawn from a bore hole to keep the auditorium temperature within comfortable limits.[MF]

Sutton Life Centre (left), Honeywood Museum (centre), Charles Cryer Theatre (right)

The LCC Schools
Ruth Lang

The post-war housing designed by the Architect's Department of London County Council is equally revered and derided for the experimental approaches they adopted with the aspiration to revolutionise the neighbourhoods Londoners live in. Yet the schools they designed to be the heart of these new neighbourhoods are often overlooked, despite being even more ingenious and revolutionary in their architectural approach. In place of the tall, monolithic Board Schools which were once so prevalent across London, the schools designed and constructed in this period were the embodiment of the government's aspirations for a modernism 'in the social, technical and economic sense, as well as the aesthetic.' The Council's Schools Division was a hotbed of ingenuity, which frequently gave new graduates the opportunity to test out cutting-edge approaches to material technologies and spatial design. Four key examples of these were constructed in Wandsworth as part of the development of the experimental neighbourhoods which brought higher densities of residents to the local area, and demanded new infrastructure to accommodate the social aims of the post-war governments.

The first of these schools might initially seem unassuming and, less charitably, undeserving of attention. Designed in 1953 to serve the Alton Estate (East) which peers over the trees behind, Heathmere Primary School was constructed from a prefabricated system originally developed by Hertfordshire County Council to facilitate rapid and economic construction. Using a lightweight steel frame structure, it is clad with a modular system of precast concrete panels, which was thought by the council's architects, Ted Hollamby and David Gregory Jones, to be 'of outstanding charm and elegance' but considered 'good, but not outstanding' by the architectural press. However, it was deemed of such significant architectural value by the Institute of Contemporary Art that it was selected to host a tour and panel discussion as part of their *Architectural Criticisms* series in the year it opened. Although the system-building approach had proven useful to the Council in enabling them to build rapidly in order to replace schools lost due to bombing, as well as to provide additional accommodation for the incoming baby boom, Heathmere School was the last of its type. From then on, there was a move away from standardisation towards plurality, and subsequent schools were able to adopt a much more inventive approach, taking time for experimentation and research as part of their design process, which was to further the Schools Division's reputation for innovation – though this was not always well received.

The design of Elliott Comprehensive School – now known as Ark Putney Academy – which was built in 1956 to serve the nearby Ashburton Estate is one such example of a much more individual approach, and has since been Grade II listed by Historic England for its architectural importance. From where they worked in the Architect's Department in the North Block of County Hall, the Schools Division's architects George Trevett, John Bancroft and James Daniel Shearer would have been able to watch the development of the innovative pavilions constructed for the 1951 Festival of Britain, which had taken place on the adjacent site on the South Bank. These have clearly influenced the architectural team in their designs for the cruciform 'monomorphic' layout of the school, which is composed of a series of interlocking sculptural forms with echoes of the aesthetics of the festival. Bold primary colours are used throughout – in the coloured spandrel panels, tiling and render – whilst the large expanses of glass curtain walling – a new technology at the time – used on the four-storey teaching block rivals that of the Fairway and Transport pavilion which had been developed by structural engineer Felix Samuely. The form of the assembly hall – which was separated from the school facilities so that it could be used independently by the public outside of school hours – is reminiscent of Wells Coates' Telekinema, which also expressed the slope of the auditorium and the ceiling within, which had been curved for acoustic reasons. The distinctive waveform structure covering the three geography rooms at roof level – which also included a small meteorological room – uncannily echoes the roof of the Thames-side restaurant by Fry, Drew & Partners, whilst the concrete balconies with slender metal balustrades also echo the Empiricist style of the Lansbury Estate, which formed the Live Architecture component of the Festival, a short boat ride down the Thames from County Hall.

The layout of the pavilions across the Festival site was planned by Hugh Casson – who had been appointed Director of Architecture for the Festival of Britain in September 1948 – as a small town which embodied new approaches to urban design, with clusters of enclosures in place of the axial arrangement of previous exhibitions such as those at Wembley and Crystal Palace. Designed in 1958 by a team led by Ken Jones, the campus of Garratt Green Comprehensive School – now Burntwood School – adopted a similar informal layout on a smaller scale but with the same intentions, breaking down the accommodation for 2,200 students

Ark Putney Academy (images by Merlin Fulcher, a former pupil)

into low rise blocks along meandering paths, in between the larger teaching blocks. As for the festival, art was an intrinsic part of school design for the LCC, who undertook new commissions and relocated pieces which had previously formed part of the festival site to the newly constructed schools. A life-size bronze sculpture, 'Drinking Calf' by Georg Ehrlich, once knelt on a brick plinth within the vast open lawn at Garratt Green Comprehensive School, but went missing while in storage awaiting relocation following the construction of a new teaching block over its original site – Historic England are still on the lookout for the sculpture.

The rhythm of the standardised structural framing system which characterised the interiors of each classroom was expressed externally, but interspersed with panels which gave each block a distinct material character – one in horizontal timber cladding, one with brick infill panels, one of glazed curtain walling affording a peek into the swimming pool, another in precast concrete panels. Amongst these, sculpturally cast concrete structural elements afforded moments of playfulness, adding to the variety of character within a standardised system; a reflection of the students' experiences which were intended in the new Comprehensive School system. The school has since been given a makeover by Allford Hall Monaghan Morris architects, whose refurbishment completed in 2014 replaced or refurbished many of these existing pavilions, giving three of the main teaching blocks a new face of distinctive, bespoke concrete panels – continuing the concrete elements which Ken Jones' team had designed – and adding six new pavilions for drama, teaching, and sports facilities. The sensitivity of the design, with its mixing of existing buildings with complementary interventions, was awarded the Stirling Prize by the RIBA in 2015. It was one of the last projects undertaken as part of the Building Schools for the Future programme which was scrapped by the government in 2010.

The same informal layout was employed in the design of Chesterton Primary School to create a 'village' of classrooms across the site, which helps break down the potentially imposing form of a large primary school into parts which would be more comprehensible to the young pupils. Each of the 14 timber roof structures creates a self-contained pavilion that opens onto a dedicated open air space for the students to break out onto. The ability of architects in the Schools Division to employ specialist engineers from outside the council enabled them to consider technologies far beyond those readily accepted in school design at the time, and Chesterton School gained renown for having used the largest recorded number of hyperbolic paraboloid structural units in its roof structure when it opened in 1964. The school's engineer, Hugh Tottenham, had been employed for his expertise in designing the first ever timber hyperbolic paraboloid roof

Chesterton Primary School (image by Open Practice Architecture)

in Britain at the Royal Wilton Carpet Factory (since demolished). This relatively new technology, which had previously been used by Le Corbusier in the Expo '58 world fair in Brussels, meant the architects could create a far more spectacular interior space within the project's budgetary constraints than they would have been able to with standardised structures. Unlike many of the LCC's schools of this period, the subsequent alterations have aimed to retain the previous character of the architecture, and complement it with expressly contemporary additions – including the new top-lit, timber clad entrance pavilion by Open Practice Architecture, which was completed in 2015.

School buildings such as these are often overlooked for their architectural merit, and many have been demolished as a result. But the manner in which these examples have been retained and reused to such success is a tribute to the LCC's legacy of material innovation, and is evidence of the longevity of good quality post-war design.

Ruth Lang is an architect, curator, and senior lecturer at Central Saint Martins. Her doctoral research into the London County Council Architect's Department explores the tension between the bureaucratic nature of the department and the ingenuity of the architecture they produced. Her work exploring the hidden influences and practitioners of architecture has formed the basis for exhibitions at the V&A in London and the Jerwood Gallery in Hastings. She writes for a number of non-academic publications, and is an editor for *Architectural Research Quarterly*.

Battersea Power Station, Giles Gilbert Scott, 1929–1955

Designed by Giles Gilbert Scott in two nearly identical phases, the first in the early 30s, the second twenty years later, this is the grandest (and certainly the largest) example of the severely reduced, mechanised brick Gothic that Scott would use for everything from universities to breweries. The power station is, as Ian Nairn pointed out in the 1960s, full of superfluities that would have made not only a modernist but also a 19th century engineer wince, particularly the fluting on those tall concrete chimneys – something compounded when they were recently replaced with replicas, despite having no plausible use whatsoever – but when you get up close, the raw power of those immense brick walls is irresistible. The building was at its most immense when commanding a gigantic swathe of nothing amidst the most expensive real estate on earth. It is now reduced to a trophy in an ugly scramble of naked property speculation. The building will always be worth seeing, however, and it gives the naff new buildings around a lesson about presence, their flimsiness making its mass all the more powerful.[OH]

Fitzhugh Estate, Wandsworth, London County Council, 1953–1956

A dry run for the 'East' part of the subsequent Alton Estate, these towers are a particularly superb example of the LCC's architecture when it was poised between epic scale and intimate detail, joining the brave new world and the integration of the past. Nothing flash, just five brick-infill point blocks with wide balconies and a community clubhouse set in a winding grove at the north end of Wandsworth Common, interspersed with tall trees. These have grown up, so that the original idea – not so much a garden city as a woodland city – is much clearer than it would have been when the planting was new. As soon as you stand in it you realise what it was the planners and architects were up to – bucolic, calm, modern, and with just enough of the sublime in the presence of the towers from the common to resist any accusations of cutesiness. The placement of the towers right next to a particularly OTT mid-19th century asylum shows modernism and Victoriana thrown together with neither sentimentality nor aggression. The asylum is now, inevitably, flats, and the shonky 'in keeping' new housing that has been built around it is far inferior as residential architecture to the Fitzhugh Estate.[OH]

Tooting Bec Lido, H.J. Marten, LCC Parks Department, 1906, renovation WM Architects, 2002, renovation, David Gibson Architects, 2017

Despite its enormous green spaces, London from the industrial era onwards struggled to provide its inhabitants with safe and convenient outdoor swimming options to replace the bucolic streams and ponds of days gone by. During the early 20th century, LCC land was surrendered to create a modern hygienic pool next to railway tracks on Tooting Bec Common, and to this day the extraordinary 91 metre-long Lido remains unrivalled as the best place for an open air dip for miles around. Recent additions by David Gibson Architects and WM Architects have upgraded swimmer facilities while protecting the grandeur of the true centrepieces – the enormous pool itself and the multicoloured 1930s changing cubicles – which become all the more vivid as they soak up the sun on late summer afternoons.[MF]

Battersea Arts Centre, Edward Mountford, 1893, renovation Haworth Tompkins, 2019

Since 1974 the former Battersea Town Hall has been home to the Battersea Arts Centre, serving as a test bed for contemporary theatre and performance. Built in 1893 according to competition-winning designs by Edward Mountford as a civic centre for the progressive-led Borough of Battersea (which elected London's first Black borough mayor John Archer in 1913) the Grade II* listed building is structured around a central top-lit lobby featuring an elegant Italian marble staircase and mosaic floors depicting the busy bees of nearby Lavender Hill. A catastrophic and still-unexplained fire gutted the Grand Hall in 2015 mid-way through a phased £13.3 million opening-up and reconfiguration of the complex led by the modern-day masterminds of theatre renewal, Haworth Tompkins. This included key additions such as a new courtyard theatre, attic office space with a rooftop terrace, and a suite of guest bedrooms for artists priced out of affordable short-term accommodation in the capital. Haworth Tompkins then also restored the Grand Hall itself where the burned-out barrel-vaulted roof is now recalled in a timber carapace below a newly-installed pitched roof, while the memory of the blaze is frozen in the walls' fire-cooked patina.[MF]

Battersea Power Station (left), Tooting Bec lido (centre), Battersea Arts Centre (right, image by Morley von Sternberg)

WEST

In Stonebridge Park
Ewan Harrison

In Patrick Keiller's 1981 film *Stonebridge Park*, a disembodied voice recounts a disjointed monologue whilst traversing footbridges that cross the North Circular. In the background the landscape of the eponymous suburb floats enigmatically, semi-detached and rain spotted. The curved double-prow of Unisys House, designed by R. Seifert and Partners on a site adjacent to the North Circular, hovers in and out of view. The footbridges themselves are no more, but the surrounding landscape is otherwise little changed. This chapter is about two fragments of the recent architectural past located in Stonebridge Park. The first of these is the aforementioned Unisys House, an example of 1970s commercial Brutalism. Travelling east from there is the redeveloped Stonebridge Estate and the Children's Centre off Fawood Avenue, designed by Will Alsop and completed in 2004.

London's surface area nearly doubled in the years between the First and Second World Wars as housing and industrial developments pushed out along the new arterial roads and railway branch lines. Stonebridge Park is the archetype of this interwar land-grab. The development of Stonebridge Park coincided with Richard Seifert's first years in practice and, although he was distinctly cagey about this period, it's likely he obtained early commissions in this area. His 1942 RIBA fellowship application records an estate of houses at Dobree Avenue in nearby Willesden as one of his first jobs. There is nothing in this typical suburban street to suggest that Seifert's would one day be one of the largest and most profitable British architectural practices.

By the mid-1970s, as Unisys House was completed, Richard Seifert had secured 'the reputation of being able to build a prestige office tower in the middle of Hyde Park if he so chooses' as *Private Eye* caustically put it. Seifert's practice was synonymous with the design of speculative offices for property developer clients. In this period the speculative office block proliferated across British cities, forming something of a janus face to that other ubiquitous expression of British modernism, the council house. The client for Unisys House was almost certainly one such property developer, and the building was almost certainly let to the American computer company that lent it its name. This tenant's need for office space and the clients' desire for profit would have been easily satisfied by a simple cubic office block. But the Seifert partner in charge – Simon Alexander – produced something infinitely more dynamic. Unisys House is formed of two seven-storey crescent-shaped office buildings. Both blocks are identical, with curved facades of navy-tinged glazing panels suspended between slender glazing bars and narrow floor plates, and return facades of precast concrete panels. A note of drama is injected by a large fold running the height of each side façade, containing staircases. The structure and interior form of Unisys House, a skin of glass covering long open floorplans, is suggested by this external detailing. The honest expression of structure was a central modernist diktat and one that the Seifert practice did not always strictly follow. But when it did, it did so with vigour all its own.

In designing Unisys House, it seems likely that Simon Alexander had in mind Oscar Nieymeyer's sinuously curved Edifício Copan in São Paulo and Gordon Bunshaft's doughnut shaped Hirshhorn Gallery in Washington DC. Bunshaft's building exerted a particular pull on the imagination of Seifert's architects in the 1970s, as is illustrated by the now-demolished Wembley Conference Centre, designed by the Seifert practice at the same time as Unisys House for a site in nearby Wembley. The influence of the Hirshhorn on the form of Unisys House is particularly clear from Conduit Road to the west, where the development resembles nothing so much as two halves of the Hirshorn cleaved apart and reversed in space.

In pursuing such a bold vision for Unisys House, Alexander must have had the kinetic views of the site in mind. Most people experience these buildings at speed, from a passing car on the North Circular or from a Bakerloo Line tube carriage on the elevated London Underground line to the south. In these views, the relationship between the two curved blocks of Unisys House rapidly changes as the splayed outer ends of the blocks hove into view and then give way to the recessive curved glass facades. None of the other buildings designed by Simon Alexander for R. Seifert & Partners approach anything like this level of dynamism.

Unisys House is redolent of the age of the car-commuter: an age that is past its zenith, in London at least. Perhaps as a reflection of this, Unisys House has been all but abandoned since the 1990s and looks increasingly spectral as a result. But the wheels of capital are still turning at Unisys House. The site's owner, the Luxembourg-based Grand Mediterranean Holdings (GMH), chaired by the convicted fraudster Nadhmi Auchi, has been in protracted negotiations with Brent Council to convert the buildings into studio flats under the permitted development rights regime: a fate that has befallen the Wembley Point tower on the opposite side of the North Circular. In 2017 Brent controversially agreed to sell GMH, and a GMH subsidiary registered in the British Virgin Islands, the adjacent

Unisys House

community-run leisure centre in order to affect a larger-scale housing-led development of the immediate area. Quite why this has stalled is not clear, although local opposition had given rise to legal challenges last year. Brent Council has no doubt been placed in an invidious position by central government funding cuts, but its decision to transfer public land to a consortium based in tax havens seems an unfortunate one for a Labour authority to take.

Heading east from the Unisys Building along the Harrow Road, lies the Stonebridge Estate. This has seen successive waves of redevelopment throughout the 20th century and the result is architecturally chaotic, though not without interest. The Stonebridge Estate, north of the Harrow Road and west of the Craven Park triangle, was originally developed as a middle class commuter suburb in the 1870s. Its prospectus boasted of 'new villas for City men,' built in an Italianate idiom – a curiously late date for such a stylistic choice. Only a few vestiges of this survive: the former Stonebridge Hotel, with jaunty ironwork, near the Tesco on the Harrow Road, and two rambling villas marooned amongst later housing at the foot of Morland Gardens. The Stonebridge Estate though, failed to take off as a smart area: the proximity of the Willesden Sewage Farm cannot have helped its prospects.

By the mid-20th century, these houses had been subdivided and sublet and municipal redevelopment was deployed to tackle the increasingly slum-like conditions that resulted. Some of the early waves of this survive on Fawood Avenue; a handful of 1930s semis and some 1950s brick-built flats. In the 1960s, these piecemeal efforts were dwarfed by the clearance of the Victorian housing and its replacement by a series of system-built tower blocks. This was a powerful composition, with much ribbed and textured concrete work, but the estate was plagued by a reputation for violence and was itself demolished and redeveloped in the 1990s. The housing resulting from this more recent phase of redevelopment, overseen by a Housing Action Trust rather than the local authority, is small in scale and not especially noteworthy.

However, a note of interest is provided at the centre of the redeveloped estate by the Children's Centre, designed by Will Alsop and completed in 2004. Located in green space off Fawood Avenue, the building provides a nursery school and play centre in a single volume enclosed by a pitched metal roof and chain-link walls: there is something simultaneously classical and archaic about this superstructure, suggestive of both the Saxon longhouse and the Parthenon. Within this, play spaces are located between classrooms housed in vertiginously stacked shipping containers, accessed by metal gantries and staircases. It recalls Joan Littlewood and Cedric Price's seminal Fun Palace project, developed

Fawood Children's Centre (image by aLL Design)

for a site in Stratford in the mid-1960s, but never built. The chainlink external envelope might also suggest Price's aviary at London Zoo. Alsop had worked for Price early in his career, and the Children's Centre demonstrates the impact that the Fun Palace had on Alsop's thinking. However, the bright colours and cartoonish appliqués derived entirely from Alsop's imagination and would be a hallmark of much of his later work.

The Children's Centre dates from the height of New Labour power and is firmly a product of that political dispensation's fondness for gimmicky architectural solutions as a panacea to complex structural problems: this must have been even clearer on its completion, when it stood at the foot of two towerblocks awaiting demolition. At the same time, the Children's Centre is clearly also a product of that period's generous funding for social and community facilities, something conspicuously lacking from the socio-architectural landscape of the last decade. Given this, its unsurprising that the Children's Centre failed to prefigure a new generation of flexibly planned and brightly coloured community facilities. Instead, in its reuse of shipping containers and in its air of impermanence it anticipates quite a different architectural development of the last decade: the pop-up street food and 'mean-time' cocktail venues of the violently gentrified inner London boroughs where the built environment is increasingly commodified and social facilities rare.

Stylistically, the Children's Centre is the diametric opposite of Unisys House: where Unisys House dominates its surroundings, the Children's Centre sits lightly in the landscape. Where Unisys House is boldly modelled yet soberly detailed, the Children's Centre is formally simple but gestural in its detailing. But there are similarities: both buildings are confident projections of recent architectural futures that have rapidly receded into the past. Unisys House dates from a period when the car was king and property developers built office blocks and largely left housing developments to the state; the Children's Centre is a remnant of the last gasp of the confident belief in publicly funded communitarian architecture as a salve to societal problems. Both these moments have passed, leaving these buildings adrift in their vastly changed contexts, overlain with a slight air of pathos.

Ewan Harrison is an architectural historian and curator with a particular interest in mid and late 20th century architecture. His doctoral thesis examined the work of R. Seifert & Partners, one of the most profitable and controversial British post-war architectural practices. He is currently working for the RIBA Library Drawings and Archives Collections on a project to catalogue the collection of Colin St John Wilson and MJ Long. He also serves as the Society of Architectural Historians of Great Britain LGBTQIA+ Network Co-ordinator.

Dollis Hill Synagogue, 1937;
Wembley Arena, Owen Williams, 1934

These two major buildings by interwar Britain's Great Engineer, creator of such masterpieces as the Boots Factory in Beeston and the various buildings for the Daily Express, are now both a little uncomfortable to visit. One, because of bigotry, the other just because of ordinary profit. Dollis Hill Synagogue was always an odd commission for such a committed functionalist, and this attempt to fuse a religious programme with his hard, glinting concrete structures has often been criticised, but I find it works rather well. Set easily among north-west London suburban semis and opposite a park with a panoramic suburban view, the synagogue is folded into a set of spiky, pyramidal roofs, with dozens of small stained glass windows, set in gleaming Central European white concrete; it has something of the strange angularity of Konstantin Melnikov's clubs and houses in 1920s Moscow. The synagogue is now part of an Orthodox Primary School, and is treated as a fortress, with high fences and round-the-clock monitoring by security guards – even the entrance is through a security pavilion, like an airport. How depressing that this is necessary, when it was not even in the London of the 1930s, when the British Union of Fascists were running riot.

At Wembley Arena, the heavy security is less invasive, given the building is so vast. It was built as the 'Empire Pool' for an imperial expo, and the interior

is not interesting for anything but its sheer size – but the elevation is still an impressive concrete hangar, with huge glass expanses between stark, straight concrete supports and two frankly industrial towers on either side. An interesting contrast, too, with Foster's new Wembley Stadium nearby, a glorious steel arch holding up a more prosaic structure below.[OH]

Ace Cafe, Stonebridge,
unknown architect, 1938

Established on the, then brand new, North Circular road surrounding London, the Ace Cafe was a simple roadside stopoff catering to travellers, particularly truckers. With its proximity to Britain's fast arterial road network, and being open 24 hours, the Ace Cafe soon attracted motorcyclists too. The building was badly damaged during an air raid and subsequently rebuilt in 1949.

In the fifties, the British motorcycle industry was at its peak just as Rock 'n' Roll arrived in London. Initially deemed too crass for radio broadcast, one of few places Rock 'n' Roll could be heard was on jukeboxes at transport cafes – cue a boom in Ace Cafe customers. The building has been used as a cafe, filling station, bookmakers office and latterly a tyre depot. It remains however, largely unaltered with large factory-like windows, a cream and brown chequered floor and a two-storey clock tower above its main entrance.[PH]

Jewish Cemetery, Willesden,
Harry Ford, Nathan Solomon Joseph,
Lewis Solomon & Son, 1873

Willesden Cemetery was opened as a burial ground for Jewish people by permission of the Home Office in 1873 under Queen Victoria. It was the first joint project of the new United Synagogue which had been established by an Act of Parliament in 1870, in recognition of the 40,000 Jewish people then living in London. The cemetery covers 21 acres with 26,000 graves making it one of the largest historic Jewish cemeteries in the UK.[Om]

The Tin Tabernacle, Maida Vale,
James Bailey, 1863

A large corrugated iron chapel, its interior transformed into a mock battleship for local Sea Cadets. The building has decks, portholes, a bridge and even a Bofors gun. The chapel was constructed as a temporary church and still has a full immersion baptismal font beneath the floorboards.[Om]

Dollis Hill Synagogue (top), Ace Cafe (bottom)

Two Public Buildings by the Borough Architect Gavin Leonard

Ealing, formed in 1965, was an amalgam of three municipal boroughs (Acton, Ealing and Southall), each with their own democratic structure and officer functions. Early committee minutes of the new council record the appointments of key personnel to new positions within the larger organisation; the town clerk as the chief officer, the borough treasurer to manage its finances, the borough engineer with responsibility for structures, roads and drainage and the borough architect, to construct and maintain buildings.

In many respects, the role of Borough Architect in Ealing dates back much further; to the appointment by the Local Board of the Suffolk-born Charles Jones as Surveyor in 1863. Jones' contribution to the fabric of the borough is enough for an Open House tour of its own, and includes two Town Halls – the first (now a branch of the NatWest bank) in The Mall in 1874 and the second in 1888, comprising the western half of the current town hall building in The Broadway. As part of this later complex, Jones designed a fire station, corporation yard and stables in Longfield Avenue, along with public baths and a swimming pool. Jones' primary school designs are exemplified by Little Ealing and Drayton Green, both of 1903. However as a municipal employee his presence was all pervading; in recreation (the laying out of Walpole Park and the avenue of horse chestnut trees on Ealing Common), street lighting (evidenced by lamp-posts at Mount Park Road and Woodville Road), sewage (the treatment works in Occupation Lane, now the site of Clayponds housing estate) and death (two cemetery chapels, South Ealing Road).

One of Jones' most significant contributions to the cultural life of Ealing is a building where evidence of his work is now almost entirely absent. Pitzhanger Manor was the country house of Sir John Soane, one of England's greatest architects and at the time of his purchase of the site in 1800, architect to the Bank of England. Soane had intended that the house be both a country retreat and a place for entertaining friends and clients. Having looked at other properties, Soane was drawn to Pitzhanger as being the site of his first significant work in architecture – the supervision of designs to the Eating Room extension on behalf of the architect,

George Dance the Younger, in whose office Soane had been a pupil. Soane's first act as owner was to tear down the existing buildings, retaining the extension for sentimental reasons.

Soane constructed a fairly modest house – albeit, with an entrance modelled on the Arch of Constantine in Rome – of only one bedroom (he never slept there) and with a greenhouse leading onto a landscaped garden and ornamental lake designed by John Haverfield of Kew. Despite the poetry brought to the house and its sculpture court and fake ruins – variously describing it as a 'dream', 'a portrait' and the family home of a dynasty of architects – he was quite prepared to treat Pitzhanger in a pragmatic fashion, as the test bed for architectural ideas and experiments. As such, the house was never finished in a conventional sense. The lack of conclusive records – in contrast to Soane's meticulous practice in his commercial work – has created difficulties for historians and restorers ever since. The Pitzhanger dream ended in disappointment, as Soane bowed to pressure of work denying him the opportunity to visit the estate, his wife's dislike of the excessive organisation required for entertaining there, and the inevitability that neither of his sons would follow him into the architectural profession. After some difficulty (and barely five years of use) Soane disposed of the house and grounds in 1810. Several subsequent owners and their unsympathetic extensions – made to the property in pursuit of greater domestic comfort – followed until Pitzhanger was bought by the politician Spencer Walpole, in 1844 as a home for his four unmarried sisters-in-law; the daughters of the former Prime Minister, Spencer Perceval, who had been assassinated in 1812.

Pitzhanger might have faced a precarious future when the last surviving sister, Frederika, died in 1900. Fortunately, the Borough of Ealing had been in negotiations since 1898 to purchase the property when it became vacant. Charles Jones was instructed to make plans to create a new library, replacing the existing facility which had outgrown its home within an extension to the Town Hall. Soane's kitchen block was demolished and a new purpose-built library building constructed to the north of the site in a simple, brick and arched-window style that took the appearance of Dance's Eating Room as its precedent. A new reading room with separate entrance was created by doubling the size of Dance's wing at ground floor level through a faithful copy of the original, even going so far as to replicate the elaborate design of the ceiling.

In 1940, Jones' successors in the borough architects' department responded to increased demand by constructing a new lending library to replace his northern extension; a simple brick box but with an elaborate classical façade and decorative ley-lights, furnished in rich materials. This became Ealing Central Library, and the hub for branch libraries in the

Design for interior of the Library at Pitzhanger Manor, Joseph Michael Gandy, 1802 (top), Ealing Public Library at Pitzhanger, 1972 (bottom)

outlying districts of Perivale and Wood End, where new buildings were put up that shared some of its details.

Thus, Pitzhanger remained an important part of the community until 1985 when the Central Library moved to new premises within the BDP-designed Ealing Broadway Centre. Again, Council officers were obliged to consider new uses for Pitzhanger and took the bold step of proposing a museum and arts centre with the restored house as its focal point. The borough architect was instructed to devise a scheme which involved removing decades of functional remodelling to reveal the forms of Soane's original designs. Early application of historic paint research techniques allowed Pitzhanger's most important rooms – the breakfast room, the library and Dance's eating and drawing rooms – to be recreated within the discipline of 'authentic restoration', followed by Soane's bed chamber a decade later, when further funds were made available. In 1996, council architects converted the 1940 library building into the largest contemporary art space in west London, linking the building to Soane's house for the first time and allowing the council's arts team to curate a number of important exhibitions that encompassed the whole site.

In 2018, Pitzhanger was transferred by the council to a new trust, amidst a major programme of research-based restoration and conjectural reconstruction by Julian Harrap Architects. From his monument in Walpole Park, Charles Jones was afforded a grandstand view of the demolition of the last piece of his work that remained; the extension to Dance's eating room. The art gallery was refurbished by Jestico + Whiles, who also designed the new restaurant within the walls of Soane's former kitchen garden.

Jones' fifty-year span as architect and surveyor to Ealing Council was mirrored by that of the borough architect, the post being deleted from the council's service in 2015. If one discounts anomalies such as the 'economy' version of Mies van der Rohe's Farnsworth House at Islip Manor Community Centre, the Aalto-esque Greenford Hall and the Horizons Centre in Hanwell, considered by the RICS to be their London Building of the Year in 2008, ahead of St. Pancras International and Wembley Stadium, the history of the Ealing architects' department is characterised by solid, functional and neighbourly buildings. Rather than the masterpieces occasionally created by other London boroughs such as Camden and Lambeth, an extensive portfolio of housing estates, schools and community buildings was created through designs that reflected their particular epoch, often closely referencing the design guides and building bulletins issued to local authorities by central Government.

As a one-off building, the Westside Young People's Centre on Churchfield Road might then be considered a final flourish of the council architects' department prior to all design being outsourced to the private sector. An ambitious brief comprising a youth centre, education and employment support, health and fitness, special needs, arts, music, conference, training and flexible workspace, suggested a building four times larger than a small site could accommodate. Seeking precedents for such a dynamic concept, the borough architect's team identified the 'social condenser' of the early Soviet Union as a means of organising multiple functional inputs to create a whole that is greater than the sum of its parts – that is, 'a generator of new and unanticipated programmes that benefit all users of the site and the wider community'.

Built Soviet precedents for the social condenser, such as workers clubs, rural education facilities and communal housing, were often compromised by technical limitations and the state's increasing hostility to radical architecture. Fortunately, the concept provided a working model of how to achieve the desired outcomes – the so-called 'functional method' developed by the architect Moisei Ginzburg and his OSA group. In the version applied to the development of Westside, individual functional requirements were considered independently of other elements of the programme, and teams of specialists were brought together to create an 'ideal' building for their needs alone. The client group and design team then analysed the outputs from the individual teams to identify potential similarities and oppositions, with representatives of each team then being brought together to discuss how their needs could be met within a community of the building's users. In this type of endeavour, local authority architects benefit from significant advantages compared to their private sector counterparts. They are able to work closely with specialists from across the spectrum of council services, the local community, and – crucially – the young people themselves, as equal partners in the design task.

As with Charles Jones' Ealing Central Library, Westside was the realisation of an expansive programme focused upon a relatively modest building of domestic character. However, whereas Pitzhanger was able to expand laterally within its parkland setting, Westside was constrained by a narrow, deep site, overlooked on both sides. Further, its situation within a conservation area dictated an exterior treatment that complemented the existing street of comfortable, Victorian houses rather than contrasted with them. Precedents in scale and massing were taken from a previous occupier of the site, the suburban drill hall, remodelled here to preserve neighbours' 'rights of light'.

The form of the building (or 'the problem of 'reassembly'' as OSA's constructivist architects would have described it) was developed by the individual teams through a series of visual prompts, not necessarily related to architecture, and concerned with function and feel as much as physical appearance. Diverse images taken from Andy Warhol's Factory, vorticism, the Hacienda nightclub, Prada shops, the Beatles' film *Help!*, surrealism, trance music and the Soviet avant-garde were used to articulate ideas concerning arrival, circulation and the transition from public to intensely private spaces.

In their citation for the RIBA award that Westside received in 2013, the judges noted that 'the architect acted as much as community organiser as designer, working with the future users, incorporating their ideas about space and how to use it'. It is perhaps only the local authority architect that would consider this to be the highest form of praise and a fitting postscript to half a century of public service.

Gavin Leonard is founder/director of E.A.R Architecture. Prior to that he worked at Ealing Council for thirty-two years, fifteen of those as borough architect leading the in-house council design team. Their work promoted forms of inclusive and collaborative design pioneered during the early period of the Soviet Union and received awards from the RIBA, RICS and Civic Society for workspace, community and youth buildings before being wound up in 2015.

Komisarjevsky featuring elaborate ceilings divided by heavy enriched beams. A restoration project is currently underway to bring the building back to its 1930s splendour.[OM]

Ealing Village, R. Toms & Partners, 1936
A glamorous interwar residential street of five blocks of flats in a Dutch-Colonial-Baroque style with a colonnaded clubhouse and adjacent swimming pool. The developer hoped to lure starlets from the nearby film studios by building a slice of Hollywood in west London but, as the celebrities of the day preferred to lodge in the West End hotels and be driven to set, Ealing Village was mostly occupied by film crew and ordinary local people. Until television became commonplace, the clubhouse hosted weekly whist and beetle drives and an annual Christmas variety show performed by residents.[PH]

Woodland Classrooms, Belvue School, Studio Weave, 2017
These classrooms, made from cedar, with an expansive concave roof, act as a gatehouse to a woodland area adjacent to the school grounds. Studio Weave held story writing workshops with the students to help devise a collective narrative for how the new space could interact with the woodland. The finished building acts as a threshold to the forest. Its frame is made from larch with cedar cladding, and birch plywood for the interiors.[OM]

Hoover Factory, Perivale, Wallis, Gilbert and Partners, 1930–1938
On the Western Avenue, and on its own, thus not quite as rewarding as the 'Golden Mile' for a walk, but a much more complete work of architecture – a grand suburban showcase of what German modernists called, approvingly, *Reklamarchitektur* – advertising architecture. Decorative concrete and steel gates like art deco objets d'art lead to the central neo-Egyptian block, nicely restored to all its picture palace polychromy on the outside, with a Tesco on the inside where the actual factory would have been. Flanking it on the left is a slightly later cafe, which is, if anything, even more fabulous than the main building, with enormous Crittall windows and ice-cream scoops of concrete. It's was loathed at the time by the cognoscenti – for Pevsner, it was 'the worst' of west London's various 'modernistic atrocities' – and certainly, this is literally 'facile' architecture, a decorated shed, but the decoration itself is majestic. As Elvis Costello says in his song about the building, 'it's not a matter of life or death, but what is, what is?'[OH]

Odeon cinema, Northfield Avenue, Cecil Massey, 1932
The defining features of this cinema, previously a theatre and nightclub, are the uses of Spanish design elements such as turrets and a tent-like roof. The interior was designed by Theodore

Hoover Factory (top), Woodland classrooms (bottom, images by Jim Stevenson)

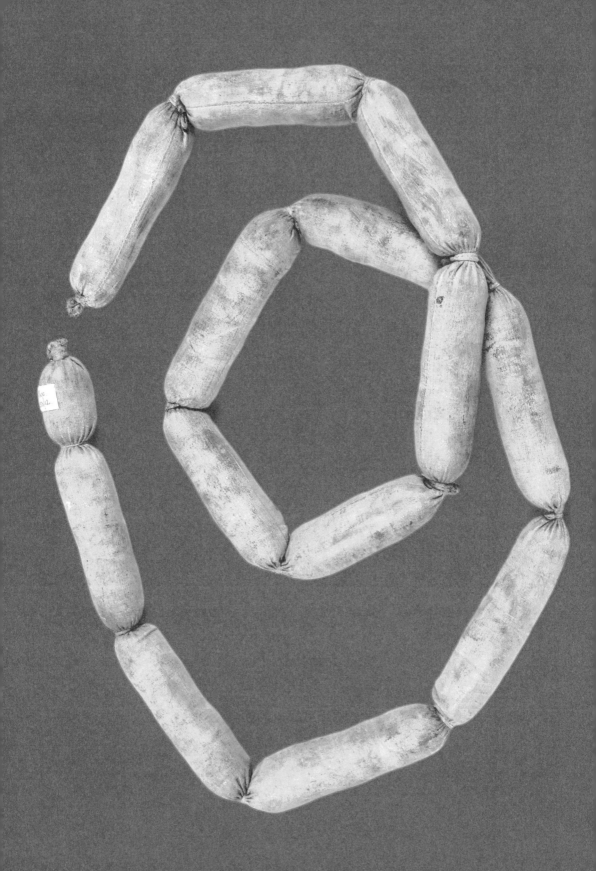

Social distancing measures pose a great threat to the livelihoods of performers in live music and theatre, with a wave of closures that may prove to be permanent. London's strong tradition of buskers and street theatre can perhaps provide some inspiration in hard times to come. One of the earliest records of street entertainment in the city is from a Samuel Pepys' diary entry in 1662, in which he describes a marionette show in Covent Garden piazza featuring a certain character named Punch. This string of sausages was used some 300 years later by Percy Press, a famous Punch and Judy performer of the mid-20th century. During the Festival of Britain in 1951, Press had a permanent theatre in Battersea Pleasure Gardens and is today remembered with a memorial plaque at St Paul's church in Covent Garden.

From barrel-organs to bagpipes, roaming bands to rappers, street musicians have also long reverberated through the streets of London. Rod Stewart, George Michael and Ed Sheeran are among those who have entertained passers-by by singing in the streets, although these days there are strict restrictions on buskers; they're banned from the City and require a permit to perform on the Underground. In the early-20th century, buskers often provided a sideshow for crowds waiting in line for the theatre or sports events. Perhaps for now, while venues stay closed, they'll be the main event.

Cotton sausage, 1925–80, 1530mm long, Museum of London (© Museum of London)

The Palace of Culture
Michał Murawski

I think I was asked to write about POSK (Polski Ośrodek Społeczno
Kulturalny, or the Polish Social-Cultural Centre) on King Street because
I am (a) Polish; (b) live in London; (c) have written a book about the
Palace of Culture and Science, a foreboding Stalin-era skyscraper which
still looms large over Warsaw today.

The connection between the Stalinist Palace and a cultural centre
created by Polish exiles who live in London *because* they ran away from
communism isn't, at first sight, entirely clear. However, the two edifices
do have a remarkable amount of quite surprising things in common.
They are both multi-functional complexes socially-condensing a diversity
of social, cultural and leisure functions under one roof; and they both
have aspirations towards *centrality*, towards being the *main* or *central* building at the focal point of a particular social world. Warsaw's architectural
ideologues intended for the Palace of Culture to function as 'the main social building of the city…its territorial and vital centre of gravity'; and the
ambitions of POSK are not far removed in terms of the will-to-centrality
driving them. As Olgierd Lalko, current POSK Deputy Chair (and former
longtime Chair) told me, 'the idea was to create a centre for all the Polish
organisations to move into, as a centre [for Polish life] not just for London
but for the whole country…all the Polish organisations would be here.'

In the case of the Warsaw Palace, it could be argued, the stated goals
were more-or-less fulfilled; at POSK, too, the multifunctional programme
was realised close to specification, although the mission of uniting Britain's
disparate and multi-layered Poles proved a formidable task. Explains
Lalko, 'you know what they say, two Polish people meet and three political
parties comes about.'

Polishness
POSK arose from several converging institutional impulses: a Polish
library in exile, established in 1942 and funded until the 1960s by the
British government, required a home and a budget; the Polish University
College Association wanted in, too; and so did the Institution of Polish
Engineers in Great Britain. Most of these émigré groups were linked to

the Polish government-in-exile, established during the German occupation of Poland in 1939 and persisting in its self-identification as the legitimate authority in the country from the formation of Poland's Soviet-backed government in 1944 until its demise in 1989. Some of these institutions found themselves in possession of a quite impressive property portfolio, the core of which was constituted by several large houses in Kensington and Chelsea. The proceeds from this real estate helped fund the establishment of POSK in 1964 and, eventually, the construction of its headquarters in 1974.

The Planning Commission of POSK – led by the institution's founding patriarch, Professor Roman Wajda – deliberated over which functions would constitute the building's programme, ultimately earmarking space for the Polish Youth Centre, encompassing the 'Pomidor' (Tomato) Club, now converted into the renowned POSK Jazz Café; the Association of Polish Veterans (still occupying offices in the building); a restaurant, cafe and bar (each still-functioning, as Łowiczanka Restaurant, Café Maya and the members-only POSKlub on the building's upper floor, where floor-to-ceiling windows provide commanding views over Hammersmith's King Street and beyond); an art gallery; and the Polish Library (occupying approximately a quarter of the space in the building); and an array of educational and community organisations. A large 300-capacity theatre auditorium, a bookshop, gallery and other functions were added incrementally over the years; and a number of Polish (and some non-Polish) entities now rent office space in the building. Etonian adventurer, sometime deputy neocolonial overlord of Iraq, advocate of extra-judicial executions and anti-Johnson Tory 'moderate' Rory Stewart planned to locate the HQ of his doomed campaign for London Mayor in an unoccupied King Street-facing all-glass shop window adjacent to the bookshop. The shopfront remains unoccupied and available today. Tenants who decide to locate their offices in POSK benefit from the added value of what Lalko describes as 'that Polish thing…the ambiance, the cultural aspects of it, the works of art on the staircases' which the building exudes, inside and out.

Socialism

This brings me to another curious thing about the idiosyncratic ambiance of POSK – with apologies to any members who may be horrified by the comparison I am about to make. To be sure, its Polishness is definitely of the émigré sort; but it really does feel like it's in, well, Poland; and it doesn't just feel like it's in Poland, but it exudes something akin – and, as an advocate for the aesthetic and affective afterlives of socialism, I mean this entirely as a compliment – to the atmosphere of a state socialist-era cultural facility in Poland, which has somehow managed to survive the onslaught of wild capitalism and remains true to its egalitarian mission of bringing enlightened culture and leisure to a diverse public (here, in implicit opposition to the aristo-centric Ognisko Polskie on Exhibition Road).

Of course, POSK doesn't at all look like the Warsaw Palace of Culture (which is decorated in a monumental, neo-Renaissance-meets-Gotham aesthetic). But it does look very much like many incarnations of the institution of House of Culture (*Dom Kultury*), which were completed in a modernist idiom in cities, towns and work units throughout Poland and other countries in the socialist world during the 1960s-1980s.

Concrete

One of the reasons for this 'still-socialist' ambiance, perhaps, is the multifunctional programme of POSK; while another is tied to the architecture of the building itself, at whose core is a neat reinforced concrete grid, albeit with a number of annexes and neighbouring buildings fairly haphazardly attached to it over the course of the decades. From the front, and from a bird's-eye-view POSK appears as a fairly coherent Brutalist edifice (very unfairly described by Pevsner as 'monstrously ugly'); but from the side aspect of Ravenscourt Avenue (on which POSK continues to own a number of properties), the building takes on a much more incremental appearance. Inside, many of the fittings – with the exception of the glitteringly-arranged 1980s theatre lobby – are 1970s originals, whereas – as several of the building's occupants and employees pointed out to me with some pride on my tour of the building – the wood panelling on the building's doors echoes the sculptural shape of the concrete pillars on the King Street façade.

People call POSK a Brutalist building, says Lalko, 'but if you look at it closely', you can see that 'someone has gone to a lot of trouble to beautify it, to make the building look more acceptable...using various mixes of aggregate, various surface finishes, to make it somewhat more attractive.' POSK compares well, says Lalko, to several more prominent buildings of the era, such as its King Street neighbour, the vast extension to the soon-to-be demolished Hammersmith Town Hall. 'I've had people from Hammersmith and Fulham council come here saying, "how do keep *yours* so well-maintained, while ours is falling down and we have to demolish it?"', Lalko tells.

Miracle

Hammersmith became the centre of London's Polish community gradually; arguably it became so because of POSK. At the time of the institution's foundation, the centre of the community was still in South Kensington but already drifting westwards as the émigré population diversified (and proletarianised). The official history of POSK, *Miracle-on-Thames (Cud nad Tamizą)* – a reference to the Miracle on the Vistula, the name given to the

Polish Social-Cultural Centre (all images by Michał Murawski)

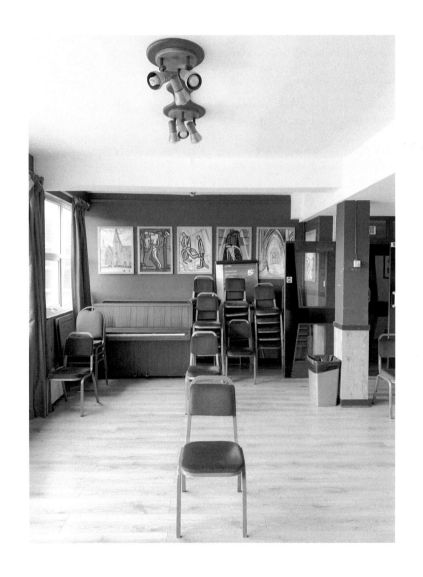

nascent Polish army's 1920 victory against the Red Army – tells the story of POSK's search for a home during the 1960s and its rejection by successive locales: first by Kensington and successively by Fulham, Shepherd's Bush and Notting Hill Gate.

'These negative experiences made us understand that we have to find a borough in which we would have a well-disposed contact within the local authorities... happily, it turned out that in the cheap and conveniently-located west London borough of Hammersmith, the borough architect was a Pole, A. Grzesik.' The mysterious figure of Grzesik – referred to in the book as A. Grzesik but in other documents as Marian F. Grzesik, a chartered architect with offices in Piccadilly, Basel and Ealing – was able to assist in gathering the necessary permissions; and it seems he was also able to leverage his position of indispensability to reincarnate an earlier, unrealised design. Recalls Lalko, 'now Grzesik's project, as I understand it, was a competition project for RIBA...which Grzesik didn't win, and he was left with this project on his hands, and he wanted to pass it on to somebody (laughs).' And thus did this community of anti-communist London Poles come to build their headquarters – the centre of Polish life in the United Kingdom – in a style resembling that of a late socialist House of Culture.

Pyzy

Life membership of POSK is £60 (members of the Polish Communist Party were once explicitly barred, but I am reassured that – 30 years after the dissolution of said party – this clause has now been removed from the statues). Non-members are welcome to visit the excellent restaurant and cafe; to attend performances or concerts held in the basement jazz club or the theatre auditorium; and to use the library. As I transcribed my interview, I sat in POSK's Café Maya, which had just reopened following the Covid lockdown. I ate a large and delectable plateful of *pyzy*, round dumplings (sort of like matzah balls, but made of potato and filled with minced pork) garnished with shavings of bacon and fried onion. The interview took a little longer to transcribe than expected, so I also helped myself to a *szarlotka*, a multi-layered, hunger-murdering but miraculously light apple pie. I did not have room to try it this time, but I have been told that the poppyseed cheesecake is even better.

Michał Murawski is an anthropologist of architecture and Lecturer in Critical Area Studies at the School of Slavonic and East European Studies, University College London. He is the author of *The Palace Complex: A Stalinist Skyscraper, Capitalist Warsaw and a City Transformed* (2019) and is currently working on a book about architecture and politics in Putin-era Moscow.

Ravenscourt Park Hospital, Hammersmith, Burnet, Tait and Lorne, 1932–1933

A mammoth project, best seen from the north side of the viaduct that carries the District and Piccadilly Line past it – as the details and interiors don't stand up to close examination, but the effect of its sheer purple mass is overwhelming. Originally the Royal Masonic Hospital and run by the NHS since the 40s, this is a cubic brick mountain in the Dutch brick modernist style borrowed from W.M. Dudok. Sprawling wings with curved concrete balconies extend around a huge and highly impressive central clock tower. The hospital grounds are also worth exploring, the placidity and precision of its gardens offsetting the stark monumentality of the hospital.[OH]

St Paul's Studios, Frederick Wheeler, 1891 and Hammersmith and West London College, Bob Giles for GLC Architects Department, 1969–1980

A juxtaposition of great lost buildings, on an unpleasant main road. On the right-hand side is a remarkable Art Nouveau terrace of artists studios at the end of Talgarth Road, with enormous insectoid windows and baroque cream faience parapets, which have been covered in grime to a degree that is now unusual in a city where the sandblaster is extensively used on historic buildings. Opposite is an unusual building by the GLC architects department,

for a Further Education College. This red brick mount of a building draws on lots of what was fashionable in the late 1960s, when it was begun – the massed mini-cities of Lillington Gardens and the industrial metaphors of the Leicester Engineering Building – and none of what was fashionable in 1980, when it was completed, after a long gestation period caused by the strikes and slow-downs of the seventies. Now, it's all gone full circle, and it looks like one of the most successful and proudly scaled of the school buildings of the 60s, that happened to have been actually opened in the 80s. The approach up Aalto-like sculptural stairwells to the asymmetrical towers and cantilevers of the entrance is ceremonial and exciting, but there's no bombast or authoritarianism about it. Currently threatened with demolition, and just refused listing.[OH]

The Ark, Hammersmith, Ralph Erskine, 1992

A curved copper and glass form makes this one of London's most striking and original office buildings, with suspended walkways, terraces and balconies that loom over the Hammersmith flyover. Despite its innovations, the Swedish firm that commissioned the Ark ran into financial difficulties and never moved in, beginning what would become a series of long-running struggles to find occupants. Named on account of its hull-like form, the building was originally designed around a large central atrium. Successive retrofits have seen this central area crossed with walkways and floors cantilevering outwards into it in a bid to increase lettable floor space.[JA]

BBC Television Centre, Wood Lane, Norman and Dawbarn, 1960

Designed by Graham Dawbarn in 1960, BBC Television Centre was the world's first purpose-built television production complex. From above, the building resembles a question mark – a distinctive shape that Dawbarn had drawn on the back of an envelope during the early stages of the design. The doughnut-shaped main block, well-known for its regular appearances on-air, surrounds a statue of Helios by T.B. Huxley-Jones and a mural by John Piper. In 2012, the BBC sold the site as part of a series of moves to reduce their property portfolio. While some production sites remain, the doughnut now houses apartments designed by AHMM.[JA]

Wolfson Institute, Hammersmith, Lyons Israel and Ellis, 1961

Often categorised as Brutalist, the work of Lyons Israel Ellis at Imperial College begins somewhat lighter, with a ribbon-windowed base, but topped by a geometric exposed concrete 'hat'. This lower building contains offices and lecture theatres and connects to the ten-storey Commonwealth Building.[JA]

The Bhavan Indian Arts Centre

Located in a decommissioned church and vicarage, the Bhavan Centre is the largest center for classical Indian arts and culture outside India. The original structure has been repurposed to transform the original church space into the 295-seat Mountbatten Auditorium, alongside a studio space and the MP Birla art gallery.[JA]

Ravensourt Park Hospital (left), The Ark (centre), BBC Television Centre (right)

Prog Rock Civic
Charles Holland

The first time I came across Hillingdon Civic Centre I couldn't quite understand what I was looking at. I'm still not entirely sure. It appears as a large, fragmented object made up of brick planes, both monolithic and light, as if the brick skin were covering a vast single interior lit by hundreds of windows, like a geodesic structure made of masonry. Arches, dormer windows and barn-like roofs are chopped up into fragments and re-assembled according to some impenetrable internal logic. If the materials – red brick and clay tiles, mostly – and the mood – neo-vernacular – are familiar from supermarkets, municipal offices and town halls across the country, the way they are used is definitely not.

Hillingdon Civic Centre is a very strange building. Its design has much to say about the recent history of the UK and the direction its architecture has taken as a result. The need for a new civic centre resulted from the 1960s enthusiasm for fiddling around with local authority boundaries. The London Borough of Hillingdon was formed in 1965 from the four smaller authorities of Uxbridge, Hayes, Ruislip-Northwood and Yiewsley and West Drayton, necessitating the building of a new, much larger municipal centre.

The building was commissioned in 1970 by a Conservative government and partially completed in 1977 under a Labour one. But it wasn't formally opened until 1979, the year of Margaret Thatcher's first election victory. Its conception, construction and completion spans a decade that saw a decisive shift in British politics from the social democratic project of the post-war period to the neoliberalism ushered in by Thatcher's government.

This political change was undoubtedly mirrored by a cultural one, a shift that exemplified the contradictions at the heart of Thatcherism. Her government's aggressive and unsentimental economic policies were accompanied by reactionary and highly sentimental social ones. This manifested itself in a form of compensatory nostalgia complete with homilies to Victorian thriftiness and the virtues of traditional family life. Architecture shifted too, moving from the welfare-state modernism of the 1950s and 60s to a postmodernism fuelled by the conservation movement and a renewed interest in traditional forms of architecture including classicism.

This is the context out of which Hillingdon Civic Centre emerged and the reason that the building became a flash point for architecture's own culture wars. Hillingdon was a building of its time, a riposte to the supposed anonymity of municipal modernism. It was controversial, held up as an example of a more acceptable and familiar form of architecture but also regarded with deep suspicion by many architects. As Historic England put it in their justification of the building's Grade II listing, its importance is 'as one of the first major works in England by a modernist architect to embrace an overtly historicist aesthetic, marking the emergence of a new architectural zeitgeist.'

But what does the building mean now, especially after a sustained period of postmodern re-appraisal? It should, in some ways, be fashionable again, part of a more pluralist landscape of architectural sources free of the bipartisan mud-slinging of the 1980s and 90s. But it is hard to think of it appealing to faux-naive Portuguese ironists or sophisticated Swiss formalists. It is too lumpy and earnest for that and its forms have none of the brittle tension or poignant flimsiness that floats current boats. It is adrift and, for that reason at least, it should interest us.

Hillingdon was designed by RMJM (or RumJum as they were affectionately known) one of the country's leading practices. Formed by Robert Matthew and Stirrat Johnson-Marshall in 1956, RMJM was a practice with impeccable modernist credentials. The project was led by partner Andrew Derbyshire, previously best known for the heroic modernism of the University of York campus. Prophetically though, it was run from RMJM's office in Welwyn Garden City.

Derbyshire's first scheme for Hillingdon was rejected explicitly for being too modernist. The overwhelmingly suburban character of the borough and a growing rejection of modernism had already soured public enthusiasm. His second attempt inflected towards the Arts and Crafts-derived architecture of the residential streets. With the formation of ever-larger London boroughs, bureaucratic managerialism had only intensified. But its expression had clearly become intolerable to his clients, so Derbyshire broke the building up into fragments, a collection of suburban motifs. The scale of the resulting building is ambiguous, an attempt to give a large, municipal office the material quality and level of detail of an Edwardian or inter-war suburban street. The late modernist megastructure has reversed improbably back towards garden cities and their later derivations.

Hillingdon has a plan that could only have been produced in the 1970s. There are a bewildering number of 45-degree corners which, taken, vertically up through the levels, results in the roofscape of angled dormer windows. The late David Dunster once claimed that the chamfered

Hillingdon Civic Centre (top, image by Piyushgiri Revagar; bottom, image by RMJM)

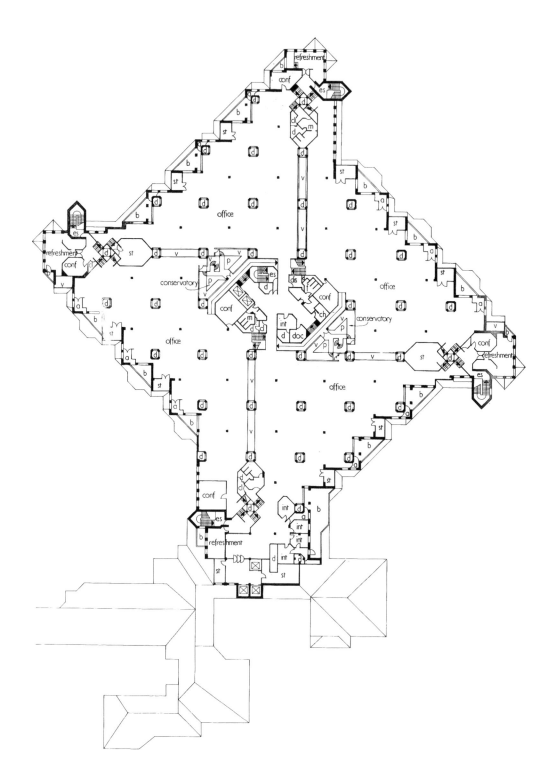

Level 4 floor plan (image via *Architects' Journal* Building Library)

corner was a peculiarly British compromise, an apology for a corner that wants to slide away from a firm change of direction and have it both ways. Hillingdon is an essay in chamfers, a symphony of compromises. It is too bulky to be charming and too formless to be striking, it is instead a loose, baggy, inhabited anthill, rising and falling, expanding and contracting not so much according to interior demands but to an abstract structural grid hidden deep within its organisational heart.

Structurally the building is made from reinforced concrete, a series of slabs supported by columns and deep transfer beams. The brick skin is stretched over this like a heavy jumper. Urbanistically it does some very odd things too. Pedestrian entry is from the High Street, but vehicle access heavily dictates the overall site plan. As a building it has the scale of the out-of-town shopping centre or the business park, and there is little attempt to form a clear front and back. Instead there are openings in the brick expanse for cars and people. Low walls and angular, cranking planters formed in brick with bullnose or 45-degree copings separate the two and define the landscape of the public realm.

The most familiar views of the building are from the dual carriageway of Hillingon Road. This is appropriately contradictory, an Anglicised version of Robert Venturi's concept of buildings relating to the scale of the American freeway. Conceived from the window of a passing Ford Cortina or an Austin Princess, the building is like a domestic pile-up, a car-crash of suburban roofs. It can be seen as the progeny of England's schizophrenic relationship to modernity, a self-image of proud individualism masking an enthusiasm for bureaucracy and a professed love of rustic bucolicism meeting a desire for the comfort and convenience of suburban life.

As a building, Hillingdon is fascinating and as a cultural product it is highly revealing. It is almost exactly contemporaneous with Robinson College, Cambridge by Gillespie, Kidd and Coisa (GKC), another building generally regarded as marking a decisive transition from modern to postmodern approaches. There are marked similarities in material – red brick – and form – set-backs and more of those 45-degree chamfers – as well a shift to treating windows as familiar elements rather than as expanses of curtain-wall.

Architectural historian, Otto Samaurez Smith has convincingly argued that Robinson College to be seen as more of a continuation of GKC's earlier work than a decisive break from it. It is harder to make the same case for Hillingdon. The imagery is more obvious, the intent to shift from the modernist language far clearer. And yet, beneath this, Hillingdon arguably holds onto modernism as a mode of working, both in its *Bürolandschaft* layout and in the processes by which it was designed. Perhaps RMJM, a more commercial and pragmatic outfit than GKC, were happier to follow a populist path, less troubled by the contradictions that arose as a consequence.

It would be a mistake to see Hillingdon as simply the product of a supreme loss of nerve. It is no beauty but it contains ideas and offers possibilities. In an optimistic mood, one could liken it to the brick expressionism of Michel de Klerk's Hembrugstraat housing in Amsterdam, a project from the early 20th century that also attempted to evoke the image of a more traditional collection of buildings. Clearly Hillingdon lacks both de Klerk's invention and his craft. If it is collage, it is a cut-up of similar objects, without tension or dissonance. If there is friction it lies in the relationship of the building to its brief and the attempt to make something large look like it is made of up of much smaller things. In this sense it is where the megastructure meets the picturesque, another English invention and another form of compromise.

Hillingdon is a product of the 1970s in other ways too. To make a musical analogy, it is thoroughly prog-rock: complex, technically demanding and yet also fiddly and twee. It is a brick-solo, both epic and whimsical. And yet, like many prog rock bands, beneath its desire for fantasy lies an organisational efficiency and commercial savvy. RMJM were masters of well-drilled, competently organised and efficient modernism. When that sensibility met neo-traditionalism it created a different kind of hybrid from the more obvious strands of postmodernism. Hillingdon remains a vast compromise, the epitome of wanting to have your cake and eat it. It is fascinating, revealing and compellingly odd. I still don't quite get it.

Charles Holland is an architect, teacher and writer. He is the principal of Charles Holland Architects, a design and research practice based in Deal, east Kent. Charles is a Professor of Architecture at the University of Brighton and a Visiting Professor at ABK Stuttgart.

Barns and Bunkers

Hillingdon is London's second largest borough and one of the greenest. Among our flagship heritage sites is Manor Farm in Ruislip. Located across 22 acres, its grounds house a unique collection of buildings. There are also archaeological remains and a varied landscape, featuring an orchard, herb garden and a moat around an ancient motte. Its Grade II* listed Great Barn is one of the oldest surviving of its type in London. It is an aisled structure, with oak posts created from trees in the nearby Ruislip Woods. Harmondsworth's Grade I listed Great Barn has one of the most intact interiors of its era. Dating back to 1426, it was built by Winchester College as part of its manor farm, and it remains an outstanding example of medieval carpentry.

One of the borough's more recent historical sites is the Grade I listed Battle of Britain Bunker in Uxbridge. Located 60 feet below the surface, it contained the Operations Room of No. 11 Group, which oversaw the defence of London and the South-East. Under the control of RAF Fighter Command, the bunker was an integral part of the world's first integrated air defence network. Known as 'The Hole' by RAF personnel, it was at the heart of major operations, including the evacuation of Dunkirk in 1940, the Dieppe Raid in 1942 and D-Day in 1944.

During Open House weekend, you can explore Hillingdon's landmarks virtually via a series of videos: for more information visit www.hillingdon.gov.uk/open-house
Contributed by Hillingdon Council

Former BOAC Maintenance Headquarters, Heathrow Airport, Owen Williams, 1950–1955

Amazing to think that this hangar was being constructed alongside Frederick Gibberd's clumsy, underscaled, timid – and now mostly demolished – original buildings for Heathrow. It does a simple functional thing – maintaining and repairing aeroplanes – but functionality can explain little of the appeal of this savage, scything arch of raw concrete, enclosing a Cyclopean vastness of space. This is instinctive Brutalism of the sort favoured by young London architects bored by the prettiness of Gibberd and his comrades, only some years before they thought of it. Hard to see publicly, but a plane departing or landing from all Terminals except 5 might well taxi past it; the closest Terminal is 4.[OH]

Lecture Theatre, Brunel University, Uxbridge, Sheppard Robson, 1966

Well known to fans of *A Clockwork Orange*, for its use as the Ludovico Institute, where Young Alex is conditioned against the old ultraviolence. The campus around is middling modern, well-planned, by the decent journeyman firm helmed by Richard Sheppard, but the lecture theatre, mostly windowless, is sculptural and daunting, with the projecting volumes of the theatres hauled up on great concrete columns – an experience of concussive mass and power. The recent painting of the stairwells but letting the concrete surfaces alone has a fittingly pop art aspect, and doesn't ruin the harsh materiality of the rest of the building.[OH]

Heathrow Hilton, Michael Manser, 1991

A similar freeze-dried, air-conditioned, perfectly controlled space to Foster's slightly earlier Sainsbury Centre in Norwich, a glass volume with rooms arranged around a giant atrium. In this placid span of steel and aluminium built into an artificial green landscape, sterility is a virtue, and the interior view is sublime – just don't go for a walk outside. (The nearest exit for the pedestrian who wants to see it is Terminal 4).[OH]

Manor Farm (top), Brunel lecture theatre (centre), BOAC headquarters (bottom)

Built in 1928 for the American tyre manufacturers, the Firestone Factory in Brentford was one of the outstanding examples of art deco and early-20th century architecture in London. Designed by Wallis, Gilbert and Partners, the building was characterised by a grand façade with ornate rectilinear columns and glazed details such as this one, as well as a decadent doorway set before a saw-tooth roofed factory floor. It was in operation until 1980 before it was demolished – a destructive act that would have monumental consequences.

'Every conservation society needs a martyr,' wrote Bevis Hillier for the Twentieth Century Society in 2014, 'a demolition so outrageous and shocking that the press and public realise the need for the society.' The Firestone Factory would be their martyr, the first high profile attempt by the Twentieth Century Society (then the Thirties Society) to prevent the demolition of a modern building. In the years since, the society has saved dozens of buildings among them the Hoover Building (Western Avenue, UB6), an art deco sibling of the Firestone factory that was Grade II* listed in the early-80s. Formerly a site for the manufacture of vacuum cleaners, the building was also designed by Wallis, Gilbert and Partners. One wing of it was converted into a residential building by Interrobang architects in 2018.

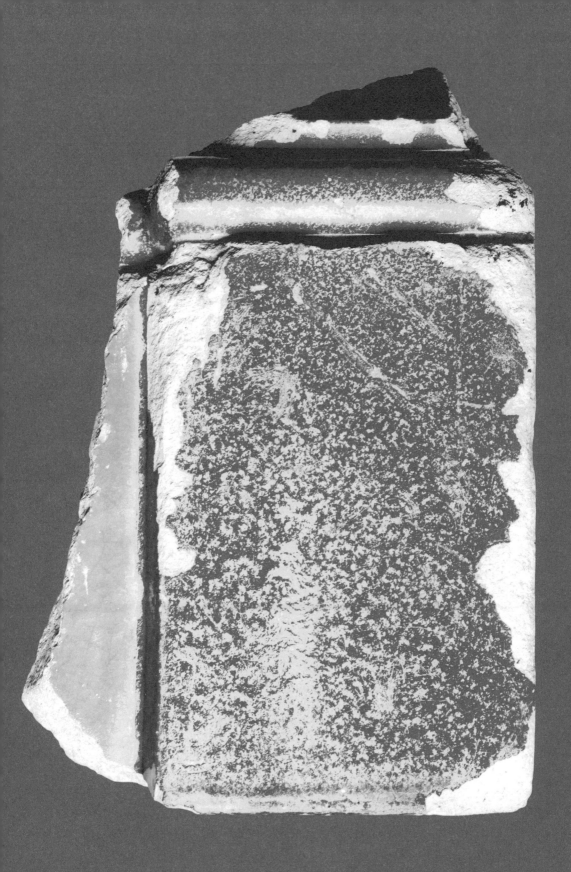

The Fancy Factories of Thomas Wallis
Gillian Darley

It was a late summer bank holiday Saturday afternoon, August 23rd, 1980. The publishers of Collins Companion Guide series had asked me (I was a cheap option) to take the photographs for Simon Jenkins's *Outer London* volume. I had chosen the holiday weekend to snap the recently redundant Firestone Tyre factory, knowing that traffic on the Great West Road (A4) would be exceptionally light and allow me to capture it from the central reservation.

Surprisingly, the site was jumping. Shoals of demolition contractors were hard at work, heavy machinery was everywhere and the wreckers' ball swung into ceramic details with careful vengeance. The job was being done at high speed since the developers, Trafalgar House, knew that the building was to be imminently listed. The paperwork was on the appropriate desk at the Department of the Environment (the antecedent of Historic England) awaiting signature. That pre-emptive strike, picking off the building's colourful decorative features in destructive dentistry, served to obliterate the ornament for which it was so well known.

Having captured the grim scene, I took my films, both colour and black and white, and ran to a phone box to ring the *Sunday Times*, where I was an occasional contributor to the Scene section. It was about 4.30pm. I spluttered that I had a bit of a scoop. 'Oh no, love,' came the friendly voice on the switchboard, 'too late, paper's gone to bed.'

This was a turning point in analogue architectural conservation. The immense frontage of the art deco Firestone factory dominated the so-called Golden Mile of the Great West Road, dwarfing the Pyrene and Coty buildings opposite, all three of them the work of Wallis, Gilbert and Partners and built between 1928 and 1932. Their more famous sibling, the Hoover Building, was a short distance away, on Western Avenue (A40) in Perivale (Ealing). The fury generated that weekend gave birth to the Thirties Society (which would become the Twentieth Century Society) and drove a rapid rollout of listing for art deco buildings around the country. It was too late for some other players in this theatrical roadside assembly, the exuberant Trico windscreen wiper blade factory (architect unknown, demolished in the 1970s) or the heroic, twenty-two pump Henly

service station, also by Thomas Wallis, gone in the 60s. The Packard
Factory had been hit by a V2 in 1945.

By the 1980s, the surviving 1930s factories facing onto the A4 or A40
were at the end of the road. Their industries had relocated or were outdated.
(In 1976 the women employees at Trico broke records for the length of their
equal pay strike). Fifty years earlier these overseas businesses had arrived
to supply the rising material ambitions of the British public. Important
components of motor vehicles and a range of domestic goods were manufactured alongside the new arterial roads while semi-detached housing
for workers had helped to gobble up the fields, orchards and farms of
Brentford. Half a century later, that parade of once confident factories was
a gaggle of redundant buildings sitting on valuable redevelopment land.

The scenographer of much of this was one man, Thomas Wallis, whose
architectural career began in government service, at the Office of Works.
From 1916 he became a consultant to Truscon – Trussed Concrete Streel
Company – an American firm with ambitions to market Moritz Kahn's
patented construction method in the UK. By 1919 British Truscon was in
business. With their reinforced concrete system, the scale and speed of
factory building had been revolutionised, starting with the American motor industry. Now Thomas Wallis set up in architectural practice, together
with the ghostly 'Gilbert', no more than a convenient two syllable name
that chimed well with his own. Convivial 'Tommy' Wallis with his comedic
'toothbrush' moustache was a bit of a joke, considered a 'character' in
the hidebound, conservative architectural profession. But flesh and blood
partners joined his office as the work began to pour in, clients arriving initially thanks to the Truscon connection but also due to Wallis's sociability.
He understood, perhaps as few others did, how architecture might help
sell the product and reinforce the pride and loyalty of the workforce. The
links to Truscon, as manufacturers rather than professionals, had circum-
vented the constraints on architects' advertising. Wallis, Gilbert & Partner,
soon Partners, were ideally placed to garner work from major businesses,
mostly American, as Britain became the bridgehead between the USA and
Europe after the 1927 Tariff Act. Many of them were surfing on the crest
of the motoring wave and a five-mile extension to London's Great West
Road, opened in 1925, offered an ideal location.

Firestone Tyres occupied the biggest site, its massive works, thousands of
square feet of saw-tooth roofed sheds, hidden away behind. Opposite it stood
Pyrene (now Westlink House) manufacturers of fire extinguishers, chrome
bumpers and trim. Beside it was the Coty factory (1932), the French cosmet-
ics firm. A slightly later addition, Currys (now J.C. Decaux), was designed
by F. E. Simkins. This bevy of pristine white factories-cum-headquarters
was essentially sleek and linear, but ornamented well beyond Bauhaus limits.

Demolition of the Firestone Tyre Factory, 1980 (image by Gillian Darley)

Popularly referred to as Jazz Moderne, the style later became known as art deco, from the 1925 Paris Exposition des Arts Décoratifs, although Tommy Wallis, son and grandson of builders, preferred the descriptive term 'fancy'. Soon, the model changed. The last additions to the Brentford industrial area, the massive Gillette works by Banister Fletcher and the factory known as Wallis House, possibly after the architect, are clad in brick.

In his heyday Wallis, with his Charlie Chaplin moustache, took inspiration from contemporary cinema design and from film itself. He titillated popular taste by alluding to events such as the recent discovery of Tutankhamun's tomb in the Valley of the Kings. The mood was Egypt, but Wallis's language remained Cecil de Mille's rather than Howard Carter's. The stylish elevations (and here the Hoover building, the most flamboyant of all, begs inclusion) were nothing if not theatrical.

Where space allowed, the approach resembled that of a lavish mansion. To the north the factories were set back, to the south they were closer to the road and so on higher ground. All were set off by expressionist ironwork, for gates and fencing, faceted light fittings and a well planted approach with graded steps and a path. This attractive, choreographed route to the entrance was for the offices rather than the factory floor, an impressive *mise en scene* offered to company visitors, salesmen and trade representatives.

The Firestone building, clad in white ceramic tiles, was announced by a columned temple front. On the pediment a clock carried the name of the firm in exuberant script. Egyptian styled coloured faience marked the bases and capitals of the columns, while the door was bordered in blue, with an 'F' monogram, horns to either side, above. As Wallis told the RIBA in 1933; 'A little money spent on something to focus the attention of the public is not money wasted but is good advertisement.' By day, the coloured highlights were like the night-time neon outlines of cinemas like the Odeon Leicester Square.

At the time, all eyes were drawn to the unprecedented cleanliness, scale and exuberant colour on the factories of the Golden Mile. J.B. Priestley noted in *English Journey* that they had been 'cunningly arranged to take the eye'. Heavy industry had moved south and everything had changed. No one driving past could miss the names of Firestone, Pyrene or Coty and externally at least, architecture had become branding. Did the entrance to the latter, boldly ribbed, perhaps allude to the Duncan, a Lalique scent bottle, presumably named after Isadora? Next door, Pyrene (1928–29) less ornamented than Firestone, depended for its effect on a lofty tower and an entrance bordered in red, green and blue faience. In newsreel footage of the opening, dozens of behatted worthies tramp up

Looking north-east along the Great West Road, 1960s

Tower entrance of the Pyrene building

the palatial double stair from the roadside. Proudly opening the door to them is a jocular figure – Tommy Wallis welcoming the eager crowd.

Of all Wallis's work, it is the Hoover factory (actually in Ealing) that has survived best. Not only does it monopolise a long stretch of the Western Avenue (A40) but it was also visible from the train line to the rear of the site where the neon sign ran the famous slogan 'beats as it sweeps as it cleans'. This architecture, with its mixture of major industry and escapist decoration, was setting the scene for a changing domestic world.

Standing on the central reservation in summer 2020, again facing the Firestone site, I see a tattered mixture of second rate 1980s glazed headquarters buildings, hungry for new tenants. Only the (listed) main gates with their 'F' insignia and a few plinths and steps offer a clue to that ambitious past. The landscaping and planting by which Wallis set such score, an aesthetic and humanising touch, is all but gone. Behind me, the renamed Pyrene building offers shared office space and Coty is the Syon Clinic. The shell of Currys (originally making cycles and radios) now houses the giant advertising company Decaux in a svelte Norman Foster makeover. (Hoover has gone through several lives but seems less vulnerable, perhaps due to location). On Hounslow's Golden Mile the economic wheel has been turning counter-clockwise for some time. Roadside retail parks and corporate headquarters – until recently Pyrene housed Carillion, the crashed construction giant – are all but extinct. Only listing, achieved on the altar of the Firestone building, gives the survivors a breathing space, but for how long?

Gillian Darley is a historian and broadcaster. Her books include *Villages of Vision* (1975), *Ian Nairn: Words in Place* (2013), *Excellent Essex* (2019) and *Factory* (2003), which also features the work of Wallis, Gilbert and Partners.

Chiswick Business Park, Richard Rogers Partnership, 1999–2003

All the contradictions in what Richard Rogers does in cities, and how he thinks about them, are encapsulated in this dreamy, limpid complex. During the 1980s, Rogers was highly critical of how the likes of Canary Wharf, or the business parks thrown up by Nicholas Ridley's 'Enterprise Zones', detracted from cities through their unplanned, car-centred, naff, sprawling and cluttered form. So here, he designs the same typology – a privately owned, privately patrolled, easily sealed-off business enclave within (but not of) the city – and makes it really nice, with public transport links, generous 'public' spaces with plenty of exotic trees, architectural co-ordination, and a lake. The buildings – standardised glass grids held up in thin steel frames, with titanium louvres and escape staircases – are the Pompidou Centre gone classical and serene, with all the pop, all the futurism, and all the melodrama taken out. Architecturally, it's completely convincing, work of real delicacy and grace. It exhibits the important virtue of knowing exactly when to stop designing, with the clarity of the module more important than expression and elaboration. It's quite gorgeous, especially in autumn. But it is what it is.[OH]

14 South Parade, Bedford Park, C.F.A. Voysey, 1890

Voysey, a designer mainly of houses, features heavily in histories of modern architecture as a bridging figure between Arts and Crafts, Art Nouveau, and modernism. His originality appears to have been a side-effect of how relaxed and functional his buildings were – comfortable, sprawling houses in the Home Counties, intended for living in rather than for showing off. The stark white walls of these houses have been claimed as a source for the early modernism of the Viennese architect Adolf Loos – here too, 'ornament is crime', though by all accounts Voysey was surprised and puzzled late in life to be pinned down as a 'pioneer of the modern movement'. The most accessible and most modern of Voysey's houses is in Bedford Park, an arty suburb planned by the protean Norman Shaw. In a sea of red brick and tile this bright white house was evidently intended to stand out. Its two storeys, tall and thin, are completely asymmetrical; there is an almost totally glazed 'ribbon window' to the ground floor, a laconic bay with a porthole window at its corner, and an almost streamlined smaller wing to the side. The only traditional gesture comes in the pitched roofs. A crisp and elegant building, and still a visibly strange and original one. It can be easily seen on the main Piccadilly Line viaduct to Heathrow.[OH]

Osterley Park House, Robert Adam, 1761

Built as a party palace for entertaining friends and clients of the Child family, bankers by trade, Osterley Park House is one of the last surviving country estates in London. Robert Adam created the neoclassical mansion by remodeling an existing Tudor house. In 1772, Adam was again commissioned to design a suite of state apartments as a sequence alluding to the elements of fire (the red of the Tapestry Room), earth (green in the State Bedroom) and air (blue in the Etruscan Dressing Room).[Om]

Adobe Village, Hounslow Heath Infant and Nursery School, Small Earth, 2011

Of all the cultural, architectural and urban UNESCO World Heritage Sites, more than 160 were built either wholly or partially from earth. For ten millennia, earth has been one of the most widely used construction materials on the planet. Despite its vanishingly small carbon footprint, earth is almost absent from contemporary British architecture. Yet in Hounslow Heath, this tiny pocket of earth construction is enriching the playground of a nursery school while protecting its user's eardrums. The school is directly under the flight path of Heathrow's southern runway and outside play for the children is dominated by ear-deafening interruptions every two minutes as landing aircraft pass a few hundred feet over their heads. Rammed earth architecture was an unlikely protagonist in this story until in 2009, the school approached designers Small Earth to create a complex of domed shelters for its students. Sound tests inside the semi-underground domes showed a noise reduction of over 17 decibels.[PH]

Chiswick Business Park (left), 14 South Parade (centre, image by Jamie Barras), Hounslow Heath Infant and Nursery School (right)

The Housing Estates of North Kensington
Emma Dent Coad

The first stop on our journey around housing estates in North Kensington is Henry Dickens Court. This was built by the council in 1953 on a Second World War bomb site under the supervision of local councillor Henry Dickens, who had a commitment to municipal housing. His grandfather Charles Dickens had written about the slum dwellings of Notting Barns. Designed by council architects, it has eight low and two high-rise blocks, set around communal gardens and play areas. Each block is named after a character from a Dickens novel, and located in alphabetical order. I have been numerous times, leafleting, canvassing or visiting. Two of our councillors live there. It is well laid out, well managed and maintained by onsite caretakers, with generous green spaces and beautiful planting.

All of this drives me into a blind rage.

While the council has invested heavily in making the estate look decent, the residents are among the most deprived in the country. Research I undertook in 2014 revealed that health deprivation was 65%, and child poverty was 57%, worse than the Gorbals in Glasgow, at 49%. The position of Henry Dickens Estate in the roll of shame has shifted slightly since 2014, but this is due to other neighbourhoods becoming poorer rather than any actual improvement. During the Cameron years I asked one of the caretakers why it was kept so pristine. He responded, 'oh this is the model estate they show ministers around, to demonstrate how well they look after council homes'. This was only five years before the fire at Grenfell Tower, just up the road.

Before we pay our respects there, we will visit the fiercely contended Silchester West Estate just five minutes away, opposite Latimer Road station. In 2015, the former garage site in front of the station was developed into mixed housing by Haworth Tompkins. It is a very elegant triangular complex, with balconies and pretty brickwork. Sadly, however, it was constructed by one of those dodgy contractors that councils rely upon. The roofs leaked regularly, damp seeped through walls, the brickwork stained from a leaky cornice. So, a mixed success.

Silchester West Estate itself was conceived in the modernist tradition by the Greater London Council (GLC) in 1969, with four 20-storey blocks, low-rise terraces and houses set around the large Waynflete Square garden. Despite the widespread deprivation suffered in the area, and the location between the elevated railway and the Westway, residents love their estate and garden. The council's pre-Grenfell development plans involved 100% demolition, with some twee 'neo-Palladian mansion blocks' (yes really), and narrow strips of grass replacing the gardens. Some of these blocks were to be built right up against the Westway flyover, clearly for the replacement social housing. The entire project was insulting to local people in a hundred different ways, including the derogatory language used to describe the area they love. A huge local campaign was fighting this very unwelcome land grab. In the event, Silchester West was saved. The event, of course, was the fire at Grenfell Tower.

Hundreds if not thousands of local residents – including myself – watched in horror for 18 hours as their neighbours burned to death in front of their eyes. So please, if you wish to visit the site and the various memorials, go with few in number and with nothing but respect. Local people are still wounded and traumatised, and know when they are considered as a spectacle. There were literally coach parties visiting in the early days, and I shouted at them too.

The low-rise Lancaster West with its three finger blocks and tower, overlooking its green lung of Lancaster Green, were first conceived by a team at Clifford Wearden and associate, Peter Deakins, in the mid-1960s. The early designs included offices and a shopping centre; these were subsequently nuked by the council architects who took over the project, due to financial constraints. The heavily engineered (if not over-engineered) concrete-framed Grenfell Tower, designed by Nigel Whitbread, was a response to the recent collapse of Ronan Point and fears about other slab block towers. It was built to be solid as a rock and impenetrable to fire. Flats and maisonettes in the finger blocks, and flats in the tower, were designed to generous Parker Morris standards, dual aspect with plenty of storage and lots of natural light. It was completed in 1974. As happened in so many estates of this period, it was planned to have on-site caretakers and decent levels of management and maintenance, but cuts bit over successive governments and Lancaster West fell into shameful disrepair, along with the Tower.

Then it was 'refurbished'.

So if you take anything from your visit, apart from a respectful and surreptitious photo, make it a lifetime commitment to demanding that safe and life-enhancing homes are built, to decent space standards, and that current homes are retrofitted to a decent and fire-safe standard of insulation and comfort.

A ten minute stroll up Ladbroke Grove will take you to Maxwell Fry and Grey Wornum's Grade II listed Kensal House. This was the first

Kensal House on a 1942 lithograph poster designed by Abram Games for the Army Bureau of Current Affairs – the caption reads 'Your Britain. Fight For it Now: Clean, airy and well-planned dwellings make a great contribution to the Rehousing movement. This is a fine example of a block of workers' flats built in London in 1936.' (Wellcome Collection)

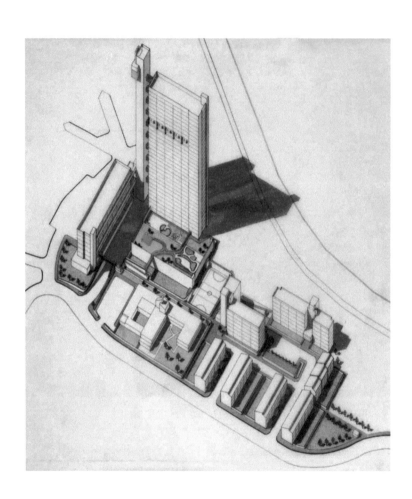

Axonometric of the Cheltenham Estate by Ernő Goldfinger *c.*1972

modernist social housing estate in London, built in 1937 by the Gas Light and Coke Company for their workers, next to the Kensal Gasworks on the site of a Sainsbury superstore. This very lovely and well-conceived project for 70 homes has two curved blocks of dual aspect flats facing south-west to catch sunlight, and designed for through-drafts to avoid 'miasmas' that brought ill-health to so many living in back-to-back slums at the time. A communal laundry and workshop, a dedicated nursery building, kick-about space and community room have all now been repurposed – this last very controversially, as the current tenant wished to extend this listed building into the tropical garden that residents enjoy. After a huge local outcry and support from conservation groups, a new application has been agreed. It is under construction at time of writing, and simply unworthy of the site.

Doubling back over the railway bridge will take you to the back of Catalyst Housing's Wornington Green Estate. On the railway side is the not quite but nearly listed, and now half-demolished, Pepler House by Peter Deakins with Clifford Wearden – such an extraordinary and clever design that I have saved its plans at savepeplerhouse.blogspot.com. The estate is half-way through a dismal redevelopment whose first phase was so badly built (with central government and Mayoral funds) that some homes leaked from above, through the floor, through the walls, via the plumbing, and the balconies flooded because they had no drainage. Five years after completion, some first phase flats are still subject to 'snagging'. The original excuse for the development – that the estate was 'unfit for purpose, overcrowded' – has been questioned by residents moved from warm dry old flats to leaky damp new ones, with larger families moved out to wait for family sized homes who may never ever return. Meanwhile, numerous privately owned flats have been let out to Airbnb – using national and London government money for profit, while not housing our homeless.

Back over the railway bridge is the 'iconic' Cheltenham Estate of 1972, comprising Trellick Tower's two Grade II listed blocks, Edenham Way's low-rise sheltered blocks, and the cherished terraced houses which, after a huge local campaign, we were able to get listed in 2012 when under threat of demolition. Edenham Residential Care Home was at the heart of the Cheltenham Estate's cradle-to-grave project. It was the only care home ever built by Ernő Goldfinger – shamefully demolished in 2009 after a long campaign, during which I chained myself to the gates. Despite what many believe, Trellick Tower is not packed with lucky architects and designers. The 217 flats are overwhelmingly still social rented, with just 27 privately owned, and some of those are lived in by the original Right to Buy owners. I have visited every nook and cranny of the building and estate, from rooftop to circulation tower rooms, community rooms, numerous flats, and the derelict semi-demolished garage. This extraordinary building was built to last and to be flexible, and still has lots to give over many years, if only the council understood and appreciated it.

Our final stop is back across the railway from Trellick Tower, the 500-unit Swinbrook Estate, planned by the GLC and Purcell Miller Tritton in 1973, a huge scheme that demolished Victorian 'slums' and attempted a relationship with the Westway to the south. This was achieved with a barrier block along Acklam Road that has its back to the motorway and balconies cascading with plants on the other side, overlooking a neighbourhood park. The estate has a long social history involving housing campaigners forcing the council to compulsory purchase hundreds of properties so they could redevelop them. This was achieved in 1969 by locking 22 councillors and officers in a church hall overnight, which encouraged a change of mind. This was one of numerous direct actions by local residents in North Kensington in the years after the riots of 1958, and there are doubtless lessons to be learnt here. Over the years I have walked many students and visitors around Swinbrook Estate, which is very pleasant, well-designed, has matured well, has lovely planting and well-maintained small neighbourhood parks.

Swinbrook Estate, according to the Office of National Statistics, has the highest deprivation scores of any neighbourhood in the whole of London.

Emma Dent Coad is the councillor for Golborne Ward and was the MP for Kensington between 2017 and 2019. She has been writing about design and architecture for 40 years.

Czech and Slovak Embassies, Notting Hill Gate, Jan Bocan, 1965–1970

The south side of Notting Hill Gate was totally redeveloped in the early 1960s, by means of some fairly indifferent commercial modernism. In the process, this monster appeared, one of the most intriguing buildings of the 60s in London. It is also a deeply odd building to have emerged during the Cold War, a full-scale late modernist Eastern European building in one of the capitals of the west. This happened because Czechoslovakia had a programme of new embassies in the 60s, showcasing socialist modernity – there are similarly ambitious structures in Berlin and Stockholm. What makes this city-block of fine grey concrete worth serious exploration isn't merely the powerful grid that faces Notting Hill Gate – though that is impressive – but in what happens when it turns the corner towards Kensington Palace Gardens, and makes various cubist plays with panels and grids. Inside, the embassy (split now into a Czech and Slovak half, and usually open for Open House) is suffused with the surrealist modernism that thrived in Prague and Bratislava between the end of Stalinism and the Prague Spring of 1968, and which persisted to a degree right up until 1989. Tentacles of glassware have been plugged into corduroy concrete, rococo chairs stand in front of walnut walls – Vera Chytilova or Jan Svankmajer meet Paul Rudolph or Marcel Breuer in uptown W11.[OH]

Cohen House, Chelsea, Erich Mendelsohn and Serge Chermayeff, 1935, renovation Norman Foster, 1979; 66 Old Church Street, Chelsea, Walter Gropius and Maxwell Fry, 1935

Two houses in a formerly arty and now oppressively moneyed corner of Chelsea by extremely important architects, neither in its original condition and neither the architects' best work, but worth seeing for the ways they've been altered. The Gropius house is compromised by the black-grey shingles added to it some decades ago – usually a building that had been so unrecognisably damaged would never have been listed, but the Bauhaus director's authority has seen it become so. Mendelsohn's house adjacent was the more impressive of the two before they were both subjected to aggressive renovations by their owners – a spatial game of long, intersecting white volumes. Most importantly, the owners' additions were a matter of addition rather than destruction – a cubic glass conservatory, well detailed and cleverly integrated with the house. It is in fact an early design of Norman Foster.[OH]

Institut Français, South Kensington, Patrice Bonnet, 1939

The cultural centre, cinema and library of the Institut Français stands in the stucco'd Italianate streets of upper class French diaspora South Ken, the area of bistros and boulangeries where Roman Polanski filmed *Repulsion*. Architecturally, it's a big break with all these white plastered facades – red brick, and in an extraordinary expressionistic variant of art deco. A small block dominated by the high, faceted windows of the library, with the brick shaped into a grand guignol version of Gothic tracery, concealing an opulent marble interior and artworks by major French modernists. The finest of these is the abstract Sonia Delaunay tapestry that adorns the stairwell; the effect is both classy and eccentric.[OH]

Czech and Slovak embassies (top), Institut Francais (bottom)

Growing Up 'in Town'
Hazel Tsoi-Wiles

'We should go into town,' my friend said to me over the phone. I was baffled. 'Where do you want to go?' I asked her. She simply repeated herself: 'Into town.' She meant the centre, we should go into central London where everything happens and where everything that matters about London is situated. I don't remember protesting her terminology but I do remember feeling shocked that my close friend could suggest such a thing to me. I couldn't go into town. I was already in town. I was always in town. I lived there.

I lived in Westminster, which meant I could say, truthfully and indisputably, that I lived 'in town'. Westminster is London concentrate; London's greatest hits, the best known, crowd-pleasing bits of it can be found in this borough. Whatever draws people to London, and whatever repels people from it, can be found here, in full colour and at slightly over 100% strength. Its landmarks are used constantly in films and TV, and the borough serves as visual shorthand for London around the world. It did not occur to me, until that conversation, that not everyone who lives in London lives in that particular London. But I did.

I lived close to Big Ben, the Houses of Parliament, Buckingham Palace, Soho, the West End, Trafalgar Square, Leicester Square, Covent Garden. I could get to Selfridges in 15 minutes on the no. 6 bus, Chinatown in eight minutes on the tube. I went rollerskating in Hyde Park, around Speaker's Corner because that was the open green space nearest where I lived. I caught the 159 bus to secondary school in the mornings and was regularly held up at the crossing outside Abbey Road Studios, as groups of early rising tourists recreated the Beatles' album cover, in rush hour traffic. In summer, after school, I walked with friends through leafy St Johns Wood to Lords Cricket Ground, sometimes hearing the crack of ball on bat, then continuing to Regents Canal, which was our shortcut to where we lived. Going 'into town' with that friend meant a regular indie club night at Astoria 2 off Tottenham Court Road, where we once saw Jarvis Cocker dancing and sometimes found Lauren Laverne and the rest of Kenickie (except the bloke) in the toilets. When our underage clubbing finished at 2am, I'd be home by 2.30am as there were loads of nightbuses going from the West End to home off Edgware Road, and I could never blame a late number 8 bus when my disappointed parents wanted to know why, yet again, I had stayed out to such an unreasonable hour.

All this convenience, sophistication, casual cosmopolitan glamour should naturally come with a Mayfair mansion flat or Fitzrovia town-house. My Westminster residence was neither: I lived in a three-bedroom council flat on Lisson Green Estate. I had all the privileges of the borough without the privileges of its private, luxury housing. We had no garden, private balcony or a door onto the street, but we did have gerrymandering and political scandal. We had no drooling photospreads of where we lived in Sunday supplements or gossip magazines, but the estate was the setting for the bleak and disturbing music video for Suede's 'Animal Nitrate'. Maida Vale and Little Venice were metres away, backdrop for many attractive period dramas. Lisson Green was backdrop for *The Bill*, providing requisite urban decay and gritty, intimidating landscapes for the police drama that worked stoically through every inner-city stereotype for ITV.

Lisson Green occupies Westminster's damaged central vision. It is a massive social housing estate sitting squarely between highly desirable, well-known parts of the borough – Marylebone, Maida Vale, St Johns Wood, Regents Park. Despite existing in the heart of it, the estate remains overlooked, and undermentioned by the borough; this grey, indistinct mass of dense, disreputable housing gets none of the glory or praise for being in Westminster. Not all housing estates in Westminster are omitted, as if to preserve the prestige of the borough, in this way – Churchill Gardens near the Thames is loved with genuine passion by architects, designers, historians, residents. But Lisson Green remains undefended, uncelebrated – and unloved. Even after major regeneration, the estate is unchanged, and with another major regeneration underway, what was done to it is proving hard to undo.

There are 23 blocks in Lisson Green, each one seven storeys high, with 52 to 63 flats per block. It was designed in the 1960s, built in the 1970s, and one name is attributed to it: F.G. West, director of architecture and planning for Westminster at the time. There is communal heating and access to rubbish chutes on each walkway. The flats are non-standard construction, all concrete but somehow different to Rowley Way or Brunswick Centre concrete. There is now pastel coloured panelling of questionable material on the blocks, and all have pitched roofs thanks to a ten-year regeneration plan that ran from the end of the 1990s to the end of the 2000s. The flats range from one-bedroom, single-storey homes to four-bedroom, four-storey maisonettes, interlocking in confusing, befuddling formation and only available by application to the council. None can be found for private rental. Flats at ground level have their own front doors from the street;

Hazel Tsoi-Wiles playing on the communal walkway at Lisson Green, *c.*1982

flats above have front doors on the third- and fifth-floor communal walkways. These walkways used to join together all the blocks, forming a grid of 'streets in the sky'. It was possible to cross from one side of the estate to the other without ever touching the ground. A lot of crime was generated by this, unforeseen but also unsurprising. The many lift shafts and multiple, unlit, pissed on stairwells where muggings, assaults and drug-dealing happened were eventually all pulled down in the regeneration plan, and the blocks have security doors and less frightening entrances now.

Gerrymandering leaves a hell of a stain though, and it will take several cycles of regeneration to remove the dark spots from Lisson Green. During the 1980s, my home was one of the homes for votes in Westminster Council leader Dame Shirley Porter's multi-pronged manipulation of the borough. We bought it after 10 years of renting it, in a too-good-to-be-true offer from the council, and we briefly became homeowners in this illustrious central London borough. Despite it being a leasehold on a non-standard construction flat in a disreputable council estate, it was an achievement for my parents who had left Hong Kong for the UK in 1970, seeking exactly this kind of opportunity. The truth of what that leasehold meant started to emerge, and it became clear we had bought an albatross: no estate agent or bank would allow it on the market. We were locked into it, while those on the waiting list for a council flat were locked out.

It did not feel like it at the time, but we were lucky that Westminster council demolished our block of flats in 1998. We did not have to campaign for them to buy it back from us, unlike other leaseholders whose homes were unfortunately left standing. Our block and adjacent two blocks were pulled down at the start of the first ten year regeneration plan; remaining blocks had cladding and pitched roofs put on, and the crime-facilitating stairways taken off. The council has been steadily buying back flats from leaseholders to complete regeneration and return the housing stock to its original purpose, but it has been a costly and demeaning process with no obvious winners.

The council had to rehome us, and gave us three – only three – flats anywhere in the borough to view. We could not go back to any flat we turned down; if we declined all the flats offered, we had to find our own accommodation in private housing and remove ourselves from the council's responsibilities. It was disorienting to be in such an enviable part of London, surrounded by beautiful, spacious period properties and shiny, tall luxury apartment blocks, not knowing where we would be moved to but only certain it would not be to the high-end homes we could see from our street.

The first flat we saw had been squatted and there was an enormous turd in the toilet when we visited. There was no flooring and everything in the bathroom was smashed. It was very off-putting but so was the entire process of being rehoused like inconvenient pets after Christmas. We chose that first flat, despite the turd, because it was a seven minute walk from our previous home. That decision summarises our experience of living in Westminster: we believed we would not get any better than that, because we were treated as if we could not get any better than that.

My parents still live there, overlooking platforms 3 and 4 of Edgware Road station. I lived in the new flat for a year, then went to university where I ironically escaped right into another giant concrete housing block (New Hall, Cambridge – designed by Chamberlin, Powell and Bon, so the good kind of concrete). And then after university, in a further ironic move, I lived in Westminster again, in a privately-rented basement of a Georgian terrace, across the road from Churchill Gardens. When I visit my parents now, I am back in the places where I grew up, and I have seen the regeneration of Lisson Green start again. The block that replaced our block has been torn down, and is being rebuilt in yet another form that will somehow still cast a shadow in the shape of a crooked councillor.

Hazel Tsoi-Wiles is a former editor of *Londonist*, a Live Art Development Agency writer in training, a repeat attendee of the Royal Court Young People's Theatre and later, the Royal Court Young Writer's Programme, and a Royal Court Theatre BEA writing group alumna. She was also one of the inaugural Almasi league writers. She currently works in university administration, and her most recent published writing is a long poem/short story in verse for the *Mechanics Institute Review*.

French House, Soho

This pub, originally called the York Minster, but lovingly christened by locals as the French House, boasts a wealth of bohemian Soho history. Situated in the Georgian street of Dean Street in Soho, it only sells half pints and over 30 different types of champagne by the glass.[ZC]

Piccadilly Circus Underground Station, Charles Holden, 1925–1928

The start of the great adventure in design that was the London Underground under Frank Pick and Charles Holden, which at this distance seems like the most significant modernist experiment in the interwar capital – never quite going all the way into continental avant-gardism, but with similar ambitions to unite art, architecture and everyday life into a well-functioning, quietly delightful whole. At Piccadilly Circus, Holden and the Underground's engineers took a typically messy old tube station and recreated it into a mirroring of the circular public space above. The use of travertine, and the circularity, make Piccadilly Circus station rather restful for a place so constantly packed – a sort of heavenly anteroom in a perpetual rotating motion. Stop at the map showing the time in all the world's cities, though, and the movement slows, as you concentrate on the dated graphic. You stand still and watch time shift, as the tourists zip around you.[OH]

University of Westminster Cavendish Campus, Fitzrovia, Lyons Israel Ellis, 1962–1970

Lyons Israel Ellis were one of several prolific and creative post-war firms – Yorke Rosenberg Mardall, Robert Matthew, Johnson-Marshall, Building Design Partnership, Chamberlin, Powell and Bon – who became the architects tasked with designing the welfare state. Unlike these others, Lyons Israel Ellis did not outlast the 1970s, so have an unblemished record, seemingly only having built to the highest grade, largely for worthy clients, with no gold-tinted glass City offices or pink Timmy Mallett palazzos at the back-end of their archives. This is one of their biggest projects, originally designed as a College of Engineering for what was then Regent Street Polytechnic. It makes an interesting contrast with the Engineering Building at the University of Leicester, by their former employees James Stirling and James Gowan. Whereas that modernist icon in the Midlands is cerebral and intriguing, the London building uses what, on the page, could seem like a similar assemblage of cantilevered lecture theatres, neo-medieval service towers and glazed workshops to far more visceral and heavy effect, raw concrete surfaces, squat and bulky forms and a much greater feeling of compressed, energetic action, hitting in the gut.[OH]

St Saviour's Church, Warwick Avenue, Paddington, Biscoe and Stanton, 1973–76

The most confident of all the modernist churches in London – not the usual wan spike on a butterfly-roofed brick box, nor the slightly sad campanile next to a monopitch prayer shed, this is a real work of architecture. A cluster of seemingly disconnected brick shards mass around what is more obelisk than spire, it is full of concentrated energy, charging right in Little Venice. It's unusual in its programme, too, joining onto a small block of Brutalist brick flats, through steps and alleyways round the back – a much more interesting and urban approach than the sad little car parks attached to so many British modernist churches.[OH]

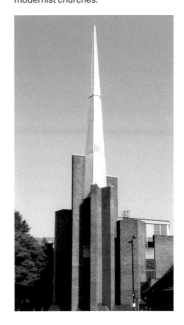

French House (top left), illustration of Piccadilly Circus (centre left), University of Westminster (centre), St Saviour's Church (right)

Afterword
Phineas Harper

I took up the role of Open House director one week into lockdown.
To say my first months on the job were tricky would be a wild understate-
ment. The last half year has been a wild ride forcing everyone at our small
charity to completely rethink their conception of what Open House
is and does. I'm enormously grateful to the ingenuity, flexibility and
dedication of our staff, volunteers, collaborators and supporters. When
the moment came, they threw themselves at the challenge of Covid with
gusto and creativity, rethinking Open House's programmes, turning live
events into dynamic podcasts, swapping guided tours for film production
and much more – not least creating this amazing book.

The pages you hold in your hand are unique to this strange year.
This is a book that Open House would probably not have made in more
normal times, and certainly it is one which few other publishers would
take a punt on. It is a paper version of the Open House festival – a critical
exploration of the neighbourhoods of London, some glamorous and
iconic, others barely investigated, even by Pevsner. It is at times unabashed
in its frank criticism; elsewhere brimming with measured praise, and
it would not have been possible without the contributions of a number
of dedicated collaborators.

I called Owen Hatherley with little other than the thought, '33 writers
on 33 boroughs'. He has turned the most cursory of briefs into a full-
throated adventure through the city assembling a coterie of writers whose
variety and backgrounds are as rich as their prose. I am enormously
grateful to Owen for his commitment to this project while juggling the
arts editoriship at the (outstanding) *Tribune* magazine and his own forthcoming book on London, *Red Metropolis*.

Rosa Nussbaum of Studio Christopher Victor has brought so much
to this project, transforming the visual language of Open House into one
which now straddles the centuries – medieval keys unlocking each chapter as
if we were passing through the gates of London's historic wall. Rosa delved
into the Museum of London archives and emerged with the enigmatic array
of objects which illustrate these pages. I am hugely indebted to her contribution without which I think the book would have little of its lush intensity.

Sian Milliner is head of Open House. Her sage advice, cool head and deep knowledge of the workings of London's boroughs have been the backbone which allowed this book to take shape, sourcing nuggets of insight from community groups and local authority staff to enrich its pages, all alongside organising one the largest architecture festivals on the planet in one of the most difficult years to do so ever.

Catherine Slessor, in addition to contributing the wonderful preface to this guide, was my first boss after university as the then editor of the *Architectural Review*. Her influence runs throughout many of my subsequent curatorial and editorial escapades including this book.

I also want to thank the Open House Friends. Covid hit our charity hard, stopping almost all our income. It's not smooth sailing yet, but a rock of stability has been the roughly 500 individuals who responded to a call for help and signed up to give small monthly donations to support our work. From all of us, huge thanks.

There are many other people to thank, their names are in printed in full overleaf, but a few in particular to single out are: Crispin Kelly, the chair of our board of trustees whose encouragement and support gave me the confidence to launch into making this book in my first few weeks on the job; Merlin Fulcher, Jon Astbury, Zoë Cave, Ella McCarron, Rhea Martin, Nyima Murry and Marianna Janowicz who wrote many of the captions, highlights and other words printed here; and Alberte Lauridsen, who supported me immensely throughout the lockdown and the hurdles it brought.

Open House campaigns to make London a more accessible, equitable and open city. The very existence of our festival, and the charity behind it, speaks to the contemporary failure of London to be truly inclusive. And yet, every year, thousands of volunteers transform hundreds of amazing buildings into the urban landscape of tomorrow – a London that is freely explored, freely interrogated, and freely accessed by all. It is in that spirit of open enquiry, debate and exploration that we present this book.

Phineas Harper is director of Open House, and chief executive of Open City, the charity behind it. He was co-curator of the 2019 Oslo Architecture Triennale and co-founded the New Architecture Writers programme. He has lived in London for a decade, traversing 15 of the city's 33 boroughs while living aboard a narrowboat on Grand Union and Regent's Canals, and the River Lea. He currently lives in Tower Hamlets, in Glenkerry House, a Brutalist housing co-operative designed by Ernő Goldfinger.

Headline sponsors

Open House
Friends and Donors

This book would not have been possible without an amazing group of individuals who, when Covid hit the UK, responded to our appeal for help by signing up as Open House Friends, and making charitable donations to support our work. We want to take a moment to recognise the huge contribution that those people make, and to sincerely thank every donor, benefactor and Open House Friend who supports us. Thanks to you, we are able to stage the annual Open House festival, to deliver educational programmes for children and young people from under-represented backgrounds, to run a year-round programme of talks, tours and events, and create provocative, adventurous films, podcasts and publications, not least this very book. They say when the going gets tough, you can rely on your friends and for Open House this difficult year has proven the wisdom of those words. Thank you.

We've made a number of gifts to thank everyone who signs up as an Open House Friend including limited edition prints, special events and the Open House silver key badge. Visit openhouselondon.org.uk/friends to find out more and become an Open House Friend.

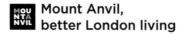
Mount Anvil,
better London living

The Baylight Foundation

The Baylight Foundation is a charitable organisation with the aim of increasing the public understanding of of what architecture can do, rooted in the experience of Walmer Yard.

Discussions around the senses and architecture are often dominated by just one primary sense – the visual one. Yet how we experience a space has to do with much more – from its temperature and acoustics, to the feel of the materials on our bodies. Spaces can be understood and appreciated through acoustic resonance, through the smells of materials and through the different moments of tactility and texture on the skin as you pass through, as much as through the visual shape. Architecture is never limited to one sense alone.

At Walmer Yard we explore this through our seasonal programme. The houses, with their unusual and tactile materials of clay walls with added straw, cast concrete, solid oak, and copper, call out to be touched. While Peter Salter's play on light and dullness offer a different experience of the spaces as the light changes throughout the day and the seasons. Sound also allows us to explore the houses differently – the staircases resonate ascending and descending footsteps and the yurts offer a moment of peace within their softened acoustic.

These are moments which can't be explored through browsing online, through a video or a photograph. During the past few months, not being able to visit or interact with architecture outside our homes has changed the way we experience architecture, and as some sensual experiences have become more taboo in light of the pandemic, we must not forget what the real experience of visiting architecture does for the senses.

Mount Anvil

Mount Anvil exists to create outstanding places where people can thrive and for them, that is all about the quality of their homes.

Keybridge is a new development by Mount Anvil and FABRICA by A2Dominion, that is transforming a corner of Nine Elms, with a collection of 598 mixed tenure homes. Located in Vauxhall, the scheme is set across six buildings of varying heights designed by architects Allies and Morrison and delivered by David Wood Architects on the site of the former BT Telephone Exchange – a building described even by Pevsner, as 'forbidding'.

Now, as the cluster nears completion, elegant brick facades scale new heights, moving from the eight-storey Keybridge House to Keybridge Lofts – which at 37 storeys is the UK's tallest residential brick tower. The project is a potent blend of past and present, integrating into the local area with references to Vauxhall's industrial heritage and providing new levels of safety and security for a modern development.

In addition to the homes, Keybridge comprises a selection of cafes, retail shops and offices that will enhance and support the local economy of the area for future generations. One acre (almost one third of the overall site) is dedicated to new public spaces, with a series of commissions from British artist, Tom Price. Price's ambitious sculptures focus on the areas' complex heritage and celebrate the River Effra – a now hidden river that previously ran through Vauxhall. These playful and poetic artworks integrate a beautiful story that weaves its way through the development promoting interactivity and an opportunity to sit, climb and explore the tactile surfaces.

Acknowledgements

Open City

Volunteers
Alasdair Bethley
Peter Bury
Bob Dawes
Catherine Day
Ola Decker
Bill Green
Rob Hurn
Alan Jacobs
Marianna Janowicz
Robin Key
Ulla Kite
Solen Fluzin
Elizabeth Nokes
Richard Purver
Leonora Robinson
Stuart Rock
Rick Smith
Alison Surtees
David Taylor
Sue Thorburn

Open House Festival
Hafsa Adan
Ella McCarron
Sian Milliner
Nyima Murry
Natascha von Uexkull

Open House Tours
Adrianna Carroll-Battaglino
Merlin Fulcher

Open House Worldwide
George Kafka

Other staff
Jon Astbury
Zoë Cave
Sophie Draper
Phineas Harper
Jeni Hoskin
Rhea Martin
Stephanie Tyler

Open City Podcast
Lara Kinnier
Ruby Maynard Smith
Arman Nouri
Selasi Setufe
Ed Ryman

Social Media Consultant
Edward Bray

Accelerate
Sahiba Chadha
Elliot Nash

Open City Trustees
Jayden Ali
Sara Bailey
Alison Brooks
Richard Ehrman
Johanna Gibbons
Stephen Howlett
Crispin Kelly
Alan Leibowitz
Alan Stanton

Special thanks
Ishwari Bhalerao
Ben Chernett
Tim Craft
Mathilda Della Torre
Caz Facey
Alisha Fisher
Solen Fluzin
David Garrand
Rosie Gibbs-Stevenson
Aiden Hall
Mark Hamsher
Kezia and Lydia Harper
Joseph Henry
Meneesha Kellay
David Knight
Ed Moss
Roz Peebles
Frosso Pimenides
Neil Pinder
Hani Salih
Akil Scafe-Smith
Maria Smith
Jim Stephenson
Leanne Tritton
Rupesh Varsani
Venetia Wolfenden

London Boroughs

We would like to thank the following London Boroughs who supported Open House this year and without whose contributions, this book would not have been possible.

City of London
Barking and Dagenham
Bexley
Brent
Bromley
Camden
Ealing
Enfield
Greenwich
Hackney
Hammersmith and Fulham
Haringey
Harrow
Hillingdon
Islington
Kensington and Chelsea
Kingston upon Thames
Lambeth
Lewisham
Merton
Newham
Redbridge
Richmond upon Thames
Southwark
Sutton
Waltham Forest
Wandsworth
Westminster

Partners

ALLFORD HALL MONAGHAN MORRIS

Allford Hall Monaghan Morris is a leading British architecture practice. They make buildings that are satisfying and enjoyable to use, beautiful to look at and easy to understand.

ROCKET PROPERTIES

Rocket Properties collaborate with clients and local communities to re-energise areas of London with innovative commercial and residential developments, with sustainability in mind.

DERWENT LONDON

Derwent London is a British-based property investment and development business whose ethos has always been distinctive and design-led.

 trowers & hamlins

Trowers & Hamlins are an international law firm who are fascinated by the future of towns and cities.

Foster + Partners

Foster + Partners is a global studio for architecture, urbanism and design, all rooted in sustainability and founded by Norman Foster in 1967.

THE HOWARD deWALDEN ESTATE

The Howard de Walden Estate is the freehold owner of 92 acres of Marylebone, central London.

London Property Alliance **WPA | CPA** Westminster Property Association | City Property Association

London Property Alliance provides a unified voice for the leading owners, developers, investors and professional advisors of real estate across Central London.

 MUSEUM OF LONDON

The Museum of London is the city's shared place in the middle of it all telling the stories of London and Londoners past, present and future.

GREENFORD QUAY

Greenford Quay by Greystar is a new waterfront neighbourhood overlooking the Grand Union Canal in Ealing.

 **Landscape Institute** Inspiring great places

The Landscape Institute is the chartered body for the landscape profession. It is an educational charity that promotes the art and science of landscape practice.

 **CANARY WHARF** GROUP PLC

Canary Wharf Group has overseen the largest urban regeneration project in Europe and is a fully integrated private real estate company.

 **JOHN LYON** HARROW·ON·THE·HILL

John Lyon's Charity gives grants to benefit children and young people up to the age of 25 who live in nine boroughs in north and west London.

Media partners

de zeen

Dezeen's mission is simple: to bring its readers a carefully edited selection of the best architecture, design and interiors projects and news from around the world.

 BBC RADIO London

The sound of London, your essential guide to London life. Proud supporters of Open House for 28 years.

ar

Scouring the globe for architecture that challenges and inspires, *The Architectural Review* is an international magazine published in London since 1896.

Editor
Owen Hatherley

Design
Studio Christopher Victor

Transcription
Marianna Janowicz

Copy Editor
George Kafka

Production
&Printed / Studio Christopher Victor

Printing
Pureprint
Colour profiles from colorlibrary.ch

Paper
Olin Regular Natural White 120 and 300gsm. Olin papers are made in the UK
by Antalis using FSC® certified, 100% elemental chlorine free pulps. Antalis
carbon balance the production of Olin via the World Land Trust.

Typography
Starling (Mike Parker, 2009) is named for William Starling Burgess, a Bostonian
sailor whose 1904 drawings found their way into the hands of Stanley Morison
and are said to have been the inspiration for Times New Roman. Neue Haas
Unica (Toshi Omagari, 2015) is Monotype's revival of Unica, designed by Team '77
for the Haas Type Foundry in 1980.

First published in 2020 by Open House, an imprint of Open City.

Open City
18 Ensign Street
London E1 8JD

www.open-city.org.uk

The Alternative Guide to the London Boroughs
© Open City, Owen Hatherley and authors 2020

ISBN 978-1-9160169-1-0